CECIL SPRING RICE

Cecil Spring Rice—Ambassador to Washington

Cecil Spring Rice

A Diplomat's Life

David H. Burton

Rutherford ● Madison ● Teaneck
Fairleigh Dickinson University Press
London and Toronto: Associated University Presses

12-23-96

Associated University Presses
440 Forsgate Drive
Cranbury, NJ 08512

Associated University Presses
25 Sicilian Avenue
London WC1A 2QH, England

Associated University Presses
P.O. Box 488, Port Credit
Mississauga, Ontario
Canada L5G 4M2

The paper used in this publication meets the requirements of the American National Standard for Permanence of Paper for Printed Library Materials Z39.48-1984.

Library of Congress Cataloging-in-Publication Data

Burton, David Henry, 1925–
    Cecil Spring Rice : a diplomat's life / David H. Burton.
       p.   cm.
    Includes bibliographical references.
    ISBN 0-8386-3395-1 (alk. paper)
    1. Spring Rice, Cecil, Sir, 1859–1918.   2. Diplomats—Great Britain—Biography.   3. Great Britain—Foreign relations—20th century.   4. World War, 1914–1918—Diplomatic history.   I. Title.
DA566.9.S65B87   1990
327.2'092—dc20
[B]   89-46135
                                                                  CIP

PRINTED IN THE UNITED STATES OF AMERICA

For Old Friends
J. E. D. — F. X. G. — J. P. M.

CONTENTS

PREFACE

More than twenty years ago, in doing a study, *Theodore Roosevelt and his English Correspondents*, I had my first serious encounter with Sir Cecil Spring Rice. I concluded that of his many English friends, and among them were Arthur Hamilton Lee, G. O. Trevelyan, James Bryce, and St. Loe Strachey, Spring Rice, *aka* Springey, was the one Roosevelt profited the most from knowing. Now, twenty years on, I have returned to Spring Rice in his own right. My purpose is to focus on his diplomatic career, significant portions of which involved relations between Great Britain and the United States.

In the early stages of researching this study I met Corelli Barnett, the keeper of manuscripts at Churchill College, Cambridge, where the bulk of the Spring Rice papers are deposited. In a good-natured way he said to me: "So you are going to write *the* biography of Spring Rice." My reply was as honest as it was spontaneous. "No," said I, "I am going to write *a* biography of Spring Rice. Others will have to determine its reputation." He seemed almost as satisfied with that answer as I was. But it is an answer requiring some elaboration.

In the preface to *Theodore Roosevelt and his English Correspondents*, I had reason to thank Lady Arthur, the daughter of Spring Rice, for her kindness in making available her father's papers, which then were privately held. At that time I described her as "the ideal proprietress of family letters, at once generous, understanding, and alert to the meaning of history." I have every reason to reiterate, and with great force, my original judgment. She and I concluded it was Spring Rice's diplomatic service that deserved to be appraised, the emphasis to center on his professional life. This means that I have discussed only those personal matters that seemed to me to bear on his formation as a diplomat and his conduct of diplomacy. The overreaching consideration from that moment of decision onward was to allow the record to speak for itself. And if, after all, there are elements of psychobiography in this study of a diplomatist, they are hardly to be avoided in an effort to understand Sir Cecil's view of life, of the society of men and women, and of the worlds in which he moved. In the main, however, *A Diplomat's Life* is biography written by a historian prepared to bring only common sense to the task of untying psychical knots.

Anyone interested in the life of Spring Rice should turn initially, as I have done, to *The Letters and Friendships of Sir Cecil Spring Rice: A Record*, edited by Stephen Gwynn. Gwynn has not told the whole story; but he has done a remarkable job of assembling letters, adding connecting links, and interpreting historical background as understood in the 1920s. His two volumes have been indispensable to me. The papers of Spring Rice go well beyond what Gwynn brought into print. Some family letters and memorabilia are retained by Lady Arthur, but the majority of primary materials are at Churchill College. Important material relating to his diplomacy is in the Public Record Office (Kew). Special thanks to Elizabeth Bennett, the Archivist at Churchill, and the assistants there, and to the helpful staff at the PRO.

The research and some of the writing of this book was done while I was on sabbatical leave from Saint Joseph's University. This is a good occasion to thank its board on faculty research and Dr. Matthew J. Quinn, Vice President for Academic Affairs, for recommending me, and to thank Rev. Dr. Nicholas S. Rashford, S.J., the President, for encouraging my work. Any number of colleagues and friends have given valuable support, especially, but in no particular order, John S. Monagan, Francis Graham Lee, James E. Dougherty, Frank Gerrity, A. E. Campbell, Thomas David Marzik, Phillip Thurmond Smith, Louis Marks, Anthony J. Joes, Richard H. Collin, Esmond Wright—and the list remains incomplete.

Pity the poor scholar who lives on academic bread alone. My wife, Gerri, succeeded in making our stay in London complete in every way, and I doubt if I would have been able to do my work otherwise. My daughters were wonderfully kind, and my brother's interest never flagged. Audrey and Eric Matkins were helpful in countless ways and in ways that counted; along with Margaret and Fred Drew, Yvonne and Chris Griffiths, and Joyce and Colin Fowler, they combined to make our stay in England a fully productive holiday. None of the above, and least of all Frank Gerrity, who has read the manuscript in its entirety and to its benefit, can be held responsible for any errors of fact or fancy, of judgment, or of interpretation.

ACKNOWLEDGMENTS

Quotations from Volume 3 of *The Intimate Papers of Colonel House*, edited by Charles Seymour, Copyright 1928, © renewed 1958 by Charles Seymour. Reprinted by permission of Houghton Mifflin Company; and permission to quote from Edith Wharton, *A Backward Glance*, Appleton-Century Co., Inc. Copyright, 1934 are gratefully acknowledged.

INTRODUCTION

Certain lives tempt the biographer to read events backward in time. This is especially so if there has been some crowning achievement in that life toward which there has been a discernible, forceful tendency, carrying with it a sense of preordination. From the point of climax there may develop something akin to a compulsion to pick through the years, isolating incidents and featuring actions that, taken all in all, suggest—if they do not prove—that there has been a spirit and a purpose combining to achieve a destiny. Cecil Spring Rice lived such a life. His long career as a diplomat attained a rare distinction when he became British ambassador to the United States in 1913, a post fraught with the greatest significance for his country with the outbreak of World War I. He served in Washington during the difficult years preceding 1918. The responsibilities of office were awesome and, in the end, extremely stressful. After a long struggle to remain neutral, during which time there were acrimonious disagreements between Great Britain and the United States, America entered the war on the side of the Allies. By no means had Spring Rice masterminded this turn of events. Indeed, few, if any, statesmen would have been able to exercise as he did the patience and the understanding necessitated by President Wilson's determination to stay aloof from the fighting. Spring Rice's conduct of affairs, a vital element contributing to United States involvement, must be ranked as an astute accomplishment.

There has been the temptation in consequence to interpret Spring Rice's first meeting with Theodore Roosevelt in 1886 as something like fate. Friendship with Roosevelt—who was truly a darling of destiny—and who was becoming more and more prominent in public affairs in the United States, can all too easily be viewed as a remote but critical factor in Spring Rice's promotion to ambassador in Washington, the predictable outcome in a series of related events. Adding force to this judgment was Sir Cecil's sudden death within a month of his depar-

13

ture from Washington. His long American mission dating from 1887 was completed; there was a time to serve and a time to die.

As persuasive or as appealing or even as romantic as such a perception of Spring Rice's life as a diplomat may appear—and no less an authority than Valentine Chirol has written that "his whole career seems to have been a preparation for the final struggle in Washington"—it is an untenable proposition, for seeing through to the heart of the matter and the man, to argue that Spring Rice was destined for that particular place in history. The Washington embassy required that the ambassador use to the full his skills and indeed the total sacrifice of self for the cause he believed in. It was his beliefs and his skills, the former in their unity, the latter in their diversity, that made his wartime assignment a success. The Washington embassy was rightfully his, however, only if the argument be accepted that destiny had been guiding his steps. A more sober assessment is offered in the pages that follow. As Francis Bacon wisely observed: "All rising to great place is by a winding stair."

The organization of this biography deserves brief comment. The first chapter overarches Spring Rice's life. It identifies his heritage and indicates the place and importance of his diplomatic assignments, one by one. The overlap that results as his work is taken up in detail in later chapters has its uses for coming to an understanding of Sir Cecil's mind in action. Whether his career is viewed generally or particularly, certain themes stand out and should be so noted. These include his contempt for autocracy, the role of the English-speaking peoples in international affairs, and a fear of German imperial ambitions. The greater the stress placed on these and like considerations, the more certainly the connection between a public philosophy and public policy can be demonstrated as a guideline to his diplomacy. To put it another way, the layers of convictions as well as of diplomatic assessments that accumulate as the Spring Rice story moves forward from the general to the particular—added to directly by accounts of his influential friendships and indirectly from an examination of his literary expression—are a way of showing just how recurring and consistent were his views on patriotism and liberalism and therefore on the conduct of diplomacy. In short, the first chapter establishes a coherent frame of reference.

In order to dramatize the literary man, I have fully considered Spring Rice's achievements in this regard. Important in itself, an analysis of his writings, and especially of his poetry, supplies more background to his life of public service.

Successive chapters take up his diplomacy and focus attention by an elaboration of his professional work, and at the same time, they bring out aspects of his personal life and private thoughts. Spring Rice was rarely able or willing to separate professional conduct from private conviction. The initial, allusive references in chapter one are more fully developed in an in-depth account of Spring Rice's diplomatic career. The second of these chapters includes the early months of Sir Cecil as British ambassador to Washington.

The climax of his career was not the Washington embassy as such, however. It was signaled rather by the outbreak of World War I, which found him occupying that highly sensitive post. Then and there Spring Rice was situated very near the center of a great historical event as the wartime measures of the British and the Germans clashed with the American policy of neutrality. His was a remarkably difficult assignment as examination of his diplomacy from 1914 to 1918 demonstrates. A final chapter takes Spring Rice's life to its abrupt end, serving also as an epilogue for a man who occupied two worlds, that of the mind and spirit and that of public service in diplomacy.

Finally, it is appropriate to say that *A Diplomat's Life* is not *revisionist* in the conventional sense of that term, largely because heretofore Spring Rice has not been the subject of a biogrpahy. Chirol called his short sketch a "memoir," and Gwynn presented his two bulky volumes as a "record." Negative assessments that historians and biographers of the period have passed on Spring Rice, especially in respect to his work as ambassador in Washington, have arisen largely from accounts of the lives of others, such as Colonel House or Lord Northcliffe. If there was controversy and disagreement between Spring Rice and these and others in the cast of characters, it may be assumed that there are two sides to every conflict. But Sir Cecil's side, when recounted here, is offered in passing, spin-offs (you might say) in pursuit of that elusive phenomenon, the real Spring Rice.

CECIL SPRING RICE

1
FAMILIES, FORTUNES, FRIENDS

Born in a year when imperial greatness was at floodtide, and dead by the time despite likely victory in World War I, British power had begun to recede, Cecil Arthur Spring Rice was both a man of his age and an individual who surveyed events with the eye of a visitor from another century and another place. He was on one hand exactly what he appeared to be: a well-born, Oxford-educated civil servant intent on promoting his nation's interests by means of diplomacy, an art in which he acquired real skill. This was the Spring Rice that most of his contemporaries and latter day historians were to recognize. There was another side to Spring Rice however, which was to remain largely hidden because it stood—or seemed to stand—apart from his career. This dimension is evident from his writings. Few people were aware while he lived that he was a serious poet, because he kept most of his verse away from the public eye. Those acquainted with him, his intimates and some others, also valued his translations of Persian poetry and legend. His two books on these subjects were published, quietly it seems, at the turn of the century. He tended to make little of them, somewhat less than they deserved, as though he were hiding from all save his closest frinds a mystical strain that inspired and motivated his literary efforts. But this mystical quality was a fundamental ingredient in his makeup, one that, if overlooked, leaves nothing but the diplomat—accomplished, capable, charming—a man of the world. For any account of the life of Cecil Spring Rice, this will not do. Poetry, story telling, and art, fusing to form a divinely driven spirit, constitute essentials of his life and work. Spring Rice's diplomacy, his skill as a political observer and analyst, and his ambassadorship are all tied to the workings of his inner self. Only the shell has figured in his place in history. Understanding the total Rice Spring, we may serve him and serve history better, bringing to light the principles he honored, the values he upheld, and the understanding of the relationship between God and man that for the diplomat was the rock upon which all else rested. The work that he did was worldly by any definition: he was chargé, commissioner, minister, ambassador, with the full complement of social commitments that are part of a diplomat's life. In viewing him from the outside, who could have known of the deeper and, in the end, the more characteristic truth?

Alive as he was to the world about him, to the political and economic changes afoot at home and in the international order, Spring Rice clung to an individualist ethic and displayed hardly any sympathy for the gathering storm of social protest that was to lead on to reform. The occasional comments that are discoverable in his writings refer ruefully to the changes pending in the kingdom and empire as popular rule prepared to replace the old aristocratic order. A classical liberal, his convictions grew more firm with each passing year. Although liberalism was central to his public philosophy, unlike that of Jeremy Bentham and John Stuart Mill, it was grounded in spirituality. It started from a spiritual point in the moral universe that was heavily, if not exclusively, Christian and in all ways religious. To put it bluntly, Spring Rice held that the individual in saving himself would save the world. As the individual was sacred, so individuals must be free to direct their own lives. In the practical order the most immediate way this could be done was by exercising political freedom. Spring Rice's liberalism was not an abstraction, not a theory to be admired like a fine Ming vase. In his day there was a struggle going on in which liberalism was threatened by autocracy. The conduct of diplomacy had therefore to proceed along these same lines. Liberalism thus became transmuted into a cause, something that people must be willing to sacrifice for and indeed to die for in order to preserve. The 1914 war was a world crisis because liberalism was fighting for its life, and history could not guarantee its survival. Such judgments on his outlook lead unerringly back to Spring Rice's roots.

1

The family name, Rice, is Welsh in origin, a variation of Rhys, but it was known in Ireland in the fourteenth century. By the time of Henry VIII, the Rices were numerous in Kerry where they prospered. Later, much of their land was sequestered by the Cromwellians, and some family members went into exile on the continent. In the late seventeenth century, Sir Stephen Rice was chief baron of exchequer in the Irish Parliament and was an ardent supporter of Irish nationalism and the cause of James II. After the surrender at Limerick Sir Stephen held himself bound by the treaty, and the family went temporarily into eclipse. With a change of creed and the passing of a generation, Sir Stephen's son helped to repair the family's condition by marriage to Mary, daughter of Maurice Fitzgerald, the fourteenth knight of Kerry, creating a link with some of the leading Kerry clans. The scion of this union in turn wed Catherine Spring, and since that day the family was called Spring Rice. Their son, Thomas Spring Rice, born in 1790, became a leading Irish politician. At the age of twenty-one, Thomas was betrothed to Lady Theodosia Pery, herself the daughter of the first earl of Limerick. An able lawyer, he was elected to the House of Commons at Westminster in 1820 as a member of Parliament (M.P.) for Limerick, and he quickly established a reputation as an active advocate of reform, especially for measures aimed at seeking relief for Catholics of civil disabilities. Later he was M.P. for Cambridge and joined the cabinet as under secretary for the Home Department in 1827. Seven years later he was named chancellor of the exchequer and raised to the peerage in 1839 with the title of Lord Monteagle of Brandon. Lord Monteagle's second son, Charles, had a promising career in the Foreign Office cut short by his death at the age of fifty-one. He had married Elizabeth Margaret, the daughter of William Marshall, M.P. for Hallstead and Patterdale in Cumberland. Eight children were born, four boys and four girls. Cecil Arthur was the third child and the second son.[1]

Such a lineage was typical of the working aristocracy that made and managed the British Empire into the twentieth century. These men (and their wives in very many instances and in their own ways) were conscious vessels bearing a tradition of love of country manifested in their service in and to its institutions of church and state. As they had inherited a past that they honored, many of them were none too sympathetic with the changes that appeared to threaten the established order of things. Winston Churchill once remarked that in Victorian times England was for the few and the very few. If Cecil Spring Rice preferred to keep it that way, he did so out of no spirit of malice but because of his confidence in the rightness of things as he had known them, an altogether human response, especially when such far-reaching changes were in the wind.

Cecil Spring Rice was born in London on 27 February, 1859. Anglo-Irish in background, he was raised an Englishman. But his Irishness persisted as he showed in these lines.

> I am an Irishman, you see,
> That is what expresses me.
> I am changing as the weather,
> You must take me altogether,
> Hopeless of distinguishing
> Which is Rice and which is Spring.[2]

With his father dead by the time he was eleven, it was his mother's house on Ullswater that he was to recall as his home. It was to be the touchstone of his love of nature, of poetry, of England itself. His boyhood days there were happy ones. He entered Eton in 1871 as a colleger—one of the ten or twelve boys admitted each year who, by reason of superior ability and promise, qualified for an expense-free education—where his older brother, Stephen, had preceded him, a colleger as well. At Eton Cecil's first tutor, William M. Johnson, described his new charge as "frail in body, gracious in manner, eager for knowledge," but he also noted a less serious side, which he thought of as falling away "into something like silliness."[3] Spring Rice's sense of humor had already begun to display itself, although in an adolescent way, a vague intimation of the wit and whimsy of his adult years. H. E. Luxmoore succeeded Johnson to become Cecil's tutor and was the most important single influence on him during his school days. Luxmoore was a father figure to a youngster who had been deprived of his own father, and whose feeling of loneliness was reinforced by the departure of his brother, Stephen, who went up to Cambridge. He could not have had a more caring tutor than Luxmoore, and they remained friends for life. As his tutor he became aware of two characteristics of Cecil that were to play significantly in later life. He was a lad often sick, which sometimes had a noticeably bad effect on his studies. Equally to the point, Luxmoore told Spring Rice's mother of his "great sweetness and tenderness of character, but I think he suffers rather from some consciousness of self. I sympathize with it but it may become very marked in time."[4] Both physical illness and spiritual strain were to work adversely on Spring Rice's diplomatic career, as Luxmoore himself would later note. Other descriptions of Cecil at Eton combine to give a good idea of his looks and likes. Bernard Holland, a year his senior, recalled him as "a rather elfin looking Colleger."[5] To A. C. Benson, Spring Rice's junior by two years, he was a hero to be worshipped from afar. "He was not a tall boy," in Benson's memory, "but he moved quickly and lightly with a decidedly abstract air . . . he had a strong, muscular development and every inch of it was under control."[6]

Mr. Luxmoore was, no doubt, more concerned with Cecil's intellectual development, and under his mentorship Cecil was soon reading *The Origin of Species* as a piece of science and philosophy while delving into theology at the same time. Luxmoore set him to reading both Augustine and Bernard of Clairvaux, and as a colleger Spring Rice did a short original essay on Thomas à Kempis. His senior essay, however, dealt with Mazzini, very much a contemporary personality. He also wrote verse and a short story, which appeared in *Out of School at Eton*, a student publication. His mind was revealing a preference not for precise knowledge—scientific and quantifiable—but much more for reflective and imaginative thinking. In a word, he was not pointed in the direction of Cambridge, which was a family tradition, but of Oxford. As he had already expressed an interest in entering government service and most probably the Foreign Office as had his father, Luxmoore was decidedly of the opinion, as expressed in a letter to Cecil's mother, that "the Oxford education would afford him better equipment for the particular type of examination to which competitors for this branch of the civil service were subjected."[7] Cecil's regrets at not being able to join Stephen at Cambridge were outweighed not only by Luxmoore's advice but by his own recognition that his best work could be done in the humanities.

Spring Rice was at Balliol in the heyday of Benjamin Jowett, its most famous master and a man who enjoyed, then and now, a reputation as a molder of statesmen, a nursery keeper who cultivated some of the finest specimens of imperial servants. If Spring Rice failed, or refused, to respond to Jowett's manner of encouraging and inspiring undergraduates, the fault lay most likely with him rather than with the master. The simple truth is, he had no very clear idea of what he wanted to do with his life, or even what he wanted to do during his Oxford years.

He had gone up to the university as an exhibitioner, no mean
feat at Balliol, his qualifying essay termed "almost the best—and
your history paper the best of the lot."[8] His promise as he commenced university life was great, and that he came to love Oxford is certain. "I don't think I could ever get tired of the place,"
he wrote his mother. "The river, the college, the trees in the
garden—I wish you could see it. But it is to be lived in, not
to be shown over."[9] What use was Spring Rice to make of this
splendid university?

To answer that question, it would not be too much to say
that he made the most of it. A double first (in Classical Modera-
tions and *literae humaniores*) shows that he had put his keen
mind to the test and had not been found wanting. Study of
Aristotle's *Ethics* and Plato's *Republic* extended and deepened
a philosophical awareness that Luxmoore had initially stimu-
lated by directing him to read the church fathers. Later thoughts
that he might choose to be a don were well grounded and no
mere flight of youthful fancy by an undergraduate in search
of a career. But intellectual distinction was not enough for Spring
Rice, who sensed, as men before him and men and women
after, that attendance at Oxford should be more than a pursuit
of formal learning, even of a double first, however fine and
useful and even necessary such an education was. He wanted
more and discovered it in various places. On the playing fields
he was a good miler and rowed in the Balliol boat. He acted
a part in *Agamemnon*. He contributed to the *Masque of Balliol*,
that collection of piquant verse satirizing personalities at the
university, an effort that won him some notoriety and some
resentment as he displayed his stinging wit. He enjoyed a wide
circle of lively and even brilliant friends—G. N. Curzon, St.
Loe Strachey, Edward Grey, J. A. Spender—all of whom later
gained distinction, Curzon as viceroy of India and Grey as foreign secretary (and Spring Rice's chief when he was ambassador
to Washington). These several pursuits fitted nicely into Cecil's
Oxford. Without consciously intending it, he had acquired a
diverse education that was to benefit him in his life's work.
Had he been more certain of his choice of careers, it is just
possible that he would have left Oxford with a more focused
and therefore a more narrow education, somewhat deaf to the
variety of choices open to a young man of his advantages. Yet
his failure to have a set purpose once he left the unversity
was disturbing. His ditty tells of this.

Can story telling be a vice
When you've an uncle like Sp   R   ?
My versatility is such
None likes me little or knows me much.[10]

He first went to France, to Tours, to improve his French, which then was the language of diplomacy. He competed for an All Souls fellowship and did poorly, then went once more back to the continent, to Paris and Dresden, travels that give a growing impression of a young man adrift. Various possibilities danced in his head: the Foreign Office, a literary career, another try at a donship, but which was it to be? As is often the case, circumstances overmastered decision making. The Foreign Office announced examinations for clerkships, and Spring Rice, now more than ever determined by the opportunity, prepared seriously. The results reflected well on his knowledge and his commitment. Arthur Hardinge, who had been with him at Eton and Oxford, wrote congratulations. "As I told you and as everybody except yourself felt certain would be the case, you were easily the first."[11] Appointment to the Foreign Office, as announced in The Times in October 1882, strangely enough did not bring an end to Spring Rice's uncertainty. Would his reflective, artistic termperament survive the routine of a Foreign Office clerkship? Was a desk his natural habitat? Could he experience a sense of satisfaction from such employment? Was Spring Rice still to look for the low door in the wall beyond which lay his magical kingdom?

The Foreign Office was organized into two main divisions, the administrative, which dealt with policy and paper, and the diplomatic, which embraced diplomats on station around the world. Ordinarily the two divisions maintained separate staffs, and personnel rarely transferred from one to the other. Spring Rice entered service on the administrative side of the fence, so there was every prospect that he would make his career in London. His first assignment was that of assistant private secretary to the foreign secretary, Lord Granville. In the early 1880s the government was much concerned with events in the Levant, and Spring Rice was expected to study and report on developments in the Eastern Department: Egypt, the Sudan, and Asia Minor. His baptism of fire was therefore in the Middle East, an area that was to play an important part in his future career as a literary figure and as a diplomat. As a junior official he took his work seriously, but there is detectable in these years

a plodding quality, if not unrest at the prospect of a desk job
for the long term.

In his personal affairs there was change. The death of his
mother meant that Stephen and he and their elder sister must
work to keep the family together. Cecil did his part gladly,
and one by one, younger brothers and sisters went out into
the world. There were bright spots too. He won a new and
much loved friend in Ronald Ferguson, who was Lord Rosebery's private secretary. When Rosebery became foreign secretary, Spring Rice was named his précis writer as he and Ferguson
deepened their comradeship.

Spring Rice's first two assignments in the Foreign Office had
given him a taste, however vicarious, of diplomacy, but they
also caused him some frustration because he was a reporter
of events rather than being in a position to make events happen.
He was unsettled in consequence, although his personal regard
for Lord Granville, who treated him kindly, and his enormous
respect for Lord Rosebery were offsetting considerations. Meanwhile, his reputation as "the wicked wit of the F.O." endeared
him to his fellows but probably did him no good with his superiors, who would be judging his career potential. Some of these
same superiors were known to look disapprovingly on his work
habits. "Springey's table—and he has a very large table—was
always a full two feet deep in paper, with his hair standing
on end," went one report. A casual if not unruly manner of
dress was another sticking point. All in all he was "offbeat"
and far from your typical junior civil servant, with even his
handwriting below Foreign Office standards.[12]

Spring Rice took advantage of Rosebery's withdrawal from
the Foreign Office to apply for leave to visit his younger brother,
Gerald, who had gone out to western Canada to farm. Several
reasons figured in his decision. Family ties had always been
strong with the Spring Rices, and Gerald's accounts of life on
the frontier must have excited his curiosity. The wild side of
nature, nature in the raw, and the very opposite of Ullswater,
beckoned to be experienced and not simply read about. Western
Canada was a world vastly different from London and important
for what it might teach him about himself. This Canadian trip
was not a lark but more like a felt necessity, not fully worked
out in his own mind, to satisfy a yearning for something new.
It is worth remembering that this urge to go to Canada was
the presupposition of his meeting with Theodore Roosevelt,
whom he encountered on his passage home in December 1886.

There is small likelihood that Spring Rice would otherwise have met TR. Much can be made of his unexpected meeting with this prime specimen of *homo Americanus*, for it ripened into a historic friendship. Conversely, too little attention has been paid to the fact that it was Spring Rice's own initiative that took him to the New World in the first place. Their meeting was accidental and fortuitous, but Spring Rice had helped bring it about.

The stay with Gerald was an exciting time. They camped and hunted, lived by their rifles and their wits, and traded with Indians and half-breeds. This first visit to North America brought Spring Rice face to face with one of the great realities of North American history—the frontier, the cutting edge of advancing civilization. This is the very sort of adventure he could share with Roosevelt, who was a historian of the frontier; it became one of the foundations of their friendship. Once returned to London, Spring Rice was enthusiastic about what he had seen and done and soon thereafter applied for an appointment to serve in the British legation in Washington. The assignment came through. Arthur Hardinge characterized it as "off the line,"[13] as it undoubtedly was. The explanation for this move may lie in a desire on Cecil's part to be near Gerald, but he was always much closer in spirit to Stephen, who was in London. Or Roosevelt may have planted the seed, which would have been typical of him, although he probably scattered a variety of ideas and suggestions in Spring Rice's direction. There may be a simpler explanation. He wrote Ferguson: "I am going to Washington for six months or a year as a change." The operative words were "as a change."[14] Spring Rice was still searching, although for what, he did not know exactly. But a clerkship from which he might rise slowly in the ranks to a position of possible importance after many years in harness had lost much of whatever attraction it once had. Spring Rice would be a diplomat after all.

2

Sketching the diplomatic career of Cecil Spring Rice as he served in posts half way around the world provides glimpses of him in unguarded moments and at the same time it provides the background against which many of his friendships were made. Such an overview also sets the stage for his role as a man of letters and as a political observer-analyst and diplomat. The variety of his assignments encouraged his skill as a geopolitical commentator, exposed him to non-Western cultures, and deepened his consciousness of the frailty of the international order. He began a lifelong education in nations and peoples as diverse as the Persians and the Swedes, the Japanese and the Russians. His gift of observation became apparent on his travels in Germany with Luxmoore while still at Eton. At that early age travel appealed to him because it enabled him to learn about the world by seeing it. The cathedral at Cologne, Dürer's etchings, Brahms's performance of his own compositions at Leipzig—these were the forerunners of a life of wandering and noting, where his observations became increasingly acute and of increasing usefulness to the Foreign Office.

Not realizing what he would find in America as he came to Washington in the spring of 1887, Spring Rice was bewitched by the country that had been a product of his own, taken aback by the public corruption he encountered there in the Gilded Age, and persuaded that in the years ahead the position of the United States in world affairs would grow rapidly in power and importance. He had his first inklings of the need of the two leading English-speaking peoples to work together for their own good and for the benefit of humanity. As foreign as America was to him, he felt strangely at home. Americans, as he met them both in the North and the South, invariably made him welcome, and that had a powerful appeal. Spring Rice was naturally gregarious and made friends easily. Although he was not given to bonhomie, he was at ease almost at once with some of the richest and most influential men in the nation. "I am getting to like this more and more," he wrote Stephen, but added, "I am not fit for the diplomatic life."[15] Weeks later he asserted to Ferguson, who had paid him a brief visit in Washington, that he did not want to make a fuss one way or the other and just let things go as the fates choose."[16] He elaborated this attitude in a second letter to Ferguson. "I hope to be back in May or June to stay in London for good. I can't take the diplomatic life at all and I only like this out of pure luxury and wickedness." In fact, he missed Ferguson more than he did London and, by identifying one with the other, left what was perhaps a false trail to his inner feelings, admitting that "I miss you more than I can say. I wish I had gone back with you." His mood was obviously still unsettled, and he did not stay on at the legation. Later he wrote to Ferguson: "And so my fate is fixed. I am glad for this. The longer I stay [in Washington] the more loath I will be to return." His affection for America, or at least for some Americans, was real. He told Stephen, "It does seem odd, I am as much at home here as in London."[17] Spring Rice was not an instant convert to America in 1887. But he was infatuated.

Once at home he had occasion to reflect on his experiences abroad. His first stint of diplomatic service had been brightened by American hospitality, which appeared to outweigh what he encountered as American vulgarity, and the United States might not be a bad place to begin to build a career in diplomacy, should he decide to stay with it. As it happened, he was selected by the Foreign Office to be secretary to an International Marine Conference that was to convene in Washington in the autumn of 1889. The conference amounted to very little, but it did bring Spring Rice back to America, and this led the minister, Sir Julian Pauncefote, to request that he remain at the legation as second secretary. A corner had been turned: diplomacy rather than Foreign Office administration would be his calling, and Washington was an agreeable place to begin seriously to learn the ropes. Pauncefote was a much respected chief, and there was the added advantage of the arrival in the capital of Theodore Roosevelt, who had been appointed to the United States Civil Service Commission. These were the months when their casual meeting of 1886 was transformed into an abiding friendship. More importantly, Spring Rice was less ambivalent about the diplomatic service as he settled comfortably into his duties. He now liked the life, and his health was excellent, although he admitted that diplomacy had its drawbacks, especially the sacrifice of a married life. "I fear I have chosen a profession that makes wandering about a necessity and I don't think a wife would have much of a time of it."[18] Clearly he believed that he had *chosen* diplomacy, that his presence in Washington was not a fluke, that his new career was a result not of circumstances but of preference. As he later made the point to Ferguson: "Life in the outside service is fuller than life in the Foreign Office because the work is at first hand." And Washington was "a grand post for interest."[19]

The education of the young diplomat continued when Spring Rice was posted to Tokyo in 1892 for a stay of somewhat less than two years. Japan was to be a hiatus in his American tour of duty. That nation emerging from its feudal past was about to burst on the international scene with victory in the Sino-Japanese War of 1894. By then Spring Rice was back in Washing-

ton and lamenting to Stephen: "I should have been in charge
in Japan and might have had some interesting work to do. Now
the chance is gone.[20] Even so, his stay there, in a country that
within a decade would be a formal partner of his own by reason
of the Anglo-Japanese Treaty of 1902, was instructive. He traveled widely in the countryside and like so many visitors was
much moved by the sight of Mount Fujiyama. His reflections
he set down in these lines.

> "Welcome," he flashes from his flaming brow,
> "Welcome to him who comes across the sea:
> The Stranger from the land that knows not me:
> Welcome the venturous keel that dares to plough
> My sacred waters:—they shall tell you how
> Once with my rage I darkened earth and sky.
> And once I tossed my fiery fountains high;
> The snow lies deep upon the ashes now.
>
> "And men that knowest not in a tongue unknown,
> High over sea and land and piléd cloud
> Uplifted on my lonely altar-throne,
> Worship the power, before whose sacred name,—
> O secret tender of the hidden flame!—
> Thou too, O stranger-heart, thou too hast bowed."[21]

From Japan Spring Rice moved on to Korea where, in the company of Curzon, he visited towns and villages, taking the measure of the things he saw. Curzon pronounced him "the best,
cheeriest, most unselfish, most amusing of travelling companions."[22] Enjoying the sights quite as much as Curzon, he also
worried about the balance of power in the Far East should Japan,
for example, snatch Korea from China from under the nose
of the Russians.

It now became a settled habit for Spring Rice to blow hot
and cold on a new assignment. He was glad, if somewhat surprised, to be returned to Washington after Japan. At the same
time he decried his lack of exposure to European diplomacy,
which, if he did not acquire it, "would be the ruin of my professional future."[23] His concern in this respect is understandable
but only to a degree. If he believed that in the near future the
United States would have a new, large place in world affairs,
especially in the Far East where America tended to focus attention and where he had seen hundreds of Americans in Japan
and Korea, then his American expertise, which relatively few

members of the diplomatic corps possessed, should advance rather than retard promotion. Hardinge, in fact, had pointed this out to him as early as 1889. "You will become quite an American specialist and be consulted on all U.S. matters."[24] It was not a bad prospect for a rising diplomat, and it was one that Spring Rice apparently did not fully appreciate.

Over the next two years America was as hospitable as ever, but American foreign policy was less so. The dispute over fishing rights in the Bering Sea was settled by an arbitration commission's award that did not fully meet United States expectations. For its part, Canada, which Americans always looked upon as a ward of the British, was bent on rejecting certain stipulations of the commission's award as too favorable to the United States. All this made for difficulties. More serious by far was the Venezuelan boundary dispute, with Great Britain cast in the image of an enemy of the western hemisphere. Spring Rice lost his composure because so much was being made over a small disagreement about a boundary line. He was entirely correct in writing to Francis Villiers, a permanent Foreign Office official and a great friend, that "in the end this people [of the United States] will not go to war unless they are clearly in the right. . . . There is no point where the interests of the United States and Great Britain are diametrically opposed and as neither wishes to take the other's territory there is no reason whatever why we should not enjoy a sort of peace tempered by newspaper articles." At which point he exploded: "But there isn't the slightest good trying to conciliate the U.S. You might just as well conciliate a jackal or a tiger."[25] As it turned out, Lord Salisbury's willingness to accommodate the United States in the border dispute contributed directly to an increase in Anglo-American cordiality. Such judgments as Spring Rice expressed on the matter were strangely prophetic of the dilemma faced by British diplomacy in World War I. At the same time it intimates his basic position after 1914: whatever the disagreement between the two powers, there was unlikely to be an irresolvable clash of vital interests.

The Foreign Office responded favorably to a request to be moved from the semitropical climate of Washington—Spring Rice had contracted malaria while in the Far East, and the hot, humid weather of the American capital he judged a danger to his health—by posting him to Berlin. There he would have the opportunity to examine the ways of *realpolitik* in its most forceful expression. Having just come out of an America whose national interests were not at odds with those of Great Britain, Spring Rice found himself at the center of a country, nay, an empire, that eyed British preeminence with envy and some hostility. The America he left behind was vulgar and publicly corrupt but democratic. The Germany to which he came was cultured and efficient but authoritarian. The leading personalities he encountered in Washington and Berlin added further contrast. The easygoing and open informality of a free society was quite unlike the stiff and ethnocentric habits of his German hosts. If a common Saxon bond and dynastic connection counted for something, a common language and cultural inheritance counted for more. For himself, Spring Rice was never bewitched by the idea of an Anglo-German alliance, whereas, within limits, he believed mightily in Anglo-American cooperation. All this may be said without any regard for history future when in 1895 he began his service under Sir Frank Lascelles, who had just been named ambassador to Germany. This suggests without proving it that Spring Rice's instinctive regard for the future welfare of his country was sound. Certainly much of what he learned of the German character and style was to influence his advice to the Foreign Office when it came to assess German moves in World War I. Referring to German propaganda in the United States as early as 1898, he called it "imperial German bombast and vituperation."[26]

The diplomatic action that Spring Rice longed for was his after 1895. The Venezuelan boundary dispute reached a boiling point in December when President Cleveland, by invoking the Monroe Doctrine, challenged the British position. "What a charming X-mas message of peace and goodwill comes to us from America!" Spring Rice exclaimed. "Well let them all go and be damned!" But American jingoism was nothing compared to German pretensions in South Africa. The Jameson Raid in January 1896, designed to intimidate the Boer farmers of the Transvaal, had, within two days, produced the Kruger telegram. The Kaiser's congratulations to President Kruger on a successful defense of independence was at once interpreted as German adventurism in a South Africa that the British had long considered one of the permanent "pink patches" on the map of world empire. Spring Rice's response to the news of the Jameson Raid was one of qualified support. "It is high time to show that whether we want to fight or not, we are ready. In this case I am sure we won't fight for we are in the wrong so far. But the outburst [of support in Great Britain] has just come in time to prevent Germany from being in the wrong on her side."[28] Part of his reasoning he explained to Villiers, saying that "there is no deep-seated hostility to England [in Germany]. We haven't yet attained the dignity of a 'natural enemy'."[29] Valentine Chirol, Berlin correspondent for *The Times* and "the most ardent advocate of a good understanding with Germany,"[30] had quickly befriended Spring Rice and at this early stage probably exercised some moderating influence on his views of the German menace. In the end, it was Chirol who came around to agree with Spring Rice's estimate of Germany as the main rival and most likely enemy of their country.

Anglo-German affairs worsened in the next years, which Spring Rice attributed to German envy of his country: the bone stuck in the German throat. Much of the trouble he thought derived from the continued unrest in South Africa leading on to the Boer War. This observation put it squarely: "The real and deep-seated object of German colonial policy is to find some part of the world where Germans can migrate and live as Germans. They look to South Africa, if ruled by the Dutch element, as such a place and therefore they will do everything possible to keep up the Dutch element."[31] There were additional reasons for Anglo-German friction. The prospect of a vast naval building program, the German thirst for colonies elsewhere than South Africa, including the Pacific, and the outlines of *der drang nach osten* were all occasions for worry.

Outbreak of war between the United States and Spain over Cuba temporarily distracted Spring Rice from his German phobia. A combination of American interests in Cuba and the demands of public opinion had made it impossible for President McKinley to resist a groundswell for war. This "splendid little war," as John Hay called it, saw all the European nations in moral support of Spain with only Great Britain favoring an American victory. Spring Rice saw immediately the implications for such an outcome in Cuba. The Caribbean would now be most definitely an American sphere of influence while possession of the Philippines also gave the United States a Far Eastern presence. In the alignment and realignment of the powers, a colonial America would enable it to shoulder some of the burden of maintaining the international status quo, a situation much to Britain's advantage. Friendship with the United States, which many in the Foreign Office now began to accept as a tiresome necessity, Spring Rice enthusiastically endorsed from his diplomatic perch in Berlin.

In America Spring Rice met many of the right people—Hay,
A. T. Mahan, Henry White, and Cabot Lodge, in addition to
Roosevelt—people who favored American overseas expansion;
he corresponded with many of them and, like them, believed
that wherever English speaking peoples took their language, law,
and other institutions, mankind was better off. It was one key
part of the cause of liberalism, and now he welcomed American
participation. Spring Rice had become decidedly pro-American.
Thus he wrote to John Hay, then serving as United States minister to London, regarding the presence of German warships in
Manila harbor well after the end of hostilities between Spain
and the United States. He said he told Prince Metternich that
America regarded the German ships as a threat and that it could
lead to unpleasant incidents. "Was Germany prepared to pay
the consequences and had his Government counted the cost?"
He went on to assure Hay that British official and public opinion
"would be opposed to any action on Germany's part which
would be unpleasant for America." These soothing sentiments
could hardly fail to touch Hay, who would soon be Secretary
of State.[32]

As Spring Rice rightly noted, the life of a diplomat involved
a great deal of "wandering about." He wrote to Ferguson from
Constantinople where in 1898 he was next assigned: "It does
seem an appalling way off [from London] but it is part of the
game."[33] His stay was a short one, but after that it was not
back to England but on to Teheran where he had been named
secretary of the legation. Whether Constantinople, Teheran, or
Cairo, he was getting a thorough immersion in Near Eastern
ways. Added together, these years from 1898 to 1903 had an
unexpected shaping effect on his life of the mind as well as
upon his *weltpolitik*. Constantinople was a unique point for
studying by observation the intrigues common to diplomacy.
Somewhere in the region, perhaps in Turkey or Persia, the vault-
ing ambitions of the Germans and Russians would clash, with
likely serious impact on the British position in that part of
the world. Spring Rice estimated that both these countries, given
their territorial ambitions, were a threat to the safety of the
empire.

Constantinople turned out to be quiet and uneventful. His
chief complaint was that he "had no opportunity of doing responsible work and the time is passed rather with the result
of making my mind rotten before it is ripe."[34] The situation
was doubly difficult because he lacked the companionship of

men and women, something he greatly enjoyed and greatly prized. He lamented to Nanny Lodge, the Senator's wife, "I am among complete strangers."[35] It was just as well that he was able to go to England for a short visit with a chance "to see my friends before diving into the wilderness." He hadn't the vaguest intimation of what awaited him in Persia.

Spring Rice was denied companionship in Teheran as he had been in Constantinople, but he delighted in the exotic and even mysterious life of ancient Persia. At first his pleasures were mostly visual. He rode each day for exercise and relaxation and what he saw and felt enthralled him. "All the circumstances here are delightful," he wrote Mrs. Lodge.[36] He retained a mirza who instructed him in Persian legend and philosophy; many of his teacher's thoughts found their way into his poetry. As his daily duties were not exacting, the time and the mood combined to allow him to indulge his passion for verse, with results that were brooding at times, or light and fanciful. And always came the release from the bondage of introspection by riding into the hills. Demavend, at 19,000 feet, "capped the mountain range with patches of snow, deep scented valleys full of running water, rocks and scented shrubs that burst their smells." He wrote to Luxmoore: "Darius passed beneath Demavend. One sees the Caspian from its top and there is Russia."[37] Ever present were thoughts of Russia and its ambitions when he stood close to the border. That aspect of Persia he did not like, sensing that "here is a universal desire for our ruin," overstated but based to a degree on what he saw of the Russians in action. Persia was weak and corrupt, and the Russians had loaned the Shah large sums of money that could not be repaid. The result was Russian ascendancy in an area where benign Persian neutrality was critical to the well-being of the British Empire. The Russian menace fed Spring Rice's pessimism.[38] He spoke of leaving the Foreign Office and government service altogether. The attractions of a literary life became an increasing temptation.

That Spring Rice did stay on may have resulted from the opportunity of serving under Lord Cromer in Cairo. Cromer, a man "who seems to know his own mind," was head of the *Caisse de la Dette Publique.* Spring Rice's appointment as the British commissioner in 1901 gave him access to one of the great colonial administrators, and it proved to be a welcome antidote to his mood in Teheran. Periods of anguish and depression are not uncommon for one of Spring Rice's temperament. In many ways he was a hopeless idealist—not an optimist, for optimism operates in the real world—who could revert to despair. As his ideals were high, his despair ran deep. Due partly to the less-than-demanding nature of his commissionership and partly to overriding personal concerns, Spring Rice now turned inward upon himself. His association with Lord Cromer lived up to expectations although his duties were routine, and the pay was excellent. Spring Rice yearned not for leisure and riches but for work and responsibility, yet Cromer's style of administration was such that he made the decisions and welcomed little assistance. He took particular notice of Spring Rice, nonetheless, and a friendship developed to the point that he sent him a copy of his book, *Modern Egypt*, and his later essays.[39]

Under the circumstances prevailing in Cairo, Spring Rice managed a trip to England as well as to America, where he was rejuvenated by seeing friends in both countries. But pleasantries were offset by the death of his brother Stephen. He wrote to Ferguson about it. "My brother was automatically a servant of the state, and naturally gave the best he had to give, because he couldn't help it. That is practically what killed him."[40] Unknowingly Cecil Spring Rice had pronounced his own epitaph.

In 1896, shortly after he began his tour of duty in Berlin, he met Florence Lascelles, the daughter of Sir Frank, his chief at the embassy. A friendship built up slowly but naturally, for they were a liked-minded couple. Theirs was truly a meeting of head and heart. Meanwhile his career took a new and exciting turn when he was named second secretary in the embassy at St. Petersburg. Romance and diplomacy were to flourish side by side.

Once in the Russian capital, Spring Rice was completely immersed in diplomacy, and this for two reasons. The embassy was of immense importance to the diplomatic game as it was then being played. The whole pace of European power politics was quickening, not to relent until the outbreak of war in 1914. Total war was the historical extension of total diplomacy. Furthermore, internal conditions in Russia, where demands for serious reform threatened to break over the barriers of law and order and come into open revolt, called for careful observation and assessment. Even as such events were taking shape, it appeared, momentarily at least, that Spring Rice might go back to Washington. Michael Herbert, the British ambassador there, had died suddenly. He was replaced by Mortimer Durand. An able man who knew little about America or its affairs, Durand might need a knowledgeable assistant. Spring Rice was an obvious choice. President Roosevelt would have welcomed the appointment, and the more so in retrospect because he and Durand were never able to get on. But the Foreign Office determined to keep one of its few American experts in St. Petersburg; Durand could be expected to make it on his own. Spring Rice made no protest or request for special consideration, reassured by Villiers that he could not be spared from the Russian assignment. Regard for his reporting of events was high at the Foreign Office, and if it was career success that more and more interested him, he had reason to be grateful to Villiers for his advice. And St. Petersburg was much closer to Berlin than was Washington. Christmas 1903 he spent with the Lascelles family in Germany, and his engagement to Florence was announced formally. Congratulations poured in from home and abroad. Mr. Luxmoore was greatly pleased, and Theodore Roosevelt was "delighted." The following June they were married in Berlin with the Imperial Guard standing in honor. During these weeks of personal happiness, Spring Rice was telling his government that there was a good chance Russia and Japan would soon be at war over control of Manchuria. "Somewhat imaginative" was one Foreign Office evaluation of this intelligence. Dated 4 November 1903, it went on to say "The Japanese have not any intention of going to war in order to turn the Russians out of Manchuria. If they do anything they would probably take some action in Corea."[41] But war did come the next year, and Spring Rice had been on target in his assessment. He was about to win his spurs as a diplomat.

The heavy defeat suffered by the Russians at Mukden in March 1905 and the destruction of their fleet at the battle of Tsushima in May propelled the new Japan to the front ranks of the powers who had a stake in east Asia. It also threatened to unsettle the balance of power there and elsewhere in the world. Theodore Roosevelt was keen to have the warring nations at the bargaining table and at the urging of Japan took the responsibility of bringing about a peace satisfactory to the combatants and other interested parties as well. In order to understand and coordinate Anglo-American moves in this regard, Lord Lansdowne agreed to send Spring Rice on a mission to Washington. Both the Americans and the British gained a better insight into the policies being pursued as a result of Spring Rice's private meetings with President Roosevelt.

When he returned to St. Petersburg later in 1905, the situation was such as to provide Spring Rice with additional responsibilities. He was chargé at the embassy from October until late May, 1906. These were parlous days in Russia. Bloody Sunday, 22 January, 1905—the protest led by Father Gapon at the Winter Palace—had ended in a hail of bullets, and soon thereafter the capital city and the nation were swept by a wave of strikes and civil disturbances. Military defeats in the Far East coupled with disorders at home gave Czar Nicholas the choice between further repression, the outcome of which was uncertain, and some concessions, the hoped-for compromise for meeeting the demands of the discontented segments in society. He chose to follow the latter course, but only grudgingly. Various manifestations of liberalization, including the naming of Count Witte as prime minister, failed to quell the spirit of rebellion. All these related events made life in the British embassy hectic and stressful. As chargé Spring Rice believed it prudent to act firmly but calmly as he settled the nerves of British residents in and near the capital and looked after a variety of British interests. This was not tea-cup diplomacy; it was more like the trenches with lives at risk unless a strong hand was applied. He had, of course, mastered Russian to the point of every day use, just as he had learned the languages of every country in which he had served. This was much appreciated by the Russian police with whom he had frequent dealings. "I have found the head of the police authority very good natured and helpful and have no cause to complain," he reported, a comment that nicely summed up the situation. Amidst the confusion and endless demands on his time, Spring Rice kept the diplomatic mail flowing and continued to write long, informative letters to his friends at home and in America. Explaining matters to Theodore Roosevelt had, by this date, become de riguer.

Reflecting the quickening pace of events in Russia, Spring Rice's career moved to this faster beat. In December he learned that he had been named minister to Teheran, thereby breaking into the outer ranks of senior diplomats. Lord Lansdowne made the appointment at the urging of King Edward VII, who had taken note of his successful mission to Washington. He was very much in "the king's good books." Apart from royal approval there were sound professional reasons why he should be dispatched to Persia as the senior British official. He understood the country and had measured the political climate there while at the same time his grasp of Russia's affairs, its psychology as well as its problems, could prove useful. This was especially so in light of the larger forces moving Great Britain in the direction of a rapprochement with Russia in respect to the balance of power in Asia Minor. An alert and able minister at Teheran was an important component in the unfolding of Great Britain's grand strategy for the area.

On 1 May, 1906, Florence Spring Rice gave birth to a baby girl, Mary Elizabeth, who quickly became Betty to the family. At forty-seven Cecil Spring Rice was older than most first time fathers but happy as any man could be at the news that his wife and daughter were doing well, that Mary Elizabeth was whole and healthy. He had sent his wife back to England from Russia. There was some reason to fear for her safety in those turbulent days, and after all, England was home. They had agreed that even barring unforeseen difficulty it was better for Florence's confinement to take place in London. With the birth of a son, Antony Theodore, two years later, the classic bachelor came to know the happiness he had discovered and envied in the families of his friends. This was no small thing to him.

Spring Rice was still in St. Petersburg when in June 1906 he learned that his name was on the King's birthday list for honors. Sir Edward Grey, who had succeeded Landsowne as Foreign Secretary, had made the recommendation, and the king was pleased "to confer . . . the Knight Commandership of St. Michael and St. George . . . in recognition of the valuable services you have rendered during the trying and arduous persual of your chargéship at St. Petersburg."[42] Again congratulations came from many quarters. The king's pleasure had set a seal of approval on him. Bernard Holland said it well when Spring Rice was given his second Persian assignment: "You are now approaching the heights of your profession."[43] Public honors and private happiness comingled as Spring Rice set off for Teheran.

The prospects in Persia were mixed, the one reassuring factor being that the new minister placed the greatest reliance on the judgment of Sir Edward Grey as foreign secretary. It was Grey as much as any individual who favored the Anglo-Russian entente that to Spring Rice remained a dubious proposition. Not even the counsel of Lord Cromer could shake Spring Rice's objections. He expressed himself trenchantly to Chirol: "As for the entente I consider it an excellent thing if it is not misunderstood. I should like to do like the county council on light bridges and put up a notice: 'This bridge is not intended for heavy traffic.' We mustn't mistake the whale for the island."[44] Yet the entente came into being and the question may be posed: was Grey or Spring Rice correct in his assessment? In the short term Grey appears the wiser statesman. When the crunch came in 1914 England and Russia stood with France. Yet in the course of the war Russia collapsed, as much due to internal decay as external attack, an event that gravely imperiled the Allied position on the Western Front. Spring Rice had spent enough time in the Russia of the Czars to be convinced that the country, or at least its government, was weak to the point of rotten. In sizing up the total geopolitical facts he was therefore distressed that Great Britain chose to put so many of its valuable eggs in a tattered basket; but such was Grey's ascendancy over his thinking that he loyally supported the foreign secretary's strategy.

Frustration at conducting affairs at Teheran derived from an awareness that strings were being pulled in London and St. Petersburg, that Persia had become a pawn in the increasingly tense game of power politics. Spring Rice's sympathy for the people of Persia and his desire to see them better governed and prosperous added to his gloomy mood. Fortunately for him, his wife and baby daughter had gone out with him and for that reason his daily routine, as he explained it to his sister Margaret, was quite pleasant. "I breakfast before eight. Then I go and give my horse an apple and then have a Persian lesson in my rooms. Then I go out and if I have time I trundle the pram. . . . We always dine alone if we can. . . . But I wish I were home; in five years from now I may have my pension. Till then I shall stick it out."[45] These last sentiments are hardly the words of a diplomat who believed that his Teheran assignment had placed him in the mainstream of British diplomacy. All in all, this second stay in Persia held little allure. He had changed no doubt since his first encounters there, and Persia was changing as well. He thought of himself as a minister unable to influence the policies of the country to which he was accredited, so far as this would best serve the interests of Great Britain.

Time in Persia took its toll in other ways. His health deteriorated to a dangerous level, and he returned home to England for a period of rest. "I have been ill—under a doctor—operated and then in a nursing home (nothing dangerous)," he informed Roosevelt in December 1907. The whole tenor of his attitude was negative, and he spoke again of possible retirement from the service: "The traces begin to rub a little."[46] England's wellbeing remained an imperative that chained him to duty. Despite official inactivity he continued to be deeply worried by international developments that menaced his country. The bugbear of Germany now came sharply into focus. Among other things he considered it vital to speak out in favor of universal military service as essential to national survival. The benefits of such training he had witnessed in Germany years before, and they had produced a lasting impression. Now, in 1907, Germany was the rival nation most to be feared. An active German enemy so well prepared for war was a sobering thought. Spring Rice's often-noted pessimism was in this instance realism of a high order, but his plea, along with that of a few other spokesmen for national preparedness, went unheeded.

Despite physical and diplomatic collapse, Spring Rice was soon fit again for duty and a fresh assignment. In July 1908, he was given the post of minister to Sweden and took up his duties shortly thereafter. "I am very much pleased with the apointment, which just suits me," he told Ferguson.[47] If this remark be taken literally, it is fair to speculate that Spring Rice judged his career to be in the descendency, that he was merely "sticking it out." Grey struck just that note when he wrote: "I hope you like Stockholm, it ought to be a comfortable place."[48] The one thing that heartened him was the frank and cordial interest shown him by the King. He was willing to take Spring Rice into his confidence, and given Edward VII's taste for foreign affairs, there remained a slim possibility of influencing the direction of large policies through communications with the sovereign.

For all of that, Stockholm was an outpost, a northern Teheran. Generally Spring Rice was in a dark frame of mind, a mood deepened by the absence of his wife and children, who did not immediately join him. Yet it was more than personal loneliness that bore down his spirit. As early as 1908 it struck him that a general European war would be virtually an irrepressible conflict. More particularly, he continued to worry about the naval race between Britain and Germany as it accelerated. The threat to British naval supremacy was real, and with it came a threat to England and the empire. Not only the dreadnoughts that were being built but the expanded capacity of the German shipyards alarmed him. Should Berlin decide to push forward, could his country afford to keep up? He also suspected that the German military command might be devising plans to drop high explosives from aircarft, as old worries and new worries combined.

Professional and personal concerns affected one another. His daughter had to return to England for medical treatment. He was distraught at the thought of failed surgery and thus greatly relieved by news that the operation was a success. Little Betty's troubles went away, but England's vulnerability remained a stubborn reality. It is understandable why some senior members of the Foreign Office found Spring Rice's pessimism defeatist in tone, or that excessive pessimism could produce overreaction. Historians have thus been moved to assess his Washington ambassadorship as flawed by the same kind of mind-set. What needs to be kept clear is a distinction between his duties and responsibilities in Stockholm and in Washington. The former was a listening post and little more, and there was not a great deal for Spring Rice to do. In his frustration he made every effort to place his fears of German aggression and British weakness before the public by contacts with some of the leading journals, including *The National Review, The Spectator,* and of course *The Times.* In Washington, in contrast, there was scope for him to act. There the same ghosts haunted him—German power, British weakness—but he was in a position to guard his country's interests by an active diplomacy.

Meanwhile there was Stockholm. Luckily Spring Rice was on leave in England when Theodore Roosevelt came to London in June of 1910, the last stop of the Teddyssey. Sadly, it was then that King Edward died, and Spring Rice lost both a king and a supporter. The vitality of Roosevelt contrasted sharply in his thoughts with the dead sovereign, and he went back to Sweden in August greatly discouraged. Adding to his woes, the Swedish climate contributed to new physical ailments. Breathing was difficult for him because of asthma and late in the year he had a severe bout with influenza and an attack of erysipelas that nearly took his life. With his health impaired and the Stockholm ministry not the prized recognition it seemed at first to imply, Cecil Spring Rice's fortunes were at a low ebb.

As months became years in Stockholm, Spring Rice was made to realize that he faced two alternatives: retirement or promotion. Turning fifty-two in 1911, retirement, except for reason of health, was premature. Yet promotion was uncertain. He had served successively in two backwaters, Teheran and Stockholm. Such appointments might be interpreted as a sign of limited confidence in his ability, traceable to a negative outlook. In late December 1911, he got the first inkling of his future. In a private letter Sir Edward Grey sounded him out on his willingness to go to Washington as ambassador. Lord Bryce, then the envoy, had indicated a desire to step down, and the foreign secretary had proposed Spring Rice's name to the prime minister. When Bryce chose to delay his resignation until 1912 in the interest of clearing up the dispute over tolls for the Panama Canal, Sir Cecil suspected the offer might be withdrawn. This was not the case. Grey explained that with the presidential election taking place, and especially in view of Theodore Roosevelt's candidacy, it would be wiser to postpone any announcement of his appointment until the political dust had settled. Once Woodrow Wilson was elected, the Spring Rice ambassadorship was formalized. As for the post itself, the ambassador-designate was cautious; he spoke his mind to Ferguson. It was, he said, "an immense relief to have got what is considered the final step in one's profession. . . . As for the post, you know as well as I do how impossible it is to 'succeed' in the newspaper sense . . . [but] I don't see that it shouldn't be possible to make a fair job of it."[49] One very important consideration was that his wife and children could live with him safely and comfortably, for as Spring Rice got older, he felt more and more the pain of separation from those he loved most. His caution about the ambassadorship contrasted sharply with the elation felt by his friends. Roosevelt gave "three cheers"; Curzon sent "earnest congratulations"; Luxmoore wrote: "It really overjoys me that you should be so honored."[50]

Even as diplomatic tensions rose and miniwars raged (the Balkan War of 1912 for example) and jingoism prevailed, few men could bring themselves to accept the idea of a general war among the powers. The potential for mass destruction was so great that hope and reason alike rejected it. Spring Rice had frequently alluded to "some grand smash-up" without beginning to conceive the magnitude of the catastrophe that it eventually became. He came to Washington in April 1913, intent on representing his country in the best way possible, which for him meant promoting Anglo-American understanding. The world war made this task exceedingly difficult as oftentimes the policies of the London and Washington governments were at odds and were perceived in both capitals as being at odds. How to respond to this divergence, how to advise his government in treating it, how best to tell the Wilson administration of the views of his government, how to neutralize hostile public opinion emanating from the German- and Irish-Americans in the United States, how to walk softly and carry a big stick in the discharge of his duties—these were among the many questions Spring Rice had to contemplate from August 1914 onward.

How he discharged his responsibilities as ambassador requires a careful review of his work. In his own mind it was certain that he succeeded, at great personal cost, by driving himself relentlessly. His quiet diplomacy, in contract to that of his German counterpart, Count von Bernstorff, had its part to play in American entry into the war in 1917. Yet his path from that of third secretary at the British legation in Washington in 1887 to embassy chief had run in anything but a straight line. Spring Rice's ultimate destiny was not ordained. Hardinge, for example, saw him as ambassador to Paris or Tokyo, and the vagaries of Foreign Office personnel policy might easily have placed him elsewhere than Washington. That he had kept in close touch with a number of highly placed Americans might imply that all along he had been priming himself for the appointment. Such a proposition would do less than justice to Spring Rice's inner need for friends. If they happened to be influential people, or were to become such, this was incidental to his genuine fondness for Ronald Ferguson or Theodore Roosevelt or Henry Cabot Lodge. He rejoiced in his friends to a degree that, as with few other individuals, it may be said: to know his friends was to know Spring Rice.

3

Until his untimely death in 1902, no single individual was a more trusted confidant than Spring Rice's older brother, Stephen. The foundation of their friendship, although it obviously was partly a kinship of blood, went well beyond that, resting ultimately on the respect and admiration of a younger brother. It is an easy matter to stress their similarities—collegers at Eton, successful university careers, conscious awareness of service to institutions they both revered, and love of country. But they were different as boys and thus as men. There may be discovered in their differences as well as their likenesses the strands that bound them together. Stephen was a person of bearing, verging on *gravitas*, who as a young man had taken up the headship of the family. Cecil, in contrast, was much less sober and predictable, which he realized did not always work to his advantage. Stephen's concern for his younger brother touched Cecil deeply. He was suspicious of the effects of study that was not serious and to the point; this very absence of imagination in Stephen supplied Cecil with the necessary balance, intellectual and emotional, to point the way to the sterner realities of living. Stephen fully approved of his brother's career in the Foreign Office. He would have been less happy had Cecil gravitated to what was for him the less certain world of *belles lettres*. Not that he was insensitive; he loved the Lake District and Ullswater but in a fashion different from Cecil. Stephen was after the manner of St. Paul's injunction that a man should put on the things of a man.

Stephen's expectations of him Cecil revealed in a letter written to his brother from Washington in 1887. "With some difficulty I have established the reputation of *homme serieux* and now can talk with an old man without being considered mad. . . . [Henry] Adams is a rather interesting sort of cynic and I had a really jolly evening with him last night talking about England and America."[51] Because he appreciated Stephen's versatility of mind, he often related stories of American politics and personalities and (displaying his yen for telling a good yarn) tales from American folklore. He was eager as well to tell his brother what he learned of American financial matters and measures taken by the Treasury Department to solve problems, as they befit writing to a British Treasury official. And he was fond of passing along the current gossip. He took delight in relating details of Joseph Chamberlain's 1887 visit to the United States, complaining at first that he thought it was a mistake as it could have an adverse effect on the British export trade but admitting that in the end Chamberlain had achieved real success. "It was great fun watching the proceedings."[52] Such was the intimacy of the brothers that when Stephen married and Cecil was unable to come to London because of legation duty, he knew Stephen would understand.

A steady exchange of letters when Cecil was first in America revealed a consistent statement of their public morality. It surfaced from Cecil's reporting of widespread corruption in American local and national politics. Regarding efforts by business to thwart legislation intended to regulate corporations in the public interest, he related the boast of one company president: "We very seldom have to spend much money—but of course in states where the legislature is hostile to us we are compelled to corrupt their politics in self-defense."[53] To the brothers Spring Rice, such conduct was simply intolerable. From accounts of his travels and stays with various families both rich and well connected, Stephen could only conclude that his younger brother was indeed getting on in a world inhabited by powerful people.

When in Japan, Cecil chose Stephen to be the recipient of his extensive journal notes describing the country's physical beauty and the people and their political system. It was an arresting account, pleasing because of what Stephen was able to learn about a faraway land, strange yet enticing. What was more important, he saw the journal as evidence that Cecil was developing skill as an observer and reporter. Having assumed the task of guiding his brother, Stephen would have been deflated if he thought his career was not progressing.

There were occasions when the government work of the two intersected. From Berlin Cecil told of "doing a large financial report which will, I suppose, be printed in time and reach you. I shall be interested to see what you think of it. I know nothing of finances but tried from a common sense point of view to understand something about it."[54] What Stephen made of Cecil's enchantment with Persian mysticism is another matter, but his involvement would not allow the younger brother to disguise his intense feelings as he translated folk tales into English along with the daily lessons with his mirza. As these comments were interspersed with mundane observations on the Boer War or the Russian efforts to suborn the Shah, Stephen had good reason to believe that the requisite balance between the routine of serious work and flights of romantic imagination remained intact. He was bemused when Cecil was detailed to Cairo as a member of the *Caisse*, well aware of his amateur's grasp of finances, and alarmed at his complaint that his governmental career might end with his service under Lord Cromer. Cecil explained to Stephen: "I have been taking lessons in finance; little I know about it."[55] He was comfortable crying on an older brother's shoulder.

In the summer of 1902 Stephen Spring Rice, exhausted by his work at the treasury, fell ill. He planned a rest and thought to visit his brother in Cairo. Cecil was delighted. "Keep up and rest and don't bother, and you will have a great time in Egypt,"[56] he wrote him. But Stephen was far too sick to travel and died within weeks of announcing his plans to visit. "This is the end of many things, I don't know what it all means, or what to think. I can't realize it at all," he confided to his sister, Margaret.[57] Family lore that Spring Rices named Stephen died young and were greatly mourned was sadly perpetuated.

H. E. Luxmoore was to become a legend at Eton College. *Letters From Luxmoore*, selections from correspondence with a number of his students who went on to accomplishment, revealed in him a range of interests and sensibilities to life's crises that endeared him to generations of old Etonians. Cecil Spring Rice was one of his favorite old boys. Legends exude an air, but they must have their beginning in time. Spring Rice encountered Luxmoore just as the legend was taking shape. Even in his mature years he could not quite divorce himself from the original tutor-student way of sharing thoughts. It is rather disarming to read His Majesty's ambassador to Washington addressing a letter: "My Dear Tutor." Spring Rice was then fifty-five years old. This particular letter, dated 24 September, 1914, contained a moving expression of his public philosophy and the cause in which he believed. He had been explaining to Luxmoore some of the techniques of German propaganda, and that led him to expound the position from which he never deviated during his years as wartime ambassador. "I am not much in favor of asking for sympathy," he wrote. "We shall stand or fall by what we do, and not by what other people think; and I don't like fierce efforts to convince Americans that we are in the right. The question is, is freedom strong enough to defend itself. A government is either too strong for the freedom of its own people, or too weak to defend them from a foreign enemy. We chose the last form. However, if there is justice or truth in the world, we shall win in the end; and if there is no justice or truth, it isn't worth living here—so we can leave it at that."[58] This was just the kind of confession of conviction that Luxmoore was still able to draw out and that Spring Rice felt entirely comfortable in making to his old tutor.

In exchanging ideas with Luxmoore, Spring Rice chose to vary the old phrase about Eton and its playing fields. He was more concerned with its "pupil rooms," which were critical to the nation and its future. "How are our future leaders?" he asked as he surveyed the world from Constantinople in 1898. "Are they physically healthy and mentally vigorous, have they the courage of body and mind?" Luxmoore was able to reassure him. "I think there is plenty of good fighting spirit left in our young men."[59] Spring Rice had no reason to believe that Etonians who came after him would not measure up to their calling as servants of the kingdom, but he needed Luxmoore's word on it as he stood in the midst of a city that once was Christian but had fallen to a foe more powerful and more determined. It was the march of history, and it filled Spring Rice with alarm.

Luxmoore was someone to whom Spring Rice might express himself fully and without restraint. His dislike of Jowett when he was at Oxford, as he explained it to Luxmoore, bears this out. "Moses and Job and Solomon and Christ lived and died that their lives might suggest to Dr. Jowett sundry platitudes and truisms, and if the facts are not exactly and correctly stated why, they make a very edifying allegory in which Dr. Jowett's young friends may live and move and have their commonplace being."[60] He had left no room for doubt about his regard for the master of Balliol. Years later he offered a candid appraisal of Lord Curzon, his wit laced with acrimony. "Is Britain great so that India may be ruled by G. Curzon?"[61] Luxmoore was not always the willing listener. Passing criticism of others he might tolerate, but he sometimes found Spring Rice's negativism too much to bear in silence. After receiving a particularly despondent letter from Spring Rice, who was then preparing to leave Teheran for Cairo—the year was 1901—the old tutor replied: "I want to scold you a bit." He saw in him a "willingness to accept the inevitable and go out to meet it." This he put down to Spring Rice's infatuation with the East, "where your largeness of sympathy puts you in touch with the Oriental submission to fate and the philosophic indifference to petty objects about which such a dust is raised in [our] society and politics."[62] Such advice filled a need in Spring Rice to combat the dampening effects of fatalism and personal detachment. On another occasion and with some asperity, Luxmoore remonstrated with him for his preoccupation with self, saying that he was "pacing the shore of your island alone,"[63] which he advised was unhealthy and uncalled for, and the intimations of which he had identified when Spring Rice was his pupil at Eton.

Luxmoore had made the point about the ravages of loneliness at the time Spring Rice was engaged to Florence Lascelles. "Always I have been hoping in later years that you would complete your life and find that other half that somewhere must be. You of all people seemed to me to need it for full achievement. . . . You will do much more with your great powers and possible opportunities."[64] Luxmoore was correct. Marriage and the birth of children meant more to him with each passing year. He thought his daughter and his son "as much pleasure as pain" because he was constantly concerned for their welfare and, pessimist that he could be, was ever fearful for their health and safety. Luxmoore knew his man well.

Luxmoore was full of pride as he watched his pupil move up the diplomatic ladder and certain that his conduct of affairs in Washington had at last brought America into the war; he described it as "the crowning success of your mission . . . the main credit is yours." It was left to Luxmoore to record in *The Eton College Chronicle* the loss suffered by Eton, by England, by Sir Cecil's wife and children, and last of all by himself with the death of Spring Rice. They would not be fellow-pensioners sharing a farm in Devon, as Spring Rice once mused, after all.[65]

Ronald Munro Ferguson and Spring Rice came together in 1886 at the Foreign Office. Their respective posts, Ferguson as parliamentary private secretary to Lord Rosebery and Spring Rice as his précis writer, brought them close as they supported the work of the foreign secretary. Ferguson was a Scot, a year junior to Spring Rice. He trained at Sandhurst and had spent five years in the Grenadier Guards. His family had a landed estate in Novar. In 1884 he was elected a member of the House of Commons for Ross and Cromarty. He was to have a distinguished parliamentary career, retaining his seat down to 1914, when he was named governor-general of Australia. With the war Ferguson put his military expertise to good purpose in the mobilization of Australian forces.

Like Spring Rice, Ferguson had a brother who migrated to the New World, but to the United States rather than Canada, and who in fact had served with Roosevelt's Rough Riders during the Spanish-American War. Like Spring Rice, Ferguson was also talked about as a possible British ambassador to the United States in 1907, when Lord Bryce was named. They saw each other whenever and wherever they could and kept up an active correspondence. Much of it concentrated on personal matters, but they also discussed affairs of state. Their letters reveal the chemical bond that linked them—never a harsh word or false note, never a straining to reach accord whether they were discussing politics or personalities. Ferguson put it well in a letter sent as a follow-up to a visit Spring Rice had paid him in Scotland. "There is no friendship I feel as close as yours, and sometimes I presume on it. God bless you, dear Springey. . . .

I was glad to see you look better . . . and I wish more than anything else I had spent the whole day with you on Monday."[66] Spring Rice's affection was gladly given. They were both tender–hearted men. When death took his old friend, Ferguson wrote to Lady Spring Rice: "You have this for consolation, that all that was worth having in friendship at home and in America, and elsewhere too, was Springey's by right. Half the world seems dead with him—at least for me."[67]

As young men in the Foreign Office they had found one another good company, sharing the hard work with lighter moments. Ferguson always said that Spring Rice wrote his campaign speeches and he merely delivered. "I hope you won't blacken your opponent more than you absolutely have to," he warned Ferguson good-naturedly when he was electioneering, "because even if you hit him some of the dirt sticks to your hands."[68] Spring Rice's influence on his politician friend could be real. On the troubling issue of government for Ireland, Ferguson conceded that Spring Rice's arguments persuaded him to support home rule.

There was no issue in British politics down to 1916 that the two did not discuss, but they concerned themselves especially with Anglo-American good will, the threat posed by likely German and Russian aggression, and the need for universal military training as the best defense of Britain's interests. As a former soldier and future military organizer, Ferguson was alive to the latter issue, and his worry increased with the ongoing German military and naval buildups before 1914. He persuaded Spring Rice of the urgency of national peacetime military service, although the latter needed little urging. Spring Rice's pessimism was goaded by Ferguson's often-expressed concerns. At the time of the Boer War, they were in agreement that the jingoes were an embarrassment but the war must be fought nonetheless. "We couldn't retire without a fight and we should have had to, the moment we got into a tight place elsewhere."[69] Spring Rice was hardly a warmonger, however. In reference to the Dogger Bank incident of 1904—the accidental sinking of a British trawler by trigger-happy units of the Russian fleet as it passed the Dogger Bank—he admitted to Ferguson, "We could not go to war because we were not sure of the facts . . . the only solution was to arrive at the facts."[70] This was a sane position to espouse and quite defensive at that.

When Spring Rice had the facts, and with his powers of divination he knew where the facts would lead, he could be outspoken. He was one of the very few in the whole government establishment who consistently warned his superiors about the threat posed by the German armaments program, and one of the fewer still who pleaded for a conscription law. "I want to see compulsory military service as the only means of saving us physically, and also of preventing us from getting into little and big wars. The people would think twice about them if they all had to fight," he remarked in what was an unmistakable barb aimed at the jingo press.[71] But his superiors thought this sort of agitation alarmist, as Ferguson had been quick to caution him. Spring Rice remained undaunted. "If I am wrong," he replied to Ferguson, "it matters only to me. If the government is wrong it matters very gravely to all of us."[72] Once he had taken the bit of universal service in his teeth, yoked with an equally determined Ferguson, he was not to let go. The question of whether the lack of a conscription law helped or hurt Great Britain at the start of World War I is no longer debatable. If the nation had been half as well prepared for ground warfare as for sea battles, it is further arguable that Germany might not have waged a Western European campaign at all or that, had it done so, the stalemate on the Western Front might have been averted. The German view of the British army—did not Bismarck once remark that if the British army landed on the German coast he would send a policeman to arrest it—was one of contempt. Had England been better prepared, as Spring Rice and Ferguson among a few others had urged, it would not have had to rely on the raw courage of the "old contemptibles." Waging the uphill battle for military preparedness brought Spring Rice and Ferguson closer together as on the eve of the Great War one set out for America and the other for Australia.

In his varied adventures in diplomacy, East and West, Cecil Spring Rice made many friends and surely one or more enemies. Of his friends, a number spring to mind at once: Edward Grey, Francis Villiers, Gerald Balfour, Michael Herbert, and, on the American side of the Atlantic, William Jennings Bryan, Don Cameron, Jack Morgan, not to mention Theodore Roosevelt, Henry Cabot Lodge (and their wives), John Hay, and Henry Adams. It would be an easy matter to extend the list. But it was left to one of his closest friends, Valentine Chirol, to write the first short account of his life and work, *Sir Cecil Spring Rice In Memoriam.*[73] As the title suggests, it was a tribute to a man Chirol dearly loved and with whom he had been a close associate since their meeting in Berlin in 1895. Valentine Chirol was a cosmopolitan. Born in England, educated in France and Germany, and a graduate of the Sorbonne, he served as a Foreign Office clerk before beginning his worldwide travels. Acquainted with Australia as well as India, Persia, and Egypt, he wrote serious books while simultaneously working as a journalist, filing stories from abroad for the London *Evening Standard* before joining the staff of *The Times*.

Two main considerations bore on their friendship. Chirol was close to the Lascelles family. He had been befriended by Sir Frank in Berlin and came to know and admire Florence Lascelles. In 1899 when Chirol was named foreign editor of *The Times*, Spring Rice gained unusual access to one of the most important newspapermen in London. Once back in England, Chirol was often at Ullswater and treated as part of the family. His abiding esteem for Spring Rice fully justified his effort to convey to contemporaries and historians the essence of the man. According to him, Spring Rice had a true sense of the beauty of things in nature, from which he drew daily inspiration; at the same time he had contempt for the ways of *realpolitik*, especially as practiced in Berlin. In commenting on the death of Bismarck, Spring Rice remarked to Chirol that the master of *realpolitik* had allowed himself just one emotion, the will to hate.[74] As a diplomat, Spring Rice took it to be his duty to promote peace, not war. Chirol analyzed one or two commonplaces about the Spring Rice temperament. His much-commented-on pessimism was, he insisted, no more than opposition to the easy optimism prevailing in Britain down to 1914. If he was "high strung and somewhat excitable," he was saved "by a keen sense of humor which he exercised upon himself as much as others."[75] Chirol has thrown light into other obscure corners of his friend's persona. He was "impulsive and somewhat impatient" in small matters, but on the great issues with which he was confronted, his judgment, based on careful study and genuine knowledge, was seldom at fault."[76] If this seems like overgenerous praise from a close friend, it is well to bear in mind two or three of Spring Rice's judgments on "the great issues." He was correct in assessing German intentions to dominate Europe by aggressive warfare, irrespective of the ententes with France and Russia to which England had made a commitment. His views of military preparedness were sound. He exercised foresight in helping to promote Anglo-American accord. How right he was, and to what degree his detractors were wrong about his conduct of the Washington embassy, will be considered in later chapters. Here it may be appropriate to quote one of America'a leading newspaper editors. Frank Cobb of the *New York World*, in a letter to Spring Rice 23 January, 1918, summed up his work neatly:

> The British and American people are under a very deep debt of obligation to you for the manner in which you handled the most delicate and difficult task since the beginning of the war. Looking at the results I do not see how it could have been better done. There was never a situation in which Talleyrand's motto, *surtout pas trope de zêle*, represented a more vital diplomatic and international policy. If you had done what some of your critics insisted upon having done in the way of propaganda, I believe a fatal mistake would have been committed. It was fortunate indeed that you have the intuitive understanding to hold the balance level.[77]

There was nothing in Cobb's statement with which Chirol would disagree.

When Spring Rice met Chirol, *The Times* correspondent was friendly to Germany. At first, in fact, Spring Rice discerned reasons to support Anglo-German accord. In a letter to Villiers he spoke of "the great mercantile circles who know what enormous interests we have in common and how fatal a war would be" with England.[78] As it turned out, it was not the merchants but the German military that both Chirol and Spring Rice came to fear. Chirol suspected the Germans once the kaiser dismissed Count Caprivi, a minister who displayed no war-like intentions. The Kruger telegram deepened his distrust. How much Spring Rice influenced Chirol's change of front is difficult to say. Drawing on his own experiences and his studied approach to foreign affairs, Chirol was more than capable of forming an independent judgment. One thing is certain, however, and that is that Spring Rice rarely missed an opportunity to denounce German ambitions.[79] Once Chirol was firmly in place at *The Times* in London, Spring Rice wrote him frequently from Constantinople, Teheran, and St. Petersburg. They were full-length communications replete with detail, reflections, and gossip, which enabled Chirol to write with added authority on foreign affairs wherever Spring Rice was posted. Spring Rice's profile of Chirol, contained in a letter to Theodore Roosevelt, is well worth notice. As he indicated to the President, Chirol "was a great traveller, has written the best small book on China and the best large or small book on Persia. He is the best informed man on European questions, especially German questions . . . whom I know. His influence at *The Times* is supreme."[80] This evaluation, given in 1904, would have been reason enough why Spring Rice was keen to have his ear, had they not also been close friends for a decade.

By any measure Theodore Roosevelt was the most esteemed of Spring Rice's American friends, and certainly the most influential public man he came to know personally. This is not to diminish in any way his friendship with Sir Edward Grey when he was foreign secretary and Spring Rice was ambassador, for they were a remarkably effective team during the first years of the war. But the Spring Rice-Roosevelt relationship was something special, in a way a microcosm of the "special relationship." They were diverse characters: Roosevelt was the man of action, Spring Rice, of reflective disposition. Born a year apart, scarcely twelve months separated them in death. The introspective vein in Roosevelt's makeup was resilient enough to provide a tangible response to his friend's poetic instinct. Roosevelt's curiosity about Spring Rice's diplomatic adventures was insatiable, so that he wrote innumerable letters rich in description of the things he witnessed, the people he met, and the historical forces that seemed to be at work shaping and at times threatening the future of their peoples. From Berlin in July 1896, Spring Rice offered his impressions of the German military. "As a matter of fact, the soldiers one sees (and regiments go by every day) look splendidly, marching proud and looking pleased and proud. It must be in the long run good for a nation to take all the young men of a certain age for two years—clean them, feed them, drill them, teach them obedience and patriotism, and train their bodies. The officers are rather different to ours. A prince (and there are a number of them) has to do exactly as the others do—that is, get up at five and work with his men and his own training until four in the afternoon."[81] Only partly did Spring Rice recount such an impression because of Roosevelt's martial enthusiasm. Equally important and equally valuable for seeing to the core of their friendship were the possible implications with the rise of the new Germany for the Anglo and American nations. In this same letter Spring Rice introduced another note that underscored his profound uneasiness about the future—the specter of Russia. "I think the Russians have got the Chinese now whenever they like . . . and when they command and drill the Northern Chinese they will be a pretty big power—such a power as the world has never seen."[82] Often in the years ahead, Spring Rice and Roosevelt would ponder together the ambitions of Germany, the destiny of Russia, the uncertainties of the Orient, and in what ways Great Britain and the United States, or the two nations working as one, must act to protect themselves.

Roosevelt's reply to this early letter disclosed further dimensions of their mutual fondness. He told Spring Rice how he and his wife had eagerly read and reread his news, and had repeated parts of it to their children. "As you know," Roosevelt wrote, "we are not fond of many people, and we are very fond of you, and if you don't come back to America for ten years, yet whenever you do, you will find us just as anxious to see you as we always were in the old days in Washington."[83] Spring Rice was witty, urbane, and keen on the Roosevelt children. In what were bachelor days for him, the Roosevelt family life was very attractive. During these years he came to value the friendship of Edith Carow Roosevelt. "Mrs. Roosevelt always refers to your last visit as one during which she really got more and more glad that you were in the house, so that she felt as if one of the family had gone when you left," TR confided.[84] As the years went by, Spring Rice wrote Edith Roosevelt frequently, especially when Roosevelt was president. He had her confidence and at times felt that it was more discreet to express himself fully to her regarding pending delicate issues, assured that the president would receive his message. Spring Rice was not merely exploiting his acceptance by Edith Roosevelt. As often, his letters dealt with family matters and the children, with tales of happy adventures or nostalgic references to past pleasures, and, because Spring Rice was a poet, an occasional romantic description of Santa Sophia or the Persian countryside. Perhaps he found it easier to write his deepest feelings about TR to his friend's wife rather than to him directly. "The more I think of Theodore, and I think of him constantly—I believe every day of my life—I think I know him as pure, high, noble and devoted character as it is ever possible to find in our present world."[85] These words leave little doubt of his affection. Occasionally sentiment did break through as when he wrote directly to TR to congratulate him on his election as governor of New York. The letter concluded: "The great thing is to retain the power of being fond of people and I have done that and most especially of you." Mrs. Roosevelt's letters reciprocated Spring Rice's feelings. "I wish you knew how often we speak of you and how much we want to see you," she wrote when he was first in Persia.[86]

Such personal feelings motivated the president to prefer Spring Rice as British ambassador to the United States when the London government undertook to name a successor to Sir Julian Pauncefote in 1903. "Good heavens, how I wish you were ambassador here!" he exclaimed quite frankly. "There are fifty matters about affairs in the Far East and you could be of great service to your own country as well as this country."[87] When the ambassadorial appointment came in 1913, Roosevelt could only say: "But now I feel horribly at not being president."[88]

"You must always remember that the President is about six,"[89] Spring Rice took occasion to advise Valentine Chirol. This remark is often quoted to expose the childishness of Roosevelt or the cynicism of its author. But can it tell something about the Spring Rice-Roosevelt relationship? The comment was made to Chirol after Spring Rice had given him a warm letter of introduction to the president. But theirs was a disappointing meeting, despite the ardor of Spring Rice's favor, so that in writing to Chirol as he did, he was trying to soothe the latter's frustration at not winning the president's acceptance. No doubt wit exceeded good judgment in the remark. Spring Rice himself must have felt let down that his two friends did not become friends in turn. A similar feeling of disappointment on the part of Spring Rice and Roosevelt became visible when some practical issue divided their two countries. England and the United States alike preferred a settlement of such disagreements along the lines of their own national interest. The controversy over the Alaska boundary was a clear illustration of this. In like fashion, Spring Rice found in Roosevelt and Chirol people of whom he was genuinely fond, but he would not allow his liking for one blind him to the other. This was the strength of the Anglo-American special relationship as conceived by both men: national advantage must be pursued even at the expense of the other partner. That diverse national interest did not finally divide England and America but curiously added strength to their informal entente was due to common Anglo-American commitments that transcended specific disagreements. As for the two friends, disagreements and quirks of character aside— Spring Rice's relentless wit and Roosevelt's frenetic ways—they were brothers by belief if not by blood.

Roosevelt was a friend of Spring Rice; Henry Cabot Lodge

was TR's boon companion. It was inevitable that Spring Rice and Lodge would meet. Unlike Chirol and Roosevelt, Spring Rice and Lodge clicked at once. They were both scholarly men, fond of books, devoted to the reading of history, and absorbed by public affairs at home and abroad. Such considerations fed a natural attraction and their acquaintanceship ripened into mutual esteem during Spring Rice's second American tour. Yet there were conflicting elements present as well. Lodge was a powerful Massachusetts politician who had a well-earned reputation as an Anglophobe. Twisting the lion's tail was a favorite compaign device of many successful American politicians, and Lodge was one of the leaders of the pack. His purpose was not simply to win votes with the old Yankees and the new Irish in his constituency. A direct descendant of revolutionaries in eighteenth-century Massachusetts, the colony that was the hotbed of rebellion, he and his state took second place to none in keeping the memories of the fight for independence alive. It was somewhat ironic that no section of the United States was more like old England than New England, with Massachusetts as its center piece. Suspicions of England ran deep, perhaps more so among the classes than the mass of people. Lodge continued to push his anti-British views well after he met and made friends with Spring Rice. When it came to politics there was hardly an ounce of sentiment in Lodge's makeup. His attitude softened eventually. In the aftermath of the Spanish-American War, he began to understand that the fates of Great Britain and the United States might well be bound together. In August 1898, Lodge wrote to Spring Rice: "The movement you describe as going on in the East is undoubtedly true and I can not but help think that our appearance in that part of the world will strengthen England, which of necessity must always remain the great eastern power. One of the general results of the war has been the coming together of the English-speaking people and I am optimist enough to think that this is going to last." As events continued to reinforce that proposition, Spring Rice told Lodge that he believed "the U.S. to be the fortress of our race and it is an infinite satisfaction to see prosperity and power [there]."[90]

Like Roosevelt, Lodge judged matters in terms of American national interest, which carried with it a touch of *realpolitik*. Spring Rice came at Anglo-American affairs in much the same way; however, he deplored the term *realpolitik*. It was for this reason that Lodge attempted to persuade the Foreign Office to

send Spring Rice to Washington in 1903. He believed that few
if any British diplomatic staff had the mastery of the American
political situation equal to his friend's; but Spring Rice remained
on his Russian assignment.

Cecil Spring Rice sought out and greatly enjoyed the company
of charming, talented women. His fondess for Nanny Lodge
gave a special character to his feeling for the Lodge family.
He certainly admired Edith Roosevelt, but he said to Mrs. Lodge:
"I adore you, as you know."[91] This attraction was intense but
not sensuous; it was profoundly moving. He was at times mes-
merized by Nanny Lodge, a woman all observers agreed was
truly remarkable. He enjoyed ready access to the Lodge homes
in Washington and at Nahant and recounted to others some
of the happy times spent there with the senator and his wife.
Their style of living became his ideal—its pleasures, its diver-
sions, its conversations, as well as in the deeper meaning Spring
Rice attached to marriage. Over this sunlit scene clouds came
in the form of personal tragedy. When Stephen died Cecil turned
to the Lodges for the solace he needed. Some years after, Bay
Lodge, the scion of the family, succumbed to food poisoning.
The Lodges were overcome with grief. In a touching letter of
consolation, Spring Rice wrote at length, never once mentioning
the death of their son, telling only of the virtue and promise
he had found in him. It was an expression of admiration, written
from Stockholm at a time when Spring Rice himself was not
in the best of spirits. As he learned later, the Lodges prized
the letter, which they read and reread many times.[92] It was such
a tribute that even Henry Adams, for all his detachment from
life and death, was moved by it.

In 1915 Nanny Lodge died. She had been an invalid for some
months, but the news of her passing struck like a thunderbolt.
It was 1915, and although the larger tragedy of the war weighed
heavily on every man and woman, it was the individual loss,
as is often the case, that brought the greatest pain. Spring Rice
reported the matter to Grey: "We have suffered a great loss
in the death of Mrs. Lodge. I don't know what the Senator
will do."[93] And to Roosevelt he wrote: "Poor Cabot. It is dreadful
to think of it."[94] The war and the death of Mrs. Lodge brought
the senator and the ambassador closer together. Spring Rice
had shared with Lodge many of his feelings about the Eastern
notion of love, and the senator was aware of his mystical-poetic
side. Sonnets that he had written to Nanny Lodge over the
years he now gathered up and presented to the senator, who

had them privately printed. This gesture of consolation quite overwhelmed Lodge. "I was dumb and voiceless because I was so deeply moved," he confessed; "your feeling so lighted with love and imagination helps me and lifts me up."[95] This was, to Spring Rice, the essence of friendship.

Roosevelt and Lodge were men of learning, but Henry Adams was the ultimate intellectual. That he welcomed a young and callow Spring Rice to that exclusive coterie that made up "the Adams seminar" is a testament not alone to Spring Rice's urbanity but to the promise his presence brought: an extra-American perspective on matters that alternately concerned and amused Henry Adams. Theodore Roosevelt brought the two together, but the young diplomat took it from there. In December 1887, he told his sister Daisy that Adams was "a great friend of mine." Henry Adams was of a distinguished American family. His great-grandfather, John Adams, helped fuel a revolution and consolidate a constitutional republic, serving as second president of the United States. Grandfather John Quincy Adams was secretary of state before serving as the sixth president. His father, Charles Francis Adams, had been American minister to London at the time of the Civil War, and Henry accompanied him as his private secretary. The most cosmopolitan of his countrymen by reason of travel, study, and residence abroad, Adams wrote history in the grand manner. His multivolume treatment of the administrations of presidents Thomas Jefferson and James Madison illuminated the era it dealt with and set a standard for later historians to emulate. *Mont Saint Michel and Chartres* was a masterpiece of history, architecture, religion, and philosophy that revealed in the author a search for happiness in the past. *The Education of Henry Adams*, an autobiography told in the third person, accented his detachment and *ennui*, familiar traits to those who knew Adams. Twenty years senior to Spring Rice, he proceeded to adopt him, after a manner, by establishing a deliberately stylized relationship: he became "Uncle Henry" and Spring Rice was "Dear Nephew." At first all this was immensely flattering, for Adams did not take to many people, but in the end their friendship was one of equals.

The Spring Rice association with Adams gives off light and shadow alike. There was much for Adams to teach the younger man. "Mostly of an evening I dine with Henry Adams who is a man about 50 who lost his wife and has retreated from the world to amuse himself by writing history," he explained to his sister Agnes. "He is full of lots of information and reads—a thing nobody here does."[96] Their table talk was no doubt stimulating. Spring Rice was aware of Adams's crochets—"He is very cultivated but rather a cynic." He thought the whole Adams clan "odd as can be. They are all clever but they make a sort of profession of cynicism." The mind of Henry Adams was a well-honed knife that easily cut through cant and hypocrisy to lay bare the realities of contemporary affairs no less than those of the historical past. In their long conversations, Spring Rice listened, gladly sharing knowledge and opinion; Adams was immensely fond of both the young Englishman and his opinion. In his letters he sometimes addressed Spring Rice as "Dear Gentle Diplomate" or simply "Dear Friend." He was prepared to offer Spring Rice the supreme compliment, framed in Adamsian malice. "I would have an hour's talk with you," he once wrote, "for in truth, my son, I am weary and oppressed by the stupidity of your class. I am desperate to tell you why I consent to talk to you. The entire diplomatic class has, in my forty years of acquaintanceship with them, supplied me with just one or two interesting specimens, and you are one. I pay you that compliment free of charge. Don't grow fat on it for it is wrung from me with bitterness of soul."[97] It was a pure Henry Adams kind of praise.

Shadows descended from this intimacy of mind and spirit. Adams was splenetic, sardonic, at odds with life, especially after the suicide of his wife, convinced not simply of the decline of Western civilization but of the extinction of the human species. He was ready to apply this negativism—cleverly conceived and phrased—to events and individuals great and small. Spring Rice, perhaps by nature and possibly by experience, was wary, hubristic in a way. He did not need an American mirza to deepen his melancholy or to aggravate a worrying mind. Quite likely this friendship thrived because of these common attitudes. Theodore Roosevelt was often exasperated by Spring Rice's bleak outlook and remonstrated with him about it. But in Henry Adams, Spring Rice discovered intellectual contours into which his own misgivings fitted virtually without effort. The results were not healthy.

Spring Rice could be so dreary at times, as when he wrote Adams from Cairo of his despair of happiness while he was serving on the *Caisse*, that Adams pronounced him "my best disciple. He shall be my successor as Chief of the C.C.A."[98] This soul searching he often displayed to his American friend, struggling manfully and in vain to convince him of the success of the Persian poet to "represent the infinite in the finite, sensual form."[99] In the end it was the pessimism of the West rather than the fatalism of the East that more commonly possessed Spring Rice. Others of his circle, fortunately for him, worked to counter the ill effects of his continual worry about the future of his race and his nation.

It can be left to Spring Rice to have the last word on the matter of his American friendships: "Looking back over my years spent in Washington the memory is one of bright vistas of friends. Whatever may be said of the relations, politically speaking, of England and America, one thing is absolutely certain—in no other country can we Englishmen make such friendships."[100] Not only had these friends added to his happiness, they had helped him gain perspectives on his race, his nation, and himself.

2

THE LITERARY IMPULSE

Cecil Spring Rice was instinctively a man of letters. That he won notice as a diplomat does not belie an artistic temperament, and part of his success at the Foreign Office was traceable to the very gifts that marked him as a literary figure. Powers of observation, insight, sensitivity to the ways of distant peoples and strange cultures, and a felicity of expression—his official reports were commended for their style as well as content—combined to make him a valuable and trusted representative of his country abroad. The strength of his artistic commitment diminished in time because of the increasingly demanding official responsibilities, yet his last poem, the one best known from the body of his work—"I Vow To Thee My Country"—was written a month before he died. Had he won the All Souls Fellowship that he dreamed of in his youth, no doubt his reputation as writer and critic would have been soon established. Once he left the embassy in Washington, there was the prospect of a mastership at one of the Oxford colleges, and that would have suited his talents and his tastes admirably. That Spring Rice chose to enter the Foreign Office and, by a mixture of ability and good fortune, to become a skilled diplomat meant his literary output would be modest in extent, yet it was striking in substance. It was to be a guide to him in his approach to people and events and his handling of diplomatic business.

Spring Rice was both a poet and a storyteller, categories into which his published work neatly falls. Yet his poems very often tell the story of mankind, historically and spiritually, while his storytelling has a poetic resonance. The art of the poet and the teller of tales appear as one. The effect of this is easier to perceive than the reasons behind it. Bernard Holland, the editor of Spring Rice's collected poems, who knew him at Eton, has recalled that "more than most men one felt in him the unseen playing beneath the seen, or the untouched below the surface. . . . One was aware that he lived in another and to him perhaps more vital world."[1] It is this other world he inhabited that comes through in his poetry and stories. Why he preferred not to share too much of this world with others than his intimates is problematical. It appears that at times he would have been willing to allow his verse to remain undiscovered and therefore unknown. That this did not come about was due to the foresight of his widow. Shortly after his death, Lady Spring Rice asked Holland to undertake an edition of his verse. The result was *Poems*, published in 1920 and suitably introduced by a long, informative essay by the editor.[2]

There are 124 poems, sonnets almost all, in the collection that Spring Rice left in manuscript form at the time of his death. Some of the poems he had written between October 1898 and December 1900 while in Persia, although he told Luxmoore that "they were gradually worked up during many years, the sediment of a good deal of thought, and the barking of one of Lucretius's pack."[3] About the same time he wrote Edith Roosevelt: "I have got to take pleasure in the old Persian mystic poets, which I see through a glass darkly. These people belong half in the world. They can escape from it into another world of their own at any moment, and so it does not much matter to them if things go badly." To which he added, as though as a Westerner he wanted to pay homage to the East: "We are altogether of this world and we make this place which is our dwelling place as happy as we can; but the other plan has its advantages too."[4] It took him but a short while to enter the Oriental mode. On first coming to Teheran, he commented on the slackness of the ways, but soon he was sitting with his mirza.[5] Together they talked of many things, of astronomy and philosophy, of human ultimates and divine mysteries. The mirza told him stories that he wrote down, intending one day to put them into English. There were poignant moments such as when his mirza said to him that the world was getting old and ready to die. "The world," he said, "thinks if the Creator sees how badly things are going, he will kill it out of anger or compassion."[6] As it happened, years in Persia provided Spring Rice with the leisure and the solitude appropriate to poetic reflection. This helps to explain the sixty-six sonnets that he sent to Luxmoore, styling them "Teheran, 1900." They were the first visible fruit of the poetry writing he had begun long ago at Eton. Now, years later in Persia, in midlife, he was to achieve a maturity of thought and expression, however inhibited he might be about letting the world have a look. In 1900 the poems were intended for Luxmoore and for him alone. He told his old tutor they "were the record of a sort of pilgrimage" that he sent as "a mark of friendship."[7]

Once Luxmoore had read the poems approvingly, his erstwhile student sought to convey in prose the idea behind much of what he had committed to verse. The concept of beauty and truth, he argued, "was Platonic, the contact of the soul with the invisible by the artifice of sense and the particular object. That is I have to love God by loving my neighbor." Whereupon Spring Rice introduced the teachings of the Bible "by which the real has revealed the ideal, the particular [has shown] the universal. But the ideal sanctifies the so called real; the universal is in the particular and makes it sacred." "It is all in St. Bernard as you taught us long ago. . . . Do you recognize St. Augustine [one of the poems was entitled "St. Augustine"] an old remark of yours in the year '75? He came up here again in Persia in 1900."[8]

A very curious note was attached to the manuscript given Luxmoore that contained the following account of the author of the poems.

> The author of these verses was born in New England in 1857—and died in Northern Persia in 1900. Shortly before the date fixed for his marriage he was attacked by severe symptoms of an hereditary malady (insanity) and left America for Japan. From there he travelled across Asia to Persia and Eastern Mesopotamia where he resided for some years. He then returned to America at the urgent request of his friends, especially the lady to whom he had been engaged and her husband, an old friend of his. On arrival he found that both husband and wife were dead. A severe attack of insanity followed, after which he returned to Persia, where he lived as a native, becoming affiliated with one of the Dervish societies. His identity was discovered through the accidental visit of a European doctor during his last illness.[9]

This was a strange concoction of fact and fiction, of hidden hope and fear. Was Spring Rice merely proposing to obscure the name of the author? If so, why did he go to such lengths? Did he wish his poems to be read even though he preferred to go unrecognized as their author? Luxmoore may have found the note perplexing, but more likely, remembering Spring Rice's imaginative nature, he did not take it too seriously.

There are other particulars about *Poems* that deserve attention.

The six sonnets entitled "Mansur" were given to Henry Adams, who made them available to Shane Leslie with permission to publish. They appeared in the *Dublin Review* for April 1918, some weeks after Spring Rice's death. These sonnets were translated from versions of the writings of the Arab mystic Hussayn ibn Mansur al Hallop, who lived in the tenth century. In the manuscript Spring Rice noted that Mansur "was condemned to death for saying he was God." Mansur the mystic fasted and experienced ecstatic visions. He preached freedom of the will, thereby arousing the wrath of the theologians. He was put to death under circumstances of the utmost cruelty. But as he died he asked aloud that his death should not shake the trust of men in divine goodness. Mansur told the world that he had been given the cup of suffering to drink. The parallels to the life of Christ are unmistakable. In writing the Mansur sonnets, Spring Rice was attempting to bind together as one the mystical elements of religion East and West. In some of his other poems a transference of Eastern and Western thought can be discerned although in the end Western religious ideas are dominant.

As *Poems* was intended to offer readers the total of Spring Rice's serious verse, the collection included sonnets written to commemorate in death the life of Mrs. Henry Cabot Lodge. Holland obtained special permission from the senator to have them reprinted. Five miscellaneous poems round out the book: a reflection called "Ullswater"; another that dealt with the famous Adams Memorial Statue in Rock Creek Cemetery, Washington, D.C.; two wartime poems—"Belgium Thanks America" and "To the American People"—published first in American newspapers; and the last entry, to which no formal title is attached, "I Vow To Thee My Country." This final poem was later set to music by Gustav Holst and has since become a favorite combination of piety and English patriotism unmatched in the hymnal.

In turning to the poems to glean insight about Spring Rice, it is useful initially to categorize his verse, although categorizing the work of a serious author may lessen the impact of a particular poem. There are obvious categories nevertheless, and awareness of them offers a means of coming to grips with the patterns of the poet's thought. The categories, while they tend to meld, are sufficiently distinct, the various associations that Spring Rice intended clear enough to be informative. The first important source of his poetry was Christianity, both scriptural and historical. Nature, as understood in the late nineteenth century as something scientifically verifiable and emotionally inspirational, acted as a challenge and a foil to Spring Rice's religious faith. As might be expected, Spring Rice drew heavily from English literature, finding special appeal in Shakespeare and Wordsworth and giving a nod to the Victorians, Tennyson, and Matthew Arnold. He also used major figures from the past, many of them religious characters, to humanize the historical story by seeing movements and events through the eyes of certain individuals. The Levant is another element of his inspiration; he employed its philosophy of life to overwrap pointed references to the East.

These several categories fail to take into account Spring Rice's need, nay, his compulsion, to express highly personal emotions. The resulting pieces, which could well be called "love songs," were notable for their intensity. Incidentally, apart from the sonnets dedicated to Mrs. Lodge, America rarely moved Spring Rice to poetic expression. This should not seem strange, for when in the United States much of his time was occupied in diplomatic business, his inner needs supplied by his many friendships. In Teheran, lacking fellowship, his poems became his companions.

Spring Rice loved the Psalms, the poetry of the Bible. In the Lodge sonnets there are versions of three Psalms, the twenty-first and the sixteenth and seventeenth in combination. This is the way he interpreted Psalm 21.

> I will rejoice in the strength of the Lord:
> He who shattered the spear and the sword,
> He who gave me my heart's desire;
> For the spoiler's castle is burned with fire.
> The mighty man hath bowed his head
> And fallen beside his captain dead,
> The bowman and the Charioteer;
> Pain and sorrow and doubt and fear;
> Death and all his ravening horde.
> I will rejoice in the strength of the Lord:
> He who crowned my head with gold
> He whose sheltering wings enfold
> Me the captive, me the slave.
> Life I craved. 'Oh, strong to save
> Strong to defend, strong to deliver,

Give me life!' And life he gave,
Long life, even for ever and ever.[10]

Not only the message but the cadences that are familiar in the Psalms became part of his rendering. In keeping with the spirit of the Old Testament, the poet sung his praise to a God of power and might, a God in whom he reposed complete, unquestioning trust. His combining of the sixteenth and seventeenth Psalms expressed the same commitment and included the lines:

Thou are my God, what can the mad world proffer,
Thou art my God, I scorn their fellowship.[11]

The Old Testament is not Christianity, however, and Spring Rice was a Christian. By no means did he possess the peasant's faith that did not doubt. He had moments of agony, only to put aside his questioning. Spring Rice was attracted to paradoxes of Christianity, which are among its striking features. "The Great Betrayal," for example, probed the incarnation and death of Jesus.

One throned in splendour on a glorious throne—
Seeing a great and perilous task to do—
Called one among His servants, whom He knew
For best and bravest—"Thee," said He, "alone
Of all the millions whom I have and own
To do this service, have I chosen thee.
Be worthy of the trust, and trust in me.
I will reward it. Go"—And he was gone.

He did the task appointed. Then, betrayed,
He died a felon's death. The mighty one
Of all his millions sent not one to aid.
"Just God, reward the tyrant!"—Nay—but see—
the throned and crowned Betrayer, who was he?
God. And the poor betrayed one—God's own Son.[12]

Such a poem underscored "the mystery of faith," a theme carried further in "The Word."

In thunder spoken from trembling hills,
In fiery letters written in the sky,
We hear and see Thy Word O Thou most High,

The Word which made and makes and rules and wills,
The Word which gave the promise and fulfills,
The law supreme which suffers no reply,
The law which bids us live and bids us die,
Which made and can unmake, quickens and kills.

"I *am*"—the dread "I *am*" in thunder rolls
His awful judgments from the heights of heaven,
And we, for whom the cloudy veil is riven,
The fiery Word is branded on our souls;
And with a humble and a contrite heart
We kneel and bow before Thee as Thou art.[13]

Here the poet has alluded to both the Word of God, his message as discovered in the Testaments, and the Word of God made flesh and dwelling among men, a bridging of the Old and the New Testaments.

To illustrate the truth that the Gospel must be lived in men's actions and their behavior toward one another, Spring Rice wanted to show that Christ had come to save the meanest of human kind, again catching the sense of paradox that he liked to dwell on. This poem he called "The Two Disciples."

I heard Him with the hearing of the ears;
I saw Him with the seeing of the eyes;
And therefore am I learned, am I wise—
Not like the watchers of the long dark years,
The idle dreamers and unseeing seers,
Whose bootless cries, importunate and vain,
Vexed the dumb heavens that answered not again,
Who searched the dark abysses through their tears,
And saw no light. And I have heard and seen—
I stood before the Master face to face;
I heard him call. But *he*, the child of shame,
The dull unlettered churl, the poor and mean,
The common fellow of the market place,
The Master bade him follow. And he came.[14]

There was in such lines the telling of parable in poetry.

Spring Rice's belief in God was highly personalized. As he wrote in one poem:

Because our tireless thoughts a busy band,

Fly through the fabric of the mighy world,
Because our curious toil has half unfurled
The mighty scroll, and sky and sea and land
Are probed with prying eye and searching hand,
Because we spell the mystic characters
Letter by letter,—can our spirit pierce
The meaning? Do we read and understand?

Make not God's temple thy museum: kneel
Down on thy knees upon the holy ground,
Pure heart and reverend mind alone can feel
That mighty mystery that girds us round,
Without whose light no mortal eye can read,
Without whose life our life is dead indeed.[15]

and in another:

'Twas He that called me from the stir and press
The kindly noises of the market place,
The Tender voice, the dear familiar face,
Who lured me with the light I loved—ah yes,
I loved and trusted wholly. Could I guess
That He who fed the hope and stilled the fear,
That He who led me here would leave me here
Alone and naked in the wilderness?

Light, in impenetrable clouds unfurled,
So great, we ask not whether good or bad,
Procurer and avenger of our sin:
Just God, behold Thy justice and be glad;
I thank Thee, Lord, that Thou has made the world
For Thee to rule, and me to dwell therein.[16]

In still another he combined a worldly love with thoughts of afterlife.

When beauty can not charm, nor ear delight,
When after all the striving comes the end,
When naught avails, nor strength, no gold, nor friend,
When Death unchallenged calls the final right,
When heaven fades before the straining sight,
And flowers and sunshine into darkness blend—
Then—when the soul makes ready to descend
The silent regions of eternal night—
Then, in that hour supreme, shall I live o'er

Those lovely days of golden memories,
Lived long ago, but ah! not lived in vain;
Then shall my spirit hear thy voice once more,
Once more thy presence dawn upon my eyes,
And dying, I shall see thee once again.[17]

These poems taken singly or altogether are evidences of the depth of Spring Rice's belief. Yet it must be remembered that he was a Victorian, born in the very year that Darwin's *The Origin of Species* was published, and he was raised in the springtime of scientific materialism. It is unlikely, if not impossible, that he was not touched significantly by the intellectual controversies of those years. He had encountered Darwin early, at Eton under Luxmoore's direction. As a spiritually serious person, he could not have been left undisturbed by the claims of an all-embracing materialism because it was a direct challenge to a faith he deeply held. A certain tension arising from this contest of minds appeared in the following sonnet.

This earth we tread on is thy work, O sea!
The architect was *thou*; 'twas thou didst lay
The strong unseen foundations: day by day,
Within thy bosom imperceptibly
The fabric grew of continents to be;
And men shall live and build and breed and sleep
Where now the waves are rolling fathoms deep
And little heed perchance will take of thee
And all thy patient toil: but some there are
To Whom, although old Neptune and his train
Are banished from the depths to realms afar,
The voice of those laborious waves of thine,
The tireless toilers of the fruitful main,
Is not less awful and not less divine.[18]

He voiced materialism in another poem:

Not for thy self, not for thy self alone
Nor for thy beauty though so bright it be
O love, fair love, do I so honour thee;
The patient architect lays stone upon stone
To build his temple—many a mingled tone
To make the finished harmony must meet
In lovely service and subjection sweet—
And does his master's work, and gives his own,

And in the mighty temple of the Earth
The deep inherent harmony of life,
Eternal in the turmoil and the strife,
Behind the whirl of birth and death and birth,
There have the gods assigned thee part and place,
And all the soul of heaven is in a face.[19]

And encountering such thoughts as follow, the grim pessimism
of Arnold's "Dover Beach" momentarily intrudes, which Spring
Rice was inclined to lighten.

Talk not of Time, I said, shut eyes and ears
To all the cruel wrong he does our bliss,
The lingering look he murders, and the kiss
He whelms beneath his weight of ponderous years.
Talk not of Time—the thought is barbed with fears
That pierce and rankle and fester—Love is his,
Is his to kill. He speaks the word,—we miss
The fruit of all our joy and all our tears.

So said I, as I watched the rosy west
Darken, and yet another day undone,
And all his glory into darkness hurled;—
And suddenly I felt my heavy breast
Lighten, and I bethought me of the sun,
Who sets to us, but never sets to the world.[20]

But on the whole Spring Rice was predisposed to glory in nature
and her ways. Pessimistic materialism he dismissed in such
poems as "Indian Summer."

The last, the dying glory of the year,
More bright than all the splendour of the spring,
On woodland and on wold was glittering;
Far off the sapphire ocean bright and clear
Gleamed, and, a double light in sky and mere,
Purple and russet, gold and fierty red,
The flaming forest all its pomp outspread
As if it surely knew the end was near.

And soon, I thought, the end will come, the doom
Will fall upon the forest and the sea,
And winter with his rage and gusts and gloom
Will spoil and tear and ravage. But for me

> The woods still glitter in the bright clear air,
> And naught is changed: and all things are that were.[21]

He would not have been drawn to Wordsworth if the message of nature was gloom and doom. Romanticism was as congenial to Spring Rice as his love of Cumberland.

It would be misleading, in consequence, to leave unresolved Spring Rice's doubts about God and nature, uncommitted to either as an ultimate. If Darwinism, when applied to man, added up to no more than a struggle for survival, a quaint adventure of the protoplasm, Spring Rice, not blind to suffering and sorrow in the world, would have none of it. And so he wrote:

> Master of earth and heaven, was this Thy boast?
> The goal of power, the crown of honour this:
> To know how deep the depth of sorrow is,
> And glory most when Thou doest suffer most?
> O mighty Master of the heavenly host,
> Beneath Thy creature's foot Thou liest low,
> And then dost glory in Thy overthrow,
> Nor count the battle won till all is lost.
>
> And therefore dost Thou bid the world rejoice,
> For Joy has risen, even from the dead,
> And being risen makes the world divine.
> O ye that sorrow, hear the Master's voice,
> 'I am your sorrow, and the tears you shed
> Blood of My veins: your grief has made you Mine.'[22]

The orthodoxy of such sentiments counts for far less than does the spirit animating the poet whose faith was convincingly real.

Shakespeare and Wordsworth were the two most common reference points in English literature for Spring Rice. He chose two separate occasions to borrow directly from Shakespeare's plays. "The man who this day sheds his blood with me / Shall be my brother, said the warrior king" taken from Henry V (4.3), were lines used to introduce a poem that continued in a way markedly like the St. Crispin's Day soliloquy.[23] In another instance he relied heavily on Richard II (4.1) in a verse that urged men to look into their hearts to find the cross of salvation.[24] More importantly, Spring Rice showed the influence of Shakespeare because of the use he made of the sonnet; he thought the model was nearly perfect. Indeed, his love of the sonnet acted as a bond with certain of his friends, especially Edith

Roosevelt, for whom Shakespeare's sonnets said it all.

Like Wordsworth, Spring Rice knew and loved the Lake District. There was no more nourishing place for his spirit when sore with distress than Old Church on Ullswater. He sang of it in "Ullswater."

> Row on, row on, the lake is still
> The stars are bright above;
> Oh, talk no more of good or ill,
> No more of hate or love.
>
> A million stars are bright on high,
> They reck not of us, they;
> Round us the shadowy mountains lie;
> How near, how far away!
>
> We cannot speak; all is too still;
> Nor smile, nor hope, nor fear,
> There is no good, there is no ill,
> Nor joy, nor sorrow here.
>
> Only the lake's unearthly calm,
> The silence of the sky,
> And in our hearts, the awe, the charm,
> The eternal mystery.[25]

The influence of Wordsworth, as with Shakespeare, is just above and well below the surface of Spring Rice's writings. What he offered in the following sonnets was not imitation Wordsworth but Spring Rice originals, drawn from the same source that inspired Wordsworth.

> Soft in the garden blows the breath of Spring,
> Sweet to his sweetheart coos the brooding dove,
> Soft to the dreamer murmurs dreaming Love,
> As soft, as sweet, as swiftly vanishing;
> Soft to the dreaming ear Love's red lips sing
> "Now is the hour to dream, and now the day:
> Swiftly the moments pass away, away"—
> And ye are brothers, Love and thou, O Spring!
>
> The Father of a million Springs art thou,
> And each the father of a million flowers:
> And Love and Thou ye reck not of the hours:

Old Time can swear that Love's as lovely now,
As sweet as Love, as swiftly vanishing—
Soft in the garden blows the breath of Spring.[26]

and

If tender wishes be but empty air,
And loving thoughts be naught but idleness,
Oh then, what hope have I in my distress,
What else were left for me but blank despair?
For when the world is dull and and dark and bare,
When loneliness and sorrow most oppress,
I feed my soul on sweet remembrances,
On many a tender thought and many a prayer.

And when from sunny seas a warm wind blows
On snowy wilderness and frozen height,
The roots that hidden sleep beneath the snows
Will cover all this waste with blossoms bright,
E'en so the roots long sown, not sown in vain,
At thought of thee, dear friend, will bloom again.[27]

There is furthermore a tenderness associated with Wordsworth (and Shakespeare) that Spring Rice captured in "The Caspian."

November

I saw a little maid with pattering feet
Who ran to me with open arms and cried
"Father!" and in my heart there swelled a tide
So strong, so deep, and oh so wonder-sweet!
I woke and heard the long slow billows beat
In ominous thunder on the shallow shore,
And gust on gust the mighty North-wind roar,
Where surge and shingle undistinguished meet.

I saw thee little maid, for thou wast here:
The sun was on thy hair, and in thy hand
Daisies—and Oh the smile! Sullen, forlorn
The leaden morning shimmers on the sand—
O little laughing maid, God bless thee, dear,
Thou ghost of one who never has been born.[28]

The "little laughing maid" was indeed born when Mary Elizabeth (Betty) came into the world.

And, like Wordsworth, Spring Rice was not uneasy in confessing his love of England:

> Follow my heart, oh follow my heart forlorn
> To where beyond the ocean breaks the morn
> Along the happy headlands of my home.[29]

Because he was abroad so much of his adult life, thoughts of England and of Ullswater welled up within him naturally.

By background and profession Cecil Spring Rice was deeply conscious of history, so that historical figures appealed to him as subjects for portions of his poetry. What is of special interest are the figures he chose to write about and, in all cases, to identify. From the Old Testament came Job, and Christ from the New; from Roman Britain came Hadrian; from the medieval epoch came St. Augustine and St. Francis of Assisi; Michelangelo came out of the Renaissance, Pascal from the Age of Reason; and finally, from English literary history, came John Bunyan and Lord Byron. All these individuals had a particular meaning in Spring Rice's understanding of the past. The sonnet dealing with Christ (unnamed but undeniably the subject) pits Caesar against Christ.

> A fractious rogue, traducer of the State,
> Sent to a rebel death; a noisy tongue
> Silenced, a slave condemned, a felon hung—
> O princes of the earth, securely great,
> High in the place of power, can this abate
> The splendour of your mailed majesty?
> A felon on the gallows, what is he
> To move your lofty souls to fear or hate?
>
> O Caesar, Lord of Lords and King of Kings
> Throned in the palace by the silver sea,
> Far have thy conquering eagles spread their wings,
> A hundred noble nations own thy sway;
> Behold, its doom is spoken from to-day;
> The dead man on the cross has conquered thee.[30]

Such phrases as Lord of Lords and King of Kings he used ironically to heighten the sense of drama by juxtaposition.

The treatment he accorded St. Augustine of Hippo is just right, historically. Augustine had witnessed the fall of Rome (and if Gibbon be acknowledged, Augustine's God had something to do with that fall). But he was allowed to see beyond the darkness that ensued.

> The crash of empires echoed in his ears,
> The shouts and curses of the ravening horde;
> Flashed in his eyes the horror of the sword,
> The blight that gnaws and spreads, the fire that sears;
>
> And dimly through a mist of hopeless tears
> He saw the old heroic blood unpoured,
> A flood of ruin, swift, deep and broad,
> That whelmed the glories of a thousand years.
>
> And even as the darkness darker grows,
> And nearer yet the tempest looms and lowers,
> Lo! where afar a strange new splendour shows
> Through storm and darkness softly glimmering;
> The shining bulwarks, the eternal towers,
> The courts divine, the palace of the King.[31]

St. Augustine and St. Francis were such different kinds of witnesses to faith that the two poems devoted to them, when placed side by side, are reminders of the range of Spring Rice's understanding of Christianity. If Augustine was able to see the City of God, Francis, true to his calling, embraced poverty.

> O gentle company of loving men,
> O fellow courtiers of the glorious King,
> With you I'll take my turn, with you I'll sing
> Of how I loved, and whom, and where, and when;
> Take the heroic sword, the glorious pen,
> Each for his love be famous, brave and true:
> And I, dear friends, I serve a lady too—
> Then hear my tale of love, ye loving men!
>
> I woo her not with gold nor deeds of fame,
> No beauty can she boast, nor fine array:
> In pride of royal rags, in glorious shame,
> We two together walk the beggar's way,
> To kneel at last, hands clasped, and side by side
> Before God's throne, the bridegroom and the bride.[32]

In this same category of historical personages, Spring Rice used two further subjects, Michaelangelo and Pascal. He wrote of the artist in light of the popular tradition that Michaelangelo, in designing the tomb of the Medicis, meant to convey a message to the future liberator of Florence. The poem he called "The Sculptor."

> Living he loathed me with a deadly hate,
> And dying willed that I should build his tomb;
> And therefore in this grave, as in the womb
> Beneath the tyrannous and brooding weight
> Of marble, Kingship impotently great,
> Pride in the stony eyes, and in his hand
> The awe-less sceptre of his lost command,
> My thought, a child unborn, shall lie and wait,
> And live and grow unknown, undreamt of, dumb,
> Through the long silence of the shameful years,
> Until the destined day at last shall come,
> And he, the child begot in shame and tears,
> Shall leap full-armed from out of the tyrant's grave
> To draw the sword and strike—avenge and save.[33]

More intriguing was the poem based on Pascal's doubt.

> I search in heaven and earth, and find no God,
> But all around me sin and want and pain
> And when my mind has sought and sought in vain,
> And cried aloud its bitter Ichabod,
> 'The world is dead, and man a soulless clod':
> A sudden glory falls upon my sight,
> Some hidden rapture, some divine delight;
> The path yet glowing where God's feet have trod.
>
> So doubt and hope alternate torture me,
> Till Faith comes near and takes me by the hand,
> And says, "Can human eyes God's splendour see?
> Can human reason God's design approve?
> Can mortal mind His greatness understand?
> Doubt not: thou canst not know: believe and love."[34]

Was this in any way an expression of Spring Rice's own doubts, a time of hesitation on the path to faith fulfilled?

There are several good examples of the persuasions of Persia in Spring Rice's poetry. "Mansur VI" tells of the end of the life of Mansur.

O poor condemned, divine and tortured thing
Who is it gave the cup and bade thee drink?
Who is it gave the thought and bade thee think?
Have I not seen the heaven of heavens descend?
Have I not heard the whirlwind thundering
Have I not felt the Shape drawn near, and bend
Toward me? It is He, the Lord, the King,
The Master,—aye, the Master and the Friend.

Slayer, I hail thee with my dying breath,
Victor, I yield the fortress of my heart;
The doors fly open, the poor lips part
Once more, and then no more world without end
The cup is poison, and the thought is dead;
And He that gives them, is he not the Friend?[35]

Plainly Spring Rice was fascinated by the Mansur legend. He
was also taken with the story of the Bab (the Gate), the founder
of a nineteenth-century religious movement in Persia. Like Mansur, Bab was put to death because he claimed to be God.[36] If
Spring Rice had done no more than translate the story of Mansur
and bring attention to the Bab, he would deserve thanks. But
in absorbing the Mansur epic in particular, he was moved to
write something original and touching. Immersion in Persian
lore is borne out further by "the Guebre Potter." The Guebre
People were survivors of the ancient fire worshippers of Persia;
they had been relentlessly put down for their idolatry. What
the poet wanted to emphasize was that this pagan sect was
able to believe in the mystical power of the flame, the wood
that did not rot but only burned. This sense of mysticism was
carried on in "Arbab-I-Shahud" (The "Illuminate"):

I lay in darkness and the vision came;
All praise to Him who makes the twain be one;
Who lit in heaven the splendour of the sun,
And in this world of darkness and of shame
Sowed the live seed of that all-mastering flame
Wherein incorporate and eternally
We two shall burn together, thou and I;
All praise and power and glory to His name!

The steel and bronze are molten into gold,
The coal and faggot glorified in fire;
No more, no more the darkness and the cold,

No more the hopeless, infinite desire—
Not all the powers of time can part us now:
He who is One hath spoken. I am Thou.[37]

There are several allusions here to an eternal oneness, a creator, monotheism, pantheism, a vision of beatitude. Such a poem demands more be known of the motivation in its composition. But the door is closed, and what is left is a poem that says too little of its purpose.

The "love songs" of Spring Rice, when taken singly, might suggest that he was no more than a troubador, singing to his lady love.

Oh, were I Lord of earth and sea and air,
I'd take the cloudy glory of the west
To robe thy beauty; Spring would bring the best
Of all her flowery store for thee to wear;
I'd set the stars of heaven in thy hair;
I'd bind the sun thy slave; at thy behest
The winds and waves should rise and sink to rest;
All lovely things for thee I'd make more fair.

The secrets of my world I'd show to thee;
I'd feed thy soul on essences divine,
Joy for thy bread and beauty for thy wine;
Earth, sea and heaven and all were thine, thine, thine
If I were Lord of earth and heaven and sea—
Alas, I have but this poor heart of mine![38]

There are in fact numerous examples of his celebration of worldly love:

And so Love gave what he alone can
A joy to live for and a life to live.[39]

In a brooding moment this same love loomed daunting.

Not love, for love has perished long ago,
Not joy, for joy with love has vanished,
Not grief, for grief itself is cold and dead.
The kindly fount of tears has ceased to flow;
Not yet despair. Despair is peace, and lo!
This tortured spirit, hurled from deep to deep,
Blind, dazed, dumb, can neither rest nor sleep,

> For ever fighting with a formless foe,
> For ever asking what no tongue can say,
> For ever struggling for a hopeless goal,
> A ghastly twilight, neither night nor day,
> Life without hope, a world without a soul,
> Not love, not joy, not sorrow, not despair,
> Not that, not yet. Oh, would to God it were.[40]

For Spring Rice, worldly love was but one expression of love that had its origin in the divine. Of love worldly and love divine, man could not always be sure; it was natural to humanity to doubt. In light of his remark to Luxmoore that the Persian sonnets were "the record of a sort of pilgrimage," his path to belief was not unclouded by doubt, "not despair / Not that, not yet."

Spring Rice greatly appreciated the company of cultivated men and women as his wide circle of interesting friends bears out. He was a special favorite of the ladies of society, but he disliked those who were frivolous or merely fashionable. As a young man he greatly admired Victoria Sackville-West and fell in love with Mary Leiter, the American heiress who later married Lord Curzon. Of other Americans, he was most attracted to Mrs. Lodge. By all accounts Nanny Lodge was the brightest jewel of her generation. Corinne Roosevelt Robinson, TR's sister, wrote that she was "patrician to the core, loveliest with the lowliest . . . one of those rare people to whom everyone accorded distinction, though she never assumed it."[41] Her fervent friend in life, Spring Rice, memorialized her passing by writing thirty-four sonnets, exquisite poems done with a mixture of ardor and restraint. He set the tone for all the sonnets in the first of them, which he styled "In Memoriam A.C.M.L."

> Come, join hands and swear
> By earth and sea and air,
> As brothers side by side;
> Troth to the sacred band,
> Troth to the sacred land
> Their love has sanctified—
> Love, inborn inbred,
> Giving, taking and giving—
> The love of the dead to the living,
> The love of the living to the dead.[42]

Any number of the sonnets were touching, perhaps none more than this.

xxx

Children, children, will you remember me,
Mother of the loved ones who loved you so?
Here on the windy shore, here by the sunny sea,
Where the merry waves dance and the merry winds blow?

Children, children, let none be sad for me,
No face be sad for me, no tear flow,
Here on the windy shore, here by the sunny sea,
Blue sky above you and blue waves below.

Here on the windy shore, here by the sunny sea,
Blue waves below you and blue sky above,
Children, children, here shall you remember me,
Not mourning tears; but in laughter and love.[43]

Two of the poems had a distinctly American flavor.

xx
1863

I heard the tramp and I heard the song,
Soldiers marching, marching along
"Glory, Glory!" I hear it yet.
My heart was hot my cheeks were wet.
"What shall I do when I am grown,"
I said, "with children of my own?"
"If I have a son and he has a son,
They shall do what these have done;
And I'll love them so, I'll love them so,
Then I'll buckle their swords and bid them go."[44]

The non-American had captured the mood of theAmerican Civil
War. In the collection this was followed by

xxi
Patria

It is not for the gifts she gave,
Nor all she has in store,
The mother of the free and brave
I'll love her more and more.

Not for the lands she has in fee,
Nor gold in millions piled;
The mother of her sons is she,
And I, my mother's child.[45]

This identity of motherhood and nationhood was one of the pieties of the era, symbolized by Queen Victoria in England and, as Spring Rice chose to say, by Nanny Lodge in America, or at least in his America. There is, furthermore, in "Patria" just a hint of Anglo-American oneness.

Death by suicide of Clover Adams, the wife of Henry Adams, was, because of its ghastly circumstances, a blow from which "Uncle Henry" never fully recovered. In due time Adams commissioned the sculptor Augustus Saint-Gaudens to do a monument to be placed in Rock Creek Cemetery. One of the renowned pieces of American sculpture, it says to every viewer what he himself finds in tragic death. The poem that Spring Rice wrote, which expressed his own feelings, included a "note by author" that is arresting in itself because it speaks of a twin dependence on Eastern and Western spirituality. Here is how the editor presented it in *Poems*.

THE ST. GAUDENS MONUMENT AT
ROCK CREEK CEMETERY

Note by Author

[It is told of the founder of one of the Sufi sects in Western Asia that, hearing of the great beauty of a certain lady, he sought her in marriage and promised her parents to build a beautiful house for her. The request was granted and the house built. The bride was brought into it veiled, according to the custom. When the veil was removed, the bridegroom saw before him, not the bride, but the angel Azrael. He fell at the angel's feet, crying, "Have mercy!" And the angel answered, "I am Mercy."]

'Son of man, behold, I take from thee the desire of thine eyes at a stroke—yet shalt thou neither mourn nor weep—neither shall thy tears run down.' So spake I unto the people in the morning; and in the evening my wife died.-Ezekiel, xxiv, 16.

I

I built my love a temple and a shrine,
And every stone of it, a loving thought;
And far and wide and high and low I sought
For sweetest fancies on the walls to twine
And deeds of gold and words that purest shine
And strength of marble faithfulness enwrought
With love's enchantment—Lady, dearly bought
Nor lightly fashioned was that house of thine.
Who came to dwell within it? Not the face
I dreamed of—not the dear familiar eyes,
The kind, the soft, the intimately sweet.
Dread presence—great and merciful and wise—
All humbly I draw near thy dwelling place
And lay the vacant crown before thy feet.

II

O steadfast, deep, inexorable eyes,
Set look inscrutable, nor smile nor frown!
O tranquil eyes that look so calmly
Upon a world of passion and of lies!
For not with our poor wisdom are you wise,
Nor are you moved with passion such as ours,
Who, face to face with those immortal powers
That move and reign above the stainless skies
As friend with friend, have held communion—
Yet have you known the stress of human years,
O calm, unchanging eyes! and once have shone
With these are fitful fires, that burn and cease,
With light of human passion, human tears,
And know that, after all, the end of peace.[46]

Clover Adams had been a troubled soul and had "known the stress of human years."

The two popular poems in the collection were less successful as poetry and probably none too effective as efforts to persuade the American people of the justice of the Allied cause at the time of World War I. "Belgium Thanks America," which appeared in many American newspapers at Christmas, 1914, was at best heavy handed. "To The American People," written after the United States had entered the war, was notable mostly because of its implied consanguinity of the British and American soldiers, an idealized and unrealistic appraisal of the personnel of the American Expeditionary Force with its multiethnic and mixed racial composition. The only consideration to be stressed is that in these war verses Spring Rice instinctively turned to poetry to express his thoughts.[47] As I hope to make clear in an evaluation of Spring Rice's ambassadorship, this was not the kind of propaganda that would satisfy many leading people in London, but Spring Rice had to be true to himself. So it appeared to the critic in the *Times Literary Supplement*, who described his work as "true poetry." This review of *Poems* went on to say: "The volume may not add to the list of the great English sonnets, but the beauty and serenity of these poems claim attention. There is a fine taste in all of them. . . . The poet uses the sonnet form with a simplicity and directness that give it charm. Into it he could put all he could not say elsewhere, and what could not be said in prose: his human love, his love of England, his feelings about life, his secret faith and conviction."[48]

Spring Rice also tried his hand at play writing. In the mid-1880s he worked on a comedy of manners. It was produced in 1884 at the Deanery, Westminster, and was a very amateur affair. The playbill for *A Knave and His Money* described the scenes and listed the cast, but his name as dramatist was not printed, probably because it was thought bad form for a junior clerk in the Foreign Office to spend time writing for the theater. As a storyteller, however, Spring Rice was a natural; which no less a storyteller than Edith Wharton has attested to. In her stately autobiography, *A Backward Glance*, she recalled meeting Spring Rice at Newport in the late 1880s. She described him as "a thin young man with intelligent eyes who appeared at a yachting party. I record our single encounter only because his delightful talk so illuminated an otherwise dull afternoon that I have never forgotten the meeting." Whereupon she unfolded the story told her by Spring Rice.

A young physician who was also a student of chemistry and a dabbler in strange experiments, employed a little orphan boy as assistant. One day he ordered the boy to watch over and stir without stopping a certain chemical mixture which was to serve for a very delicate experiment. At the appointed time the chemist came back, and found the mixture successfully blent—but beside it lay the little boy, dead of the poisonous fumes.

The young man who was very fond of his assistant was horrified at his death, and in despair at having involuntarily caused it. He could not understand why the fumes should have proved fatal, and wishing to find out, in the interests of science, he performed an autopsy, and discovered that the boy's heart had been transformed into a mysterious jewel, the like of which he had never seen before. The young man had a mistress whom he adored, and full of grief yet excited by the strange discovery, he brought her the tragic jewel, which was very beautiful, and told her how it had been produced. The lady examined it and agreed that it was beautiful. "But," she added carelessly, "you must have noticed that I wear no ornament but earrings. If you want me to wear this jewel, you must get another one like it."[49]

The story had, of course, all the earmarks of a tale with hidden meaning that Spring Rice did not supply, leaving that to his listener. Whatever Edith Wharton thought of it, she knew she had encountered a gifted storyteller. Since this took place well before he lived in Persia, the incident underscores his natural bent for exploring the deeper caves of the imagination, which time in the Levant would foster.

The storyteller often amused his friends in this way, and he was especially adept at engaging children with accounts of make-believe. In his bachelor days in Washington, he delighted the Roosevelt youngsters with stories that were long remembered and often repeated by those who heard them. Years later, while serving in Sweden, his daughter had been sent back to England because of sickness. She was only three at the time. To cheer her up during her convalescence, her father wrote her long letters about the adventures of her favorite toy animal, a bear called James. Composed in a childlike dialect, it told how James set out to find the "healing water" that would make Betty well. After a series of exciting encounters with a big fish, an eagle, a puffin, a sea lion, and a polar bear, along with other strange creatures, James succeeded in making his way to the palace of the Blue Queen, who guarded the precious liquid, and he procured the healing water to make Betty well again. To add to the story, which was later published in book form for private distribution, Spring Rice supplied some charming line drawings of the characters he had created, to the delight of Betty and all children who read about James.[50]

Well before his stay in Sweden, Spring Rice had written two books based on Persian lore, *Songs from the Book of Jaffir*(1900)[51] and *The Story of Veleh and Hadijeh* (1903).[52] The first of these he published anonymously because he remained fearful that such literary efforts might not reflect positively on his professional position. *Songs from the Book of Jaffir* consisted of three fragments of an old Persian legend adopted, as he explained, "from the Persian translation of Jamshid of Yead, The Guebre." The plan of the little book is simple. There is a short introduction in which is described the desperate state of the Guebres, the fire worshippers who had been put down in ancient times. By means of *Songs from the Book of Jaffir*, the Guebres sought to keep their beliefs alive through chronicles of the people and in the books in which their songs were written. What follows is three extracts from the *Book*. For each extract Spring Rice provided a brief explanation of the setting of the song and story behind it.

The first of these tells of Tyra, the slave girl, and of how King Ephta loved her only to cast her aside. Tyra then beguiled Apt, a servant of the king, a former slave from the same tribe as Tyra but now a trusted aide. When Tyra was called upon to dance for the king's pleasure, her words stirred Apt to slay Ephta, for Apt had fallen under her spell. The second extract speaks of Bindra, King Artabas's jester. He was able to slay Artabas, by using his comic ways as a disguise for a man bent on revenge for the king's cruel treatment of his tribe. The song of Bindra shows the strength of his faith and that of the others who conspired against the king.

> Strong from its birth from its mother, the earth
> Rejoicing it came to the fire and flame.
> The Wise one has sought it, the Strong one has wrought it:
> Oh, you who have known it in old days and new,
> Who is worthy to own it? The brave and the true.
>
> The Earth is its mother, the Fire is its brother:
> And woe to the land, and a curse to the land,
> If a traitor has worn it, a coward has drawn it.
> Oh, say, who will dare it: my friend, is it you
> Who is worthy to wear it? The brave and the true.[53]

The death song of Artabas, in contrast, had a certain coyness about it, the barest intimation that he is marked for destruction saved until the last line.

The light foot that dances,
The light lips that kiss:
The bright eye that glances,—
He cares not for this.
The juice of the vine,
The rapture divine,
He knows not, he shares not:
He feels not, he cares not
For love or for wine.

His spirit is braver,
Our hero and king:
The song must be braver
His servants shall sing.
Then honour the word
Of our master and lord:
What boon shall we bring him?
What song shall we sing?
The song of the sword.[54]

The final extract deals with a great and powerful king, Oreb, who was grief-stricken by the death of his wife Yramith. The love song of Yramith, the queen, is particularly affecting.

God lit a star in heaven
  To make the darkness bright:
God lit a star in heaven:
  He shone, and there was light.

He shone, but his heart was lonely,
  And he prayed and sorrowed sore.
And the Lord of Heavens had pity,
  And lit him a million more.

Each star had a million brothers
  To keep him company:
Each star had a million brothers,
  And each as bright as he.

So shining each to other
  About God's throne they move,
And sing God's praise together,
Together sing His praises
  Who gave them friends to love.[55]

Blind with rage at the loss of his beloved, the king threatened

destruction over the land. The god Athra spoke to Oreb through
a vision of his dead queen, her spirit urging him to heal and
not to wound the people. And so Oreb was persuaded by the
shade of Yramith and became celebrated as a wise and compas-
sionate ruler.

Songs from the Book of Jaffir shows the grip Persia took on
Spring Rice's imagination. He admitted to Chirol that while
it was a "slight and rather ridiculous thing it has given me
an infinite amount of amusement . . . and all rendered in fifty
pages which I am the only person in the world who will ever
understand." He expressed a different and somewhat precious
estimate of it in writing to his sister, Margaret. On congratulating
her on the birth of her first child, he went on to say: "In a
sort of way, I have had a child too. If you see a booklet called
Songs from the Book of Jaffir, published by MacMillan, you
might read it as a sort of nephew. But don't give me away
as it would be very awkward."[56] An Eastern mystic in the Foreign Office simply would not do.

Spring Rice was soon to alter his attitude. When *The Story
of Valeh and Hadijeh* was published in 1903, his name occupied
a prominent place on the title page: "Translated from the Persian
by Mirza Mohamed and C. Spring Rice." This was an extraordinarily important enterprise. He described it as "the story of
a gentleman who was in love with a beautiful cousin. . . . The
book is from the author's own copy with his notations and
extracts from the lady's own letters and precious seal. . . ."[57]
Awe and enthusiasm had not abated when some months later
he explained to Stephen, as the work was progressing, "It is
a curious idea to write a unique book, have it copied in the
best possible handwriting with illuminations—and then send
it as a memorial. There is no story in it—only two cousins
in love with one another and not allowed to marry and then
one of them is sent away to India and dies there after sixteen
years in Delhi."[58] When the book was about to come into print,
Spring Rice wrote Luxmoore about it. "The Eastern idea—that
knowledge is a revelation really possible only through love as
we call it, and not by any means possible by logic or reasoning,
which is only, as Ruskin would say, the horse which carried
the cart to the gate—this idea is worked out so naturally and
from so many new points of view, that it seems to me a very
curious and interesting phenomenon.[59] Sir Edward Grey wrote
to congratulate Spring Rice on the translation. "I like very much

the author's saying that the mark of a holy man is his holiness. There is depth in that."[60] Spring Rice's absorption with an English rendering of *The Story of Valeh and Hadijeh* makes it the center-piece in the Persian phase of his career as a man of letters.

For all its Levantine influences one can not help but notice the parallel between the philosophy of the mirza and that of the Greek idealists.

> A poet has said that even such [a clear pond] is the mirror of thought in which man sees the reflection of things as they are, of the branches of the tree of life. But he sees only the image. A light green leaf fluttered from the willow into the pond. And sometimes, as you see, a leaf from the tree, a real leaf, falls onto the mirror and hangs between the mirror and him who looks. And then he knows there is a real tree as an image.

So spoke the mirza as he told the story of the lovers; so Plato might have written in *The Republic*.[61]

The scholarly dimension of Spring Rice's infatuation with Eastern thought is well illustrated by the seventy-two footnotes that he worked up to explain quotations and obscure points in the text. To the untutored, they take us further into the maze of Persian life and legend. There is a trace here, perhaps more than a trace, of the Oxford don Spring Rice never became.

The value of this translation was acknowledged at the time. Edward Browne, the Cambridge University authority on Persia, spoke of Spring Rice as an accomplished student "with an extraordinary insight into the Persian mind."[62] The total of his literary output indicated wider horizons, indicated that he not only possessed a rare perception of both Eastern and Western spirituality, but by his investigations had, from time to time, discovered a common ground between them. But Spring Rice was not a reclusive mystic; he had to express his deep-seated spirituality in secular ways—in the pursuit of patriotic diplomacy and liberal politics.

3

OBSERVER AND ANALYST ABROAD

As an apprentice diplomat, whether in America, Germany, or Persia, Spring Rice gained a reputation as an acute judge of men and events and a persuasive reporter of a point of view. His ideas at times were at variance with general impressions or at odds with official thinking higher up in the Foreign Office chain of command, but he tried to provide well-developed evidence to substantiate conclusions. Admittedly, he operated with certain set objectives in mind, the chief of which were the safety of England and the empire, and the advancement of the liberal cause. These were his paramount considerations, distinct but inseparable: could liberal England survive in a world of competing autocratic nationalism? This general proposition he viewed in terms of practical questions. For example, would it be to Great Britain's advantage to reduce Russian power in Persia? Did American presence in the Philippines benefit the empire in the long term? His assumptions about the nation's vital interests were not greatly different from those of others in government; it was in the policies to be pursued and in the means to secure the world position of his country that he often parted company. He was ahead of others in advocating the Anglo-American special relationship and more or less behind official thinking respecting Persia because of strong doubts about power sharing with the Russians. And to close the circle, Russia posed an enduring threat to the development of a liberal regime in Persia. In all such situations, Spring Rice was the close student—involved, intense, intent—and in turn, these attributes were recognized by successive foreign secretaries. Some admired his outlook more than did others, but they all took Spring Rice seriously. After a while his reputation preceded him as he took up each new assignment. But to meet him, to hear him urge his views by presenting the facts with utter conviction, was to recognize his undisguised patriotism. A sense of duty, from which others might have been distracted by poor health or the Weltschmerz that on occasion appeared to overcome Spring Rice, was paramount to the diplomat.

To a large extent his success in reporting rested on an ability to assimilate rapidly the variety of persons, places, and policies he had to deal with. An Eton-Oxford education had opened windows on the world, and he learned to relate quickly and critically to fresh, even exotic situations. He had come away from school and university with a mind receptive to ideas, combined with a determination to separate truth from falsehood, the desirable from the undesirable, the workable from the impractical. Sharp differences that he encountered in various cultures and societies and an ability to size them up and convey their meaning in terms of British diplomatic advantage all attested to his natural skills.

Spring Rice also maintained a deep curiosity about nature and its ways, about the spirit of man and the meaning of life. A yen to see and to know took him to the far corners of the earth and the heart, where the less daring might not care to tread. That he undertook travels into the hinterlands of continents and the recesses of the soul speaks of a restless energy and a stern character. In spite of his earliest doubts about wanting to remain in diplomatic service, he did continue; he conquered, or at least beat back, the allure of ease that retirement held forth, and that, in a thoroughly human way, he toyed with from time to time.

What Spring Rice observed and noted was often not to his liking, but this was incidental to his commitment to diplomacy. After but a few years he came to understand the raw material of his profession: the world was a disagreeable place, with British interests under threat. This may account in part for his official pose as the ever-suspicious Englishman abroad. Only in America did he find his refusal to trust other nations and other peoples awkward. Everywhere else there were dubious allies such as Japan and, later on, Russia, or there were enemies. Valentine Chirol thought him unjust when he insisted that Japan was not a stable friend.[1] But it was in the United States he first had to face disagreeable reality. If American politics were unsavory, American politicians could be of the utmost interest. He hated the sin but learned to love the sinner.

It is sobering to realize how little Spring Rice knew about America—its history, its laws, its government, its ways—when he first arrived in 1887. The fault was not necessarily his. En-

glish education gave little or no attention to the American experiment, and British diplomacy made no concerted effort to study
the republic one hundred years after its birth. Books on the
subject were not at hand. James Bryce's *American Common-
wealth* was not published until 1888, and, in fact, Bryce exchanged views with Spring Rice respecting the Irish in America
just as he was rounding off his study.[2] There is no indication that Spring Rice was aware of, much less had read, De
Tocqueville's *Democracy in America*, which had been long
available. The history of France, or Germany, or even of Russia was one thing; the history of the United States—if it had a
history, which too many otherwise well-informed Englishmen
doubted— was another matter. Even granting his time in western
Canada and his brief encounter with Roosevelt, Spring Rice's
knowledge was slim. Yet as a junior officer he would be expected
to write reports for the Foreign Office, assist the minister, who
at the time was Sir Lionel Sackville-West, and do whatever
other work that might be assigned. Canadian-American affairs
was made his primary responsibility although his work was
in fact quite miscellaneous. In light of this, he would need
all his ability and natural curiosity and his openness to new
ideas to do the kind of job required by the legation and satisfying
to himself.

In giving an account of Spring Rice's American education
the use of categories is better avoided. To cull, for example,
the full range of his observations and judgments on such topics
as trade, political machinery, or foreign policy, setting each
category aside for separate discussion would take on the flavor
of a set of exercises. Such a method, enlightening to a degree,
would be devoid of the sense of growing sophistication that
Spring Rice gained. To avoid making a wooden image, a mere
receptacle of information, it is better to follow his response
to America as he came to know the country. Chronology is
more useful than category, just as life is spontaneous rather
than analytical. At least it was for Spring Rice: the theory was
less to his liking than feeling the pulse of life.

Once in America, he quickly perceived that the machinery
of the national government was designed to conserve conditions
rather than change them. He termed the divisions of power
between the legislature, the executive, and the judiciary a "word-
padlock, and unless all the rings are arranged in the right way,
it won't open. This is all very well if you want anything maintained. But is isn't if you want something done."[3] This arrange-

ment, he believed, had an impact on foreign policy by placing the secretary of state in the anomalous position of having little or no power. New to the business of diplomacy, Spring Rice went too far in saying that dealings with the secretary of state were "simply a farce . . . he has no power and he knows it."[4] Lacking the practical evidence that the secretary of state, in this case Thomas F. Bayard, could wield as much authority as the president might accord him, the head of the State Department appeared to be only an administrator. At the time, however, President Cleveland was much more concerned with domestic affairs than with diplomacy, so that Bayard's influence was considerable. It would not always be that way; Cleveland was the formulator of American policy at the time of the Venezuelan boundary dispute (1895). On the other hand, John Hay, when serving as McKinley's secretary of state, had a formative policy role. As Spring Rice was to learn, the machinery of American government was run by people, and even a structure of rule intended to conserve could get things done by the interaction of politicians and political parties.

Spring Rice began making comments on public corruption almost as soon as he arrived at his post, and his willingness to describe its variations was, he found, hard to curb. In New York City he noted that one-half of the electoral officials were in the pay of the candidates. When his cousin, Allen Rice, stood for office but refused to pay for votes, he was roundly defeated.[5] At higher levels Spring Rice was fascinated to watch the wire-pulling. He told of dining with Whitelaw Reid, the owner-editor of The New York Tribune, in the company of Roosevelt and Lodge. The table talk turned to James G. Blaine as a possible presidential candidate for the Republicans in 1888. Reid was well disposed to the Blaine candidacy, but both Roosevelt and Lodge had serious reservations. Blaine had a towering reputation as a corruptionist and had lost to Cleveland in 1884. The powerful editor and the two junior working politicians were feeling each other out. In the end the party rejected Blaine and nominated Benjamin Harrison, who went on to defeat Cleveland and claim the presidency.

Unversed in the history and geography of the United States, Spring Rice learned much from his travels both in the North and in the South. His observations were bound to be colored by the opinions and prejudices of his hosts, but they could be acute nevertheless. He went south in the late spring of 1887, where he sensed the quickened cadences of the New South.

After telling Ferguson about the carpet-bag governments of re-
construction, he curiously set the date 1870 as the year after
which the region began to work out its own salvation. Lately
there had been talk about "the white men of the New South,
'unified America' and all sorts of manifestations of brotherly
love. Together with that," he reported, "there is an enormous
commercial boom and money from the North is flowing down
South on the most significant scale. The change is rather wonderful and seems to astonish even Americans. . . . And yet the
difference in character between the North and the South must
be very great. Yet managing their own businesses seems to cure
their differences, now that the question of relative strength has
been settled beyond a doubt."[6] There are misconceptions in the
foregoing account along with shrewd observations. More importantly, Spring Rice was beginning to accept the complexity of
America, that it did indeed have a history. His simplistic view
would gradually give way as stereotypes crumbled.

For the most part, Cecil Spring Rice associated with Americans of wealth and power. It could not have been otherwise,
given the status of diplomats in the nineteenth century. Yet
he never suffered the dullard gladly and often complained that
far too many of those he met were lacking in dimension. He
also noted that the average successful politician lacked facility
of expression, something he had been raised to expect from
men who governed. Nonetheless, he was comfortable with many
beyond his immediate circle, from the Camerons of Pennsylvania
to the Carrolls of Maryland. There was a disadvantage in all
this, as his grasp of American affairs was often circumscribed.
The only countervailing source of opinion was the popular
press. This he read regularly but without approval. The popular
press as the voice of the people was an idea foreign to him.
The penny press was yet to have significant impact in England,
whereas many American newspapers had adopted a rough and
ready style. He held pretty much with Lord Rosebery's often-
quoted remark that the penny press was written by morons
for morons. Spring Rice's blind spot was no more apparent
than in regard to Ireland's struggle for independence. He found
there was "an intense unwillingness" on the part of the papers
"to say anything hostile to the Irish." His explanation ran as
follows: "This of course comes from the fact that a very large
number of newspaper writers are Irish and that the papers themselves depend largely on the bar-room and liquor saloon which
are almost wholly Irish."[7] Such a remark would seem to imply

a high literacy rate for the Irish-American population, whatever its drinking habits, which was not what Spring Rice had in mind. Then there was the Irish-American practice of bloc voting, which displayed an anti-British animus whenever the occasion permitted. In Great Britain Spring Rice favored home rule, but apparently he did not like the taste of the real thing in America.

One of the most ambiguous of his early observations of domestic America had to do with the Knights of Labor, an association of workers founded in 1869. From the first it was a general labor organization with all workers invited to join, skilled and unskilled, men and women, young and old. Only bartenders were excluded. It was a brotherhood and a sisterhood for all the laboring class. Blamed for the Haymarket riot of 1886, it went into decline soon thereafter. But Spring Rice misread the structure of the Knights along with its rationale. He described it as a union whose members were divided into trades. He was also incorrect to conclude that during strike action, discipline among the workers broke down because one craft union would not support the demands of a different craft, that the workers "did not possess the power of self-denial."[8] He was quite right in pointing out that since large numbers of workers were in no union, there was a ready supply of workers to replace the strikers. In other words, Spring Rice saw labor for what it was at the time, one more commodity to be exchanged in the market place. He was, in effect, learning about socioeconomic America by trial and error, a luxury a junior diplomat was better able to afford than a mission chief.

Further, he rightly discerned that New York City, for all its financial preeminence, was not the de facto capital of the nation. "New York is not anything of the kind," he told Ferguson, and "this is one of the commonest mistakes into which foreigners fall."[9] Spring Rice always applauded the honest politician, and there were undoubtedly more of this type than the reputation of politics in the Gilded Age might imply. Respecting President Cleveland's move to reduce United States tariff rates because of growing government monetary surpluses and the considerable expense the tariff added to the cost of living for average Americans, he thought the president "had the added advantage of an honest chief of an honest party pledging himself in an intelligent manner to a simple, straight forward course of action."[10] Such an appraisal is especially significant in light of Spring Rice's growing Republican propensities.

It was the fight over the tariff in 1887–88 that gave Spring

Rice some intimation of the workings of the committee system in the United States Congress. He was disheartened by it and spoke of it to Stephen. ". . . Here the committees have charge of a bill; they elaborate and decide by vote. The minority introduce a minority bill. The two go before a Committee of the Whole House. An amendment is finally moved by the chairman of the original committee, entirely altering the whole. This is, of course, entirely compromised in the debate. The bill is then voted or vetoed [sic]. You see the despotic power of the small standing committee which takes evidence, etc., just like a department with clerks and other fixings—and gives orders to the Treasury whose Secretary reports to them as if they were the real executive. The confusion is immense and results in almost absolute deadlock as the existence of the government is never dependent on a vote of the house."[11] In the comparision that formed in his mind the parliamentary system appeared to promote desirable legislative change efficiently, while holding the government to a responsible course of action, which the American congressional system did far less well. "There is no where in the world I should think such a base system of politics and politicians. I see it more clearly everyday. . . . The battle is mainly for places, on which the real seriousness of politics depends.[12]

From his evaluations Spring Rice extracted a remarkable insight. "The reverse of the model is better. There is little danger of any real attack on the condition of labor or of property. The country is happy and does not care what goes on in Washington."[13] His judgments on features of American politics were incisive and in some ways prophetic, although he was quoting, in agreement, Mayor Cooper of New York City, "'We found that the only way universal suffrage could be made compatible with good government was by getting a vote not for a ticket but for a man; people were interested in that and we could get a good man to stand. Into his hands we confided the whole of the responsibility.'"[14] What a remarkable commentary on leadership and its place in the political system that enjoyed universal manhood suffrage before the voters were prepared to decide elections on great issues of the day. It is significant, further, because the cult of personality at the presidential level was soon to make its appearance in the tenure of Spring Rice's great American friend, Theodore Roosevelt. No doubt his admiration for good men serving in office, individuals like Roosevelt and Lodge, added justification to Cooper's contention about the workability of manhood suffrage in a still unlettered population. At the same time Spring Rice was cognizant of the cult of personality and the dangers that inhered in a blind hero worship: "Every four years here become simply the lowest form of demogogueism."[15] As he prepared to return to London and a desk at the Foreign Office at the end of 1887, he offered this comment: "I don't know what I shall make of English politics after the experience I have had here. I think I shall be reconciled even to the Irish members."[16] Lesson number one in American life was finished. He little realized how quickly lesson number two was to follow.

Respite from hard American political realities and separation from a growing circle of American friends was short lived. Spring Rice was soon back in the United States in official attendance at the International Marine Conference meetings in Washington. Once the conference had come to its inconclusive end and he joined the British legation as second secretary, again it was Congress that caught and held his attention. At the start of 1890, the Senate was engaged in an emotional controversy over the condition and treatment of blacks in the South. They were being lynched for crimes, alleged or otherwise, with Southern senators supporting the vigilantes and Northerners decrying lynch law as an offense to justice and humanity. Spring Rice followed the senatorial debate with great interest, as he had spent some little time in the South on his first visit. His evaluation of the matter was straightforward. "The dangers must increase as the years pass, and in time there will be the devil to pay."[17]

1890 was a year that saw three major pieces of legislation before Congress, proposals dealing with a regulation of corporations, the unlimited coinage of silver, and a renewal of the tariff. Spring Rice watched the progress of all three pieces, the Sherman Antitrust Act, the Sherman Silver Purchase Act, and the McKinley Tariff. Restrictions on corporations contained in the first bill added up to "strong measures," and he thought its effects would be very far-reaching unless the corporations could somehow evade it. The likelihood of evasion was, in his judgment, great because of widespread collusion between business and government, but he failed to take into account, at least explicitly, the sanctity of property, as then understood in American constitutional law, as a further reason for frustrating the antitrust legislation. He was perhaps too engrossed by the corruption in public life to assess the legalities. Spring Rice took only a passing interest in the money question, content to make an analysis of the divisions within the country created by the Western demand for free silver.[18] But he reckoned with the political implications. "A new party is coming up which seems to carry everything before it." He referred to the newly formed Populist party, and he was not alone in thinking that Populism might hold the key to the American political future.[19]

In matters of trade and commerce he was deeply involved. "I have been making a study of trade relations and sending home long reports which no soul will ever read and which will enrich the record office," he wrote Ferguson.[20] Time thus spent was not wasted. The first hard evidence of what in his view was an advantage, if not a necessity, of firm friendly relations between England and the United States emerged from his investigations. He had been explaining to Ferguson the wisdom of compromise on the issue of fishing rights in the Bering Sea, insisting that "one is naturally anxious to come to a friendly understanding with the U.S.A." Why? Spring Rice stated the case frankly and with some anticipation of things to come. "It is a question of supply. We get an enormous proportion of our food supply from the U.S. In case of war in Europe our enemy will attack our food supply. Under the rule accepted by France, Germany and Russia, the necessities of life are contraband of war; this doctrine is protested against by the U.S. and ourselves. So in case of a European naval war in which we are engaged, the U.S. navy is bound to protect our commerce and our food supply, which is an important consideration. Besides this our trade with them is six hundred million out of a total of sixteen hundred. And our interests are bound inextricably up."[21] Considering that these opinions were set down in 1889, twenty-five years before the reality of Britain's dependence on the United States hit London with full force, Spring Rice's reputation for prescient analysis is well deserved. No less important to note is that the basis of Anglo-American friendship was Spring Rice's estimate of the vital interests of the two countries, matters of fact and not of sentiment.

This line of reasoning led Spring Rice to more general conclusions. He continued to dismiss much of American upper-class society as dull and fatuous, as repellent to him; and in the cross section of the population the indigenous prejudices were repugnant. Yet some of his very best friends were American, and his fondness for them and their numbers would increase with the years. Neither love nor hate did he allow to impinge on his judgment about the advisability of Anglo-American cooperation in world affairs. "I think the policy of Wolsey and Elizabeth towards France is the sort of line we should adopt [toward the United States]. To keep friends at almost any cost. . . . I can't help think our offensive power is vastly overrated. . . . I am sure peace we must have, our tempers we must keep. A break of our relations now [with America], might mean almost any disaster—in the Pacific, or the Atlantic or Europe too."[22] Such a contention, along with its foreboding tone, would have struck almost any ranking Foreign Office person as grossly overdrawn. In 1892, when Spring Rice offered the foregoing prescription, Great Britain was thought of as enjoying unsurpassed power. "Rule Britannia" was no idle phrase. Yet within four years, London would be yielding to the "logic of the Monroe Doctrine" in Venezuela, and within ten years the Boer War was to demonstrate that "our offensive power is vastly overrated." By no means did Spring Rice possess some occult power of divination; what he did have was a clear-headed awareness that dangers lurked in the world to which England and the empire were not immune.

Time in Japan as legation secretray—no more than eighteen months from the spring of 1892 to the autumn of the next year— provided Spring Rice with an opportunity to compare and contrast three political systems: British, American, and Japanese. Things he learned were both amusing and instructive. He was not favorably impressed by the state of Japanese politics. Japan had the trappings of a constitutional monarchy but little of its substance. There was a premier and a cabinet, and parties and politicians—all under the banner of the emperor. The emperor was the final authority in the kingdom, if not personally and actively, then through the coterie that surrounded him. The party in power, that is, the government, wanted things to remain as they were. The opposition, termed the *Radicals,* sought to introduce ministerial responsibility step by step.[23] The Radicals wanted to give parliament power over the purse, a proposal the government "thought to be out of the question."[24] As far as Spring Rice could determine, it was not parties that counted in Japan but clans, the mere embryos of political parties as understood and practiced in the West. "Parliament is the devil and unsettles everything."[25] The chaos of the American Congress stood in stark contrast to the powerlessness of the Japanese legislature, with the House of Commons the alternate model of sanity and responsibility.

While resident in the Far East, Spring Rice understandably turned attention to a consideration of Japan's still-to-be-determined place in the international order. Japanese designs on Korea he readily detected. Korea "was sinking deeper and deeper into debt to Japan and it is believed that Japan now wants to annex the customs administration."[26] The issues raised were far larger than dominance over Korea, however. It was "an important branch of the great Pacific question," namely, which nation or nations would control the Far East, commercially, militarily, strategically? Was it to be Japan or Russia? Spring Rice reported that Russia had clearly earmarked parts of Korea for exploitation. He was also mentally lining up sides, not for the Sino-Japanese War of 1894, but for the Russo-Japanese conflict ten years on. How was Russia to be stopped in its quest for territory and influence? By Japan and England "acting in concert," was Spring Rice's answer.[27] "The great feeling in Japan," as he saw it, "is that England is her natural ally; not out of love for us but out of hatred of Russia."[28] He would not predict Japan's actions in the future at home or abroad. Would it evolve into a true constitutional monarchy, or would it remain a feudal oligarchy? Would it expand into China or outward into the Pacific? He called these prospects a "toss-up." Regardless, Great Britain could ill afford to be indifferent to Japan as a power in Asia. It could make a needed counterweight to Russian ambitions and a useful ally in the preservation of British interests generally. As Spring Rice remarked to Ferguson, all this gave him "plenty to think about."[29] He admitted that in London Japan was regarded as a "practical joke" and there are "a good many arguments in favor of that point of view," to which he added cryptically, "I should not wonder if it [this view] turned out to be wrong."[30] Of course it did.

By the time Spring Rice had returned to Washington in 1894, the political climate there had changed markedly, and not to his liking. Grover Cleveland, who had lost his reelection bid in 1888, regained the presidency in 1892 possessed of a different outlook on public affairs. The Panic of '93 and the ensuing depression lasted most of Cleveland's second term. Economic disaster had split the Democratic party between the radical free silverites and the conservative "gold-bugs." As the leader of the latter faction, the President was battling both western Democrats and the Republicans. It was not a good time for him, or for the nation. The happy, prosperous America that Spring Rice had often remarked on was in deep trouble. Protests over economic and social conditions among the masses took on the coloration of a class struggle. This was reason enough why Cleveland's confidence was shaken with the country on edge. It explains in part at least why the president took a truculent attitude toward the boundary dispute in Venezuela. His hard-line defense of the Monroe Doctrine was an effort to distance himself from domestic woes. Whatever the justification of his posture in this and in other matters, Spring Rice was downcast by much of what he observed over the next two years. His high praise for Cleveland in his first term fight for a lower tariff now turned bitter. He thought Cleveland less capable than Harrison—historians would surely disagree with him—which may be explained by the president's antagonisms to British inter-ests. Cleveland "was bound to show that he was not elected with British gold by being as disagreeable to us as possible," Spring Rice predicted shortly after his election.[31] As a British diplomat who was becoming pro-American, he favored an ex-pansion by the United States across the Pacific, and Cleveland was to curb this movement temporarily by blocking annexation of the Hawaiian Islands. The Democratic chief did not fit the mold common to Spring Rice's Republican friends.

Although he made the statement apropos of circumstances in 1892—"For England the Republican administration is best"— Spring Rice was expressing an attitude that had wide implica-tions.[32] He quite honestly preferred Republicans to Democrats on most counts. His fondness and friendships with Roosevelt, Lodge, and other highly placed Republicans in government and business were neither exceptional nor indefensible. The Repub-lican was the stronger of the two parties and tended to dominate from the Civil War on. Grover Cleveland was the only Democrat elected president between Lincoln and Woodrow Wilson, a span of more than fifty years. It was a matter of cultivating the ruling class; ranking Republicans were likely to have more to say in shaping United States policy toward Great Britain than were Democrats. Perhaps because he was aware of his own prefer-ences, Spring Rice went out of his way to urge avoiding trouble with the second Cleveland administration. The Bering Sea dis-pute is a good example. He went so far as to ask Ferguson, who was once again Lord Rosebery's parliamentary private sec-retary, to urge his chief to push for a settlement of the issues favorable to the United States. The reason he advanced is inter-esting because it was so undisguised. "England has steadily gained in public estimate here by her integrity. We do not wish to destroy the U.S. sealing interests—nor to annex Hawaii. . . . Can we afford to throw away this advantage?"[33] His desire for American friendship and support was not bounded by the Republican party.

Impressions of America in the toils of a deep economic slough had lasting effects on Spring Rice. He wrote about it to Stephen. "I hear railroad property is in a bad way for some time to come. . . . Congress can't agree on a tariff. . . . The old sectional feeling is growing again. . . . There is a strong feeling against the Senate which is called America's House of Lords. . . . As for silver, the hope here is that England will be forced to accept bi-metallism. . . . The state of depression is astonishing. . . . There are said to be a million men out of work. . . . A coal famine is imminent. . . . The general explanation is that it is the demonetization of silver which has caused the trouble. . . . As a matter of fact, as far as I can make out from the business men, the real reason is uncertainty."[34] Very likely in the last portion of his assessment of the impact of the Panic of '93, Spring Rice had put his finger on the deep cause of the economic inertia that was related to the perceived unreliability of a Democratic administration.

Despite growing proficiency as a young diplomat, Cecil Spring Rice was not yet fully convinced that he should remain in the profession. He had done useful work at the legation with a promise of more to come. He had the respect of his chief, Sir Julian Pauncefote, who insisted that if he had had any success in Washington it was due to his two assistants, Spring Rice and Michael Herbert. And Spring Rice certainly enjoyed the perks of office. It is disarming, therefore, to read in a letter of October 1894 to Ferguson: "I hope to leave this before very long; and if not to find work here, literary if possible—only, it is so infernally difficult to begin."[35] The two worlds that Bernard Holland said Spring Rice occupied, that of the spirit and that of work, had not yet come together in 1894.

Had Spring Rice turned to literature he would have had ample material, based on what he had seen and heard of American politics, to allow him to write several novels of satire and indictment in the style of Henry Adams's *Democracy*. Politics continued to fascinate him as long as he remained in America. He still found it hard to believe how long it took to get important legislation through the Congressional mill; four years of study and politicking is what he estimated the typical tariff law required.[36] He sometimes felt that the fault was in the bicameral legislature, but he also knew that Americans believed that a two-house legislature was essential to rule. Pennsylvania had experimented with a one-house body, and he admitted it "proved to be a disaster."[37] He needed no reminders that the purpose of governmental machinery was to conserve and not to promote easy change. On a lighter note he told his sisters of the visit of Rudyard Kipling. One of the things they did was go to the zoo in Washington. "Kipling was like a child and roared with laughter at the elephants and the bears." From there he took him to "another sort of Beasts' show, the Congress." So put off was he by the scene of confusion in the House of Representatives—noise, smoke, loud conversation, and the un-availing bang of the speaker's gavel—that Kipling "resolved not to take his wife to see it, as she was an American and he wished to respect her country."[38] It was the spring of 1895, and Spring Rice, grown restive again, asked for reassignment.

When he arrived in Berlin that year, Whilhelmine Germany was in a state of relative political calm. The man who had replaced Bismarck in 1890 was himself a soldier, General Count Leo von Caprivi. He proceeded to conciliate the Socialists, the Radicals, the Centrists, and the Poles in advancing many reforms having to do with trade, local government, schools, and military service; at the same time he encouraged his cabinet ministers to take initiatives. The Reichstag, because it feared the return of Bismarck, at first cooperated. The German domestic ship of state was on even keel. Whether the seas would remain calm and whether adventurism in foreign parts would agitate domestic politics were considerations the British ambassador and his staff would be watching closely, and certain among them apprehensively. Spring Rice was very much the worried second secretary. As it turned out, Germany abroad rather than at home became his preoccupation. The net effect of his observations was to identify Germany as Britain's most dangerous potential enemy.

Unlike the United States, there were no enclaves of feeling in Germany sympathetic to England. Spring Rice's first reaction tended to stress the hostility that greeted his government's policies.[39] He returned to this attitude from time to time over the length of his stay in Berlin, and put it down to envy of England as a great power by a less great power.[40] In a letter to Stephen, dated 2 November 1895, he said, almost in passing, that the Germans were preparing to "grab S. Africa."[41] It was as though he had a nose for trouble. The Jameson Raid only a few weeks

later thrust Anglo-German relations to the forefront of official
minds in London and Berlin. The Kruger telegram worked only
to confirm Spring Rice's November premonition. With the British press playing the developments for all they were worth,
jingoism appeared to carry the day.[42] He well realized that jingoism was a frail basis for formulating a foreign policy, but it
was something the Germans understood, a cry for action. Still
reflecting concern about England's envied position as the great
power, Spring Rice "firmly believed" there was a "European
plot" to divest Britain of parts of its empire. He pointed an
accusing finger at Germany because of all the advanced industrial states, it alone lacked colonies to satisfy its colonial thirst.
The fear of a plot persisted in Spring Rice's thinking. "No one
who has read the official German press during the last month
[January 1896] could doubt there was a plot against England
on an enormous scale," he told Villiers at the Foreign Office.
He was equally certain that talk of a Franco-German rapprochement was idle: "It falls to the ground as soon as you try to
build on it." This last statement evinced Spring Rice's conviction that Germany was thrown "more completely than ever into
the arms of Russia."[44]

There are two ways of interpreting Spring Rice's intense concern with power politics. One is negative, excessive worry to
the point of paranoia, the "plot syndrome." With the probable
exception of the United States, was any other country worthy
of England's trust? But, to sound a positive note, it is very
likely that by residing in Germany and in Berlin, the seat of
a government given over to power politics, Spring Rice began
to think more and more in geopolitical terms. H. S. Chamberlain
and Sir Halford MacKinder, by advancing the heartland thesis,
had provided a rationale for German expansion that could not
be dismissed as mere theory. Spring Rice's American exposure
had given him a taste for geopolitics. He knew Captain Mahan,
who was a friend of Roosevelt and was welcomed in the Adams
circle. In 1890 Mahan had expounded the influence of sea power
on history that every British naval and diplomatic person had
taken to heart. The Kaiser too was much impressed by Mahan's
writings. Would Germany pursue simultaneously the heartland
thesis and that of sea power to dominate the twentieth-century
world? Spring Rice feared it might. He was at the nerve center
of real politik in Berlin. It was a natural environment for the
growth of a geopolitical approach to designing British strategy

for the new century. Without proposing to dismiss Spring Rice's suspicions about a plot—perhaps better understood as caution— a geopolitical theme would be more and more evident in his thinking on the diplomatic front.

This geopolitical frame of reference was nicely stated not in spite of a steady preoccupation with the developing crisis in South Africa but because of it. Japan was at the time seeking to regularize her position in East Asia, hard on the heels of victory in the Sino-Japanese War. From contacts made while he was in Tokyo, he reported that Japan wanted British cooperation in the regeneration of China. British investments were needed. "Something must be done from without," otherwise Russia could be expected to move into north China, he told Villiers. But "Japan's army and England's fleet are a combination quite invincible." Why not agree with Japan on the settlement of "the problem of Asia" as Mahan's phrase had it. The settlement might consist of England, or England and Germany, advancing money sufficient to pay off all of China's debts and charges to justify a takeover of the administration of the country, "which they should manage with the friendly assistance of Japan." Spring Rice favored such a line of action as he continued his account of the informal Japanese proposal. "If necessary England should occupy Chusan and Shanghai. Japan then would be safe from Russian occupation of Korea . . . at present with Russian superiority at sea and the degeneration of China Japan acting alone had no hope of preventing the inevitable catastrophe. But England ought to take steps soon" was his final piece of advice to Villiers.[45]

Another expression of Spring Rice's geopolitical turn of mind concerned the Ottoman Empire, whose failing health England had long ministered to. On the one hand, the Germans were showing interest in the domains of the empire in southeastern Europe. In Asia Minor, collusion between the sultan and the German press, which had discounted the seriousness of the Armenian massacres, might signal the start of a formal combination, with Germany becoming a power at the straits and beyond. On the other hand, Russia, keen to be the big Slavic brother, might dispute Ottoman Balkan suzerainty also with an eye to the Dardanelles. In both scenarios, Spring Rice perceived a threat to England's position at Suez and in Asia Minor. Furthermore, he believed that the highly autocratic rulers of Germany and Russia might have enough in common philosophically and

institutionally to keep them on good terms and make them enemies of liberal England at one stroke.[46] Whatever the permuta-
tions of geopolitics, his country appeared at risk.

Spring Rice's fears were also aroused by German designs in
Africa, especially when Great Britain decided to commit troops
under Kitchener to pacify the Sudan in 1896. Spring Rice knew
that South Africa would be hard to defend. He dismissed German interests in northern Africa as inconsequential compared
to their interests in South Africa, convinced that the push would
come among the Boer farmers, who had reason to look upon
the Kaiser as their patron.[47] His correspondence with Theodore
Roosevelt demonstrated his large view of international affairs.
"I wonder what you think of the European situation," Spring
Rice began one letter and thereupon transmitted his own analysis with a gloomy prefatory remark. "It looks like the gathering
of great forces for a struggle, not in the immediate future (that
would be better) but in the more distant future." He then made
the following points. "Only Russia of the great European powers
is self-sufficient." He believed that peace at the time was absolutely essential to Germany. "Owing to Alsace and Lorraine
Europe is hopelessly divided and it looks as if commercial and
colonial jealousies will divide England and Germany in a similar
manner." He worried that Europe may become a continent "at
the mercy of a really barbarous power but with a high military
organisation. . . . If America disintegrates, as some Americans
maintain is possible, or if it goes mad like South America, the
future of the world is not improbably in the hands of the Slavs."[48]
Drawing on the intimacy of their friendship, Spring Rice wrote
philosophically about the past as a clue to the next century.
Brooks Adams's *Law of Civilization and Decay*, a book with
a message of the inexorability of decline, had set Spring Rice's
teeth on edge, and he launched an attack on theories of history.
"The Roman Empire fell because there was no one left to fight
for it; as long as we are born, live free and are prepared to
fight in sufficient numbers, I don't see the present world much
like that of the Antonines."[49] "And I don't think the Ten Com-
mandments are played out, and I don't believe that people who
say so are pleasant people to live with. . . . I always write to
you because I think you are one of the people with fixed ideas
. . . and that you don't think them subjects of argument."[50] With
the fall of Rome still in his mind, he was confident that economic
conditions did not portend the decline of England. Wealth had

been accumulated in large amounts by a relatively few individuals, but the little people also had established a stake in society. "The most striking increase is in the sums in safety banks—deposits in small amounts. . . . The small people share in the profits."[51] Socioeconomic salvation was not dispensed by the state but gained by the individual; of this Spring Rice was certain. England and America would do well, he thought, to worry less about the distribution of wealth and more about fecundity if they were to secure their future.

During his stay in Germany, Spring Rice did not neglect domestic affairs there. Having learned the language, he began a study of public institutions. He monitored the press and came to resent it, not because it was popular as in America, but for the opposite reason: papers were government "inspired." His dislike was magnified because the daily journals never spared England or its policies regarding South Africa or any other place in the world. It was "curious to see the anxiety displayed by a newspaper in connection with the government to estrange England from France, Italy, or Russia, to suggest to Turkey, to inspire the Amir, etc., etc."[52]

Looking at the imperial government in operation, Spring Rice concluded by the time he left Germany in 1898 that the kaiser had taken full control, "as absolutely as Louis XIV did, only the Germany of today is not the France of Louis's time. You can't crack your whip over an engine with much effect."[53] Not that the emperor was everywhere popular; there was one difficulty in particular to be studied. Wilhelm was the hereditary king of Prussia, but he was not emperor by divine right. Whenever his behavior was unduly rash, the other princes expressed displeasure.[54] Even so, Spring Rice did not incline to take the kaiser lightly. "There is no doubt he is an able man although he is vain and exaggerates everything he says or does. But a man does not necessarily lie because he talks loud. We may very well undervalue him." At any rate, the emperor was at the center of public affairs as well as the government itself. "Nothing in the machine must move unless it is at his personal request. He is like the cock who said the sun rose to hear him crow."[55] Then there was the Reichstag in the process of trying to enlarge its powers despite fierce rivalry between the parties. Behind the parties stood public opinion, which was on occasion known to stay or force the hand of the emperor. To Spring Rice this appeared to say that "the Empire, however strange its constitution to our notions, belongs to the countries in the main governed by public sentiment."[56] But once that sentiment hardened into support of government action, the kaiser's likeness to Louis XIV became more pronounced.[57] What was troubling in all this was an absence of genuine freedom to express opinions in the face of a policy once set. German society was too conforming; liberalism was too faint. Liberalism, Spring Rice deduced, was what the ruling classes in Germany feared the most, a condition he termed "a striking fact."[58] Germans "would not catch the mange but when exposed to Liberalism at home or abroad it could be highly contagious," so that liberalism was accounted "the most dangerous system of all."[59]

This study of politics at home was overshadowed by Spring Rice's more constant occupation: German foreign policy. Because they were derived from the same source—the nation as a living embodiment of the race—he was fully aware that domestic affairs mixed inextricably with international plans and ambitions. This was borne out in a long, essay-like letter to Henry Adams, written from Berlin and dated 7 November 1897. In it he saw through to the core of the military-industrial complex as it operated in Germany at the close of the ninetenth century, and shared his forebodings for the twentieth. Here I will allow Spring Rice to speak for himself, and at some length, in this analysis of the German situation.

Germany is in a peculiarly exposed position from the military point of view, which the years succeeding Jena have brought home to the national consciousness. She may have to fight a war with two fronts and if she does not win she may be absolutely extinguished. How to face the danger? By a great army which has had to be increased time and again, and also to be fed and armed. For this she has to find men and money. From the agrarian point of view it seems to be true that the agricultural districts in Prussia at any rate supply the best men. There is no doubt whatever that the system by which one class alone supplies officers to many of the regiments is a great thing for the *esprit de corps* among the officers and discipline among the men, especially those that come from the country and are accustomed to look up to the landlord. It is also the fact that the officer's pay is not sufficient to support them and that life is getting more expensive; and that the burden falls on the landed estates which are thus instrumental in keeping up the army to its present state of efficiency. It is also true that Germany does not provide enough food to feed its population and that in case of war with certain countries, Germany in default of a sufficient navy may run a risk of starvation. From this it should follow that (i) in the interest of the army the landed estates should not be allowed to go into insolvency, and (ii) that every thing ought to be done to prevent the cultivated area going back. I leave out a, no doubt, important factor, the absolute devotion of a whole class to the civil and military service of the state and the danger of doing anything to turn this feeling into bitter disappointment and a sense of undeserved wrong.

Now for the other side. The last time that it was found necessary to increase the army, the new Chancellor, Caprivi, was assailed by a new factor in German political life, the economist. It was explained to him that the expense necessary could be borne if German industry was assisted, and that this was not to be done by protection properly so called, but by what might be termed promotion; that is, by providing better conditions. Industry wanted the home market (to be secured by moderate protection) but it wanted also a foreign market for its products, and it also wanted cheap food for its labourers and cheap raw material. The solution was to obtain and secure your foreign market by allowing the foreign nation to give you what you desired to receive; that is, wanting two things, you use one as a condition to getting the other. It is Cobden's principle sanctioned by treaty. This was the policy which Industry desired and which was accorded. The result was that Agriculture found at once that there was an enormous importation of foreign food and agricultural products while landlords were being ruined in all directions. This came at a time when money had been extremely cheap and when the landlords had been raising money everywhere on mortgages. The effect was a degree of personal exasperation which I suppose, short of civil war, has hardly anywhere been equalled. A ferocious campaign of denunciation and calumny was conducted against the chief promoters of the new policy and now the last of them, Marschall, has been hunted out of service.

What is the ruler of men, a heaven-sent and guided Emperor and King, to do under the circumstances? He is King of Prussia and has been taught history. He knows what his house owes to the Junkers. He is also chief of the army and he knows what is the value of good material and of discipline. But he wants to be able to pay his army and also to build a fleet. How can he do it unless Germany is rich? and Germany can only be rich by manufacturers. He is therefore in a continual dilemma which he generally solves by giving the agrarians everything they want except the essential thing. They hate Caprivi and Marschall; both are got rid of, but their policy is maintained. Every sort of subsidiary legislation is introduced which can appear to assist agriculture—financial facilities, railway rates, agents abroad, etc., etc. If a measure is desired which can gall the dignity of the mercantile classes without doing them much harm, it is probably passed, if not too outrageous. But nothing is done either to save agriculture in the way it desires to be saved, or to inflict irretrievable ruin on industry. Nor is there the slightest chance that anything will be done. But the result is that Industry is furious and Agriculture not satisfied; and that the Government will have to face a general feeling of discontent.

In the meanwhile there is the fourth estate, which has been growing while the others have been fighting. Every year the Socialists have been becoming more numerous and more determined. And they have been faced, not by really repressive measures (for these had to be abandoned), but by insults that did them no harm, and by half measures that Catholics or Liberals in their own defence were obliged to make innocuous. Like the Industrialists, the Socialists have been irritated but not injured. The Government has been always showing its teeth and growling but has hardly ever dared to bite. The Industrial, galled and exasperated, is apt to say, The worst Socialist is the man who has the ear of the Government and wants to take away my property, not the man who preaches a doctrine in meetings and hasn't the smallest chance of carrying it out. This autumn these two were very nearly acting in unison in matters of elections. The Catholics remain. The memory of the Kultur Kampf, Bismarck's confessed blunder, makes them, naturally the conservative element, one of the most determined of the Government's enemies. They can make a bargain, not an alliance.

In the face of all this opposition, what is the Government's strength? Bismarck had hardly ever a parliamentary majority. This Government has certainly not one. Every one in the country seems to have their grievance. It exists because it is the Government, represents union, order, police, money, peace. The Germans seem no less unable to conceive of not accepting the Government as the Government because they object to its policy than a Hindoo would be of not worshipping the Ganges because it had overflowed his crops. Perhaps the reason again is the immense and tremendous pressure from without, which makes a German regard his Government as a sailor does his captain when the ship is in a cyclone.[60]

From beginning to end, Spring Rice displayed a firm grasp of German affairs and a genuine worry about German devotion to the fatherland. This was coupled with what in his judgment was a hatred of England, as the following lengthy extract from a letter to Villiers states.

I should say that the desire here was to organise a common course of action against us—less perhaps for the sake of Asia, than for Europe, to unite in China what Europe had disunited: to establish themselves in China, to have a *point d'appui* so as no longer to be treated as a negligible quantity by the two allied powers: but at the same time to avoid a direct conflict with us until they are ready—which will certainly not be yet. The way to attack England is Napoleon's—to attack her trade—and this can be done as easily in peace time as in war. If she fails in commerce, she must gradually be extinguished politically, and then the rich inheritance can be divided. And indeed England would richly deserve the fate unless she is prepared to fight. This sounds extravagant and it may be so; but that it is the common sense of the people and politicians of Berlin no one who reads the papers can deny. An overt action on our part might lead to a retreat on the part of Germany, but it is almost certain to lead to the powers drawing nearer together, and more closely approaching a union against us. An overt action on Germany's part is, as I said, very unlikely. But Germany is arming both with the military and the commercial arm, and there can be no excuse for us not to arm too. When his neighbour keeps cats, the milkman locks the dairy."[61]

What may indeed have "sounded extravagant" in 1897 was what nearly came to pass after 1914. As Gerald Balfour wrote him in May of 1915, "All your warnings about a coming war with Germany have been realized."[62] There were few surprises for the British ambassador in Washington once World War I commenced.

In 1898 the United States not only smashed Spain in Cuba but conquered the Philippines and picked up the Hawaiian Islands by peaceful annexation, both stepping stones to the China trade. America was thereafter a significant presence in the Pacific and had a stake in the Far Eastern balance of power. The pace of the Anglo-American special relationship quickened, with Lodge, the long time antagonist of Britain in the world, now talking cooperation between London and Washington. Spring Rice was writing him to the same effect. The two governments must work together to protect and promote their common civilization: institutions, language, literature, and a liberal concept of man in society. Lodge held these to be "common possessions to be defended as they were won, in common—and to be enjoyed in common too."[63] He furthermore welcomed any step his country would take "outside her own continent" because it would tend to increase the common good. In context, "outside her own continent" meant Asia and its outer approaches, but it might well include Europe should conditions require. At all events, Germany was to emerge as the common Anglo-American enemy once the twentieth century began to unfold.

To some one of Spring Rice's background and disposition, Constantinople was likely to awaken in him the meaning of its long history: the rise of civilizations and empires, and of those who founded them, and their decline as new empires arose to conquer them. With the onset of the new century, the city of Constantinople continued to occupy a strategic position vis-à-vis modern empires: British, German, Russian. It was a listening post for diplomats and a nesting place for spies. Its climate was that of the underside of realpolitik, swollen by rumors, in short, a city quite contemporary in its antiquity. For Spring Rice it was only a way station along the diplomatic road, as Cairo was to be a detour afterwards, both between Berlin, where politics had consumed him, and Teheran, where the spiritual fires touched his soul. Way stations and detours were likely habitations for his thoughts.

Spring Rice's contemplation of the Levant was not an idle one. Always he needed to apply the historical lesson to the immediate situation. If Byzantium went under, was it not that it was unable and unwilling to defend itself against a barbarous but manly foe? "All the science and gold of the old world availed nothing; they couldn't be honest and they couldn't fight."[64] There stood Santa Sophia, "the most marvelous building" Spring Rice ever was to behold, and sloth, mental and physical, had undermined what it represented, a magnificent Christian shrine surrendered to the infidel. Shall we, he asked over and over, be prudent enough to avoid a similar fate? Often he doubted that England was alert to danger, or possessed of sufficient will to fight the ultimate battle, should it come to that. The darker his mood became, the more likely he was to look to the United States for support.[65] This growing trust in America was all the more remarkable because he knew at first hand the strong anti-British bias in some sections of American society. Such thoughts came flooding in on him in Constantinople as he recalled his Washington days with a mixture of fondness and uncertainty. One reason he was glad to go from Washington was that it had been heartbreaking to be in a country he so much favored but which did not return the compliment as completely as he offered it. But he could not forget or think it unimportant that he "never enjoyed himself so much" as in America.[66] This feeling for the republic was bolstered as public opinion in the United States began to change, and friends occupied high political office. He expressed the hope that no new difficulty would arise that would upset or reverse the new, official friendship. Major obstacles did in fact bar the way to a workable Anglo-American accord, including the renegotiation of the Hay-Pauncefote Treaty allowing the United States to fortify any canal that it built in Central America, and the Alaska boundary dispute, which in its resolution once again showed Britain's willingness to appease American pretensions. On the settlement of the latter issue Roosevelt wrote Spring Rice: "It has been a very fortunate and happy thing to get the question decisively settled and out of the way," which, understandably was the way he wanted his English friend to view the concessions made by London.[67]

At Constantinople, where the shield of the Prophet covered the frescoes of Santa Sophia, Spring Rice dwelled at length on England's vulnerability. He found it "rather disagreeable in that part of the world to be an Englishman. We are closing up our accounts here. The situation is notorious."[68] But why this bleak assessment? There were several factors. The Ottoman Empire, the institution England had gambled could maintain stability in southeastern Europe, as well as in Asia Minor, was yearly getting weaker. Prospects were that it would soon break up, giving Germany in Turkey and collaterally Russia in Persia their long awaited opportunity to dissect the Ottoman corpse with its breath still faint on the mirror of history. Germany and Russia were "powers of darkness" arrayed against liberal, enlightened nations. Put that way, Spring Rice, who strangely was not much impressed by France and its great accomplishments, came to see that Paris and London were natural allies, whereas the Franco-Russian entente was a combination of opposites . . . the product of realpolitik. Yet that entente was a diplomatic fact. Diplomacy was at sixes and sevens with principle. Meanwhile, Spring Rice was much relieved that Britain and France had not gone to war over Fashoda; he was ready to welcome negative evidence if need be to support his contention that like-minded liberal nations must establish and hold a common front.

Spring Rice allowed his fear of Germany and Russia to become obsessive. "The policy of Germany and Russia to divide Europe and Asia between them" became clearer and clearer, "the basis being that Germany is to help Russia by keeping her rivals [England and Japan] quiet . . . while Russia guarantees Germany's peace in Europe and a market in Asia."[69] What Russia was to gain from all this he never explained. This was to prove a wrong-headed analysis at the end of the day. Spring Rice never trusted the Russians and thought the Anglo-Russian entente of 1907 wholly at odds with his conviction about a common front by liberal powers so that no further explanation seemed called for.

Why did Spring Rice believe that England alone, or in concert with other liberal states, might be unable to parry the thrust of Germany and Russia acting singly or in concert? By 1900 no alliance of liberal nations was in place, and the prospects for such an alignment were not in sight. But his deeper concern centered in his own country and its habitual complacency. "We believe that all is for the best and that the best survive." Living in Constantinople was a constant visible reminder that the best did not always survive. "Civilization is neither made or maintained by accident," Spring Rice insisted, or by leaving things alone; "It must think and struggle to maintain itself. We seem to be going light-heartedly into terrible times."[70] His sense of impending doom was a fixed idea.

When this worrying mood was heavy upon him he was more likely to seek solace not from Stephen or Ferguson, but from Theodore Roosevelt. With TR he was no less pessimistic about the fate of liberalism but more analytical, and thus less emotional in voicing his fears. Spring Rice's penetration was acute. He focused on the problem of a free people acting—and fighting—effectively against an enemy population conditioned to believe whatever it was told. In a closed society it was easy enough to explain away inconsistencies. "A word of explanation is enough." Free societies were governed not by decree but by public opinion, which could itself be volatile. Between free nations "a single newspaper article can create bad blood." "The coast of Asia Minor was studded with free cities that quarrelled with one another and were absorbed by a barbarous empire."[71] That might well be the fate of free but quarrelling nations of the near future. For Spring Rice, and he believed for Roosevelt also, there was the obvious need to retain "the fighting edge." Nor could he refrain from contrasting the virtues he imputed to the races speaking English with what he saw daily in Constantinople. The Turks were brave but savage, the Greeks clever but dishonest. It was good, he told Roosevelt, that their two nations had at last begun to come together, his one reassuring thought as he departed Constantinople for Teheran.

There is much that is revealed about Cecil Spring Rice from his first Persian interlude, 1899–1901. It was an unpredictably moving time for him as he drank deeply from the wells of Persian mysticism, half convinced as he was that in the West men were drinking from the mirage of faith. While he came to respect greatly the view of life—"The Asiatic looks with a quiet eye on our restless emotions"—he did not quite succumb to its allure.[72] Indeed, among other things, Persia taught him that it was possible to unite an other-worldly love with a very worldly object, his country, which he once remarked to Roosevelt he loved "in the same absurd way that you love yours."[73] By nature, Spring Rice was a man who gave, and gave gladly. It was not out of expectation that he gave but out of a need for fulfillment. In his private world he gave to his wife and family and especially to his children; he gave to friends and to his country as loyalty shaded into a public sphere of duty and his profession. It was his depth of feeling to such commitments that caused him pain and disillusionment when his country seemed to him careless of its destiny.

In Teheran Spring Rice served under Sir Arthur Hardinge, with whose diplomatic outlook and habit he often disagreed. As Hardinge had to be away from his post for as much as a year, Spring Rice acted as chargé, although not formally designated as such. The experience was valuable, good training for future service in a like capacity and under more trying circumstances in St. Petersburg. At Teheran, Persian politics was immediately in front of him, with officials easily accessible. But Spring Rice thought the Persian people were abused by their rulers; the great part of the population was poor and neglected. The price of food, for example, was controlled by the merchants who were patently profiteers. With his ear to the ground, he picked up vibrations that seemed to portend outbreaks and riots but no revolution. Banks might be threatened by an angry crowd but the people remained largely unpoliticized.[74] When the people had recourse to the authorities to demand a redress of grievances, promises were made but rarely kept. The bureaucracy was a honeycomb of corrupt officials. Spring Rice quickly apprehended that corruption was a way of life, among the poor no less than the rich, and that dishonesty carried no stigma. The official who took no bribes was deemed foolish, and he who offered none was wicked.[75] Yet the sun shone every day, the people somehow survived, and Spring Rice concluded that the lower classes were probably less desperately poor than their equivalent in England.[76] To cheat or not to cheat was not the moral question. Was it then, Spring Rice wondered, that the whole of the people along with the religious and political leaders saw life as a game, perhaps a cosmic joke, and that it was enough if "Allah be praised?"

The government of the Shah survived on loans, which it considered a form of bribery, and it expected to borrow money from England, that is, be bribed by England, because it was a rich country that wanted Persian favors. At the same time it thought nothing of being in debt to Russia, which also was seeking advantage. Spring Rice feared the final result could be subornation by the Czar because St. Petersburg was more willing to lend money than London. It followed that once deeply in debt to Russia, Persia would be a diplomatic ward. There were tangible signs of Russian ascendancy. There were a thousand cossacks in the northern part of the country who were officered and armed by Russia, the only cohesive and disciplined force in the whole of Persia. Equally troubling to Spring Rice was the lack of a clear-cut, positive British policy to counter Russian influence and maintain Britain in the area. The result was a decay of the British presence and a corresponding rise in the threat to their interests. The Russians were seen as wanting all of Persia as a sphere of influence. The "Persian problem" went deeper still. British policy was not well thought out, Spring Rice arguing that there was little planned coordination between the military and naval forces and the Foreign Office. The disaster of the Boer War, and quite possibly the war itself, was to bear witness to that. In Persia, he contended, the problem was "almost purely military." Troops in large numbers must be sent in to offset the Russian penetration, something to which he was sure the Foreign Office had given little attention. He could not help but compare English complacency with German planning methods in similar circumstances. The Germans studied a case in itself, and then in what ways it related to other elements in their general policy, should they proceed to act. In Berlin political and military requirements were treated as one. The Germans, furthermore, would say nothing, would make no noise unless it had been determined that the action contemplated would benefit them overall. If good results were promised they were prepared to act.[77] Spring Rice's frustrations remained unrelieved all the time he was in Persia, causing him to utter some very adverse comments about his government and his superiors. By

the end of his stay, he was looking "to get out of the service
. . . in some decent way." He had a less-than-shining reputation,
and he would not have been honest with himself had he not
admitted it. Perhaps the diplomatic service was no place for
an outspoken junior officer.[78]

The question may well be put: What did Spring Rice want
his country to do in and for Persia in order to reclaim its position
there? If English officers were retained to train the Persian army,
if Parliament would vote funds to keep the Shah content, if
investments were encouraged to promote the construction of
railroads and the development of natural resources, then England would have a reasonable expectation of an influential
place in Persian affairs.[79] But instead the Foreign Office neither
planned nor acted. Spring Rice advocated a reorganization of
the diplomatic machinery. There was need for experts in Middle
Eastern affairs, men who spoke the languages and understood
the cultures. Tenures should be long enough to enable officials
to gain expertise on the ground, thus improving effectiveness;
but there should be turnover as well to prevent the blight of
indifference born of overfamiliarity. And there must be chiefs
of mission who were dynamic in contrast to what he encountered in Hardinge's do-nothing style.[80] Such discontents as
Spring Rice expressed must be read in conjunction with the
Boer War, which England stumbled into, in his judgment, and
then became mired in because there was lack of coordination
between the army and the Foreign Office.

This Persian experience intensified the contradiction between
the ideal and the real that was to trouble Spring Rice most
of his life. Because the two were sharply at odds, he contemplated abandoning the service and withdrawing to private life.
That he did not do so must not be attributed entirely to the
opportunity to join Lord Cromer in Egypt. In fact, his options
were severely limited. He had no head for business; conceivably
he might have gained a place as an Oxford don had the offer
been made; and it was, as he remarked, "infernally difficult"
to start up a literary career. These limitations apart, Spring Rice
stayed in the diplomatic service because unconsciously it had
become his life's work. It continued to offer the best prospect
for the union of his two worlds. With or without Cromer's invita-
tion to come to Cairo, he would have continued as a diplomat,
yet his position on the *Caisse* gave him time away from worrying
duty, which he badly needed. Conflict between the ideal and

the real as he had known it in Persia had worn his spirit peri-
lously thin.

Once in Cairo, Spring Rice rejoiced that he had put Teheran
behind him—"How glad I am to be here!" he exclaimed.[81] Assignment to the *Caisse* added up to a restorative two years. He
was detached from the diplomatic service, and his work was
anything but stressful. Leisure time he employed in translating
The Story of Valeh and Hadijeh, an uplifting but demanding
task. Leave in England and a visit to his old chief, Sir Frank
Lascelles, in Berlin were happy occasions. Furthermore, time
in the United States enabled him to commune with his friend
Roosevelt, who was now president of the United States. Incidentally, this repaired his reputation somewhat at the Foreign Office,
for few if any there could boast of so close an association with
the White House. All in all, Spring Rice had good reason to
recall his official connection with the *Caisse* as pleasant.

Anticipating his return to the diplomatic service he kept a
watchful eye on the activities of the Foreign Office. He was
especially hard on Lord Rosebery, whose character he now described as an "enigma." He was disturbed that Rosebery saw
no need for the reform of governmental procedures or policies,
changes Spring Rice believed essential for Great Britain if it
was to maintain its place in the international order. Things
would not improve by themselves; complacency was the beset-
ting sin of the English. He related inaction to poor leadership
and more than once declared that what England needed was
its own version of Theodore Roosevelt.[82] By distancing himself
from the Levant, by going to England and America, he gained
a new sense of equilibrium, substituting detachment for disillusionment. If he continued to believe power in Persia was a
key to an overall strategy in the Middle East, he became less
irritable in stating his views.

In Egypt Spring Rice remained the observant analyst. Egypt
was the East, and as he watched the fallaheen working the
land as his ancestors had for past millennia, he wondered: "Is
all politics the fringe of the *real* reality, the ripple on the deep?
And the curse of men and women (which is also their strength)
as written in Genesis—the real thing?" He described himself
as "full of all sorts of vague feelings chasing each other like
ghosts in a haunted house."[83] Such thoughts came to him early
in his stay. He would eventually reveal a more prosaic turn
of mind, noting the rise and fall of the Nile and how it affected

the Egyptian harvest, and the construction of the great dam at Assioul, referring to it as an engineering experiment that turned into an engineering feat.[84] Fortunately, Spring Rice returned to everyday reality and did not stay fastened overlong to the reveries of the spirit.

Time spent in England was like a tonic to him, and he was content, "enjoying the still uncorrupted beauty of the wonderful country . . . to feel one's feet on the chalk turf and to see the fields and woods fading into the mists under the branches of the beeches on top of the downs," in a happy land where one did not have to bribe the station porter to procure his services.[85] Such playful thoughts contrasted sharply, when he brought his mind back to diplomacy, with what he had discovered of German manuevers in Washington. The kaiser's government was making a strong pitch to keep relations close between the fatherland and the millions of German-Americans. Methods consisted of anti-English press releases and threats that if certain measures were not passed by Congress, it would mean a loss of German-American votes. It appeared that Berlin was trying to control the immigrant electorate whenever it was to Germany's advantage.[86] As Florence Lascelles shared his misgivings about Germany and its intentions, she, along with Chirol and Roosevelt, were sounding boards for his worst fears. The German menace was the bad penny that always came back to haunt him, even at the Caisse. Spring Rice remained a diplomat in his interests and outlook during this brief separation from the service. Others, including Francis Villiers at the Foreign Office, were aware of this. Villiers valued his talents and believed he was wasting his time in Cairo. Appointment in February 1903 as secretary to the embassy at St. Petersburg, in which Villiers had had a hand, marked both a return to the service and an important step in Spring Rice's career. He might well have been posted to Washington where the newly named Michael Herbert had bid for his services. But he was pleased to go to Russia. It would bring him face to face with czardom.

This Russian assignment was the culmination of Spring Rice's diplomatic apprenticeship. The Russia of 1903 was "very interesting, most absorbing and fascinating at times." Fully aware of Russian expansionist tendencies in a world characterized by shifting diplomacy that had produced half-wrought alliances, there was much to be reported to the Foreign Office from St. Petersburg. He informed his superiors, for example, that the

Russians appeared ready to make some accommodation respecting spheres of influence in Asia. A few months before, Lord Lansdowne had taken a stiff line in defense of the Persian Gulf as a peculiarly British preserve, the exact kind of action Spring Rice had urged from Teheran. The results of this tough stance were clear. An exchange of views with Sir Louis Mallet, Lansdowne's précis writer, gave indication that Spring Rice's opinions were now being studied carefully, his despatches making a favorable impression over a period of months.[87] More important recognition would follow, but such were his suspicions of Foreign Office administrators that he badly needed early reassurance.

Meanwhile he had begun to examine czardom at first hand. Initially he was impressed by appearances. "The people here are so accustomed to misery that what we would think abominable, they don't mind in the least," he told his sister Margaret. "I can understand the intense mournfulness of Russian literature. Their history is so sober and their country so ugly and their climate so intolerable they must be marked out by nature to bear and inflict suffering."[88] In taking the long view of their history, he felt that "the average Russian, unlike the average Englishman, was glad he did not live in a free society, but rather preferred the order imposed on him by his government, even though he might grumble."[89] There was no sign of social upheaval visible, from what he could tell. The peasants were quiet, the industrial workers less restive than in either England or America. The overconcentration of wealth in the hands of a very few was incredible. As in like situations, Spring Rice came up with a penetrating judgment. Russia must remain at peace. Should she go to war with any power, the consequences would be dire, possibly fatal.[90] But war with Japan did ensue, one of the sources of the Revolution of 1905.

This kind of analysis earned him a new aura of importance at the Foreign Office, and he had few regrets that he had not been assigned to Washington to assist either Michael Herbert or Mortimer Durand, however much he was flattered that the president and Senator Lodge preferred to have him in their midst.

4

VETERAN DIPLOMAT

If diplomats are made, not born, Cecil Spring Rice was no exception to that rule. The truth of this is obvious. Many of his interests and much of his instinct ran counter to the demands of a diplomatic career; and the evidence abounds that he thought of throwing it over on occasion out of distaste and frustration. Every life has within it elements of conflict and uncertainty—the "could-have-beens," the "might-have-beens"—that have a way of bringing these to the surface. Spring Rice indulged in retrospective self-analysis defensively. Nevertheless, he learned well the craft of the diplomat, sharpening his skills and, it must be said, gradually acquiring self-confidence and thereby gaining the confidence of his superiors. Nothing nurtured his self-confidence like associating with Americans of the highest rank. To be the intimate of the president, a powerful senator, and the secretary of state, and welcomed into their families, of this no other British diplomat could boast, although Spring Rice boasted quietly for all of that. To imply that acceptance by these and other Americans ordained that he be ambassador to Washington one day remains unconvincing. There was no deciding event or set of events developing into a pattern that led on to the embassy. Spring Rice did not believe it, nor did his friends in either England or America believe it—however much the latter group may have labored for it—and historical judgments should be so shaped. What may be claimed is that Spring Rice carried out his appointed assignments, his ability as a diplomat became more widely acknowledged, and on these bases he would advance from secretary at St. Petersburg to minister at Teheran, to minister at Stockholm. Finally in Washington he joined that corps of senior officials upon whom fell the responsibility of representing Great Britain worldwide.

Spring Rice had worked hard to acquire a sound sense of history. In 1904 he had alerted Roosevelt to the world being "on the verge of great change." Although the particular reference happened to be to the Far East, he knew that a power shift in one area of the international network would necessarily cause repercussions elsewhere. He was especially sensitive to the future of Japan, Britain's Far Eastern ally, but he also kept a sharp eye on Germany's maneuvers, England's natural, if not actual, enemy. Sitting in the Russian capital, he kept a book on the world, determined to put his views (and those of his government) before his powerful friends in the United States. Perhaps it was only out of friendship that he wrote the president so regularly, but whatever his motivation, his arguments had a shaping effect on TR's outlook.

The difficulties confronting a common Anglo-American strategy for East Asia arose from several sources, some but incidental to Japan's new military prowess. One such difficulty was Sir Mortimer Durand, the British ambassador that Roosevelt was not comfortable with. This was a purely personal matter, but it may have been aggravated by the president's expressed preference for Spring Rice. Another was the uncertainty of the United States regarding the large policy England was pursuing in the Orient. This was due mostly to a lack of communication. More specifically, what should be the Anglo-American response to Russian ambitions in that part of the world? Roosevelt wanted clarification of British intentions, confident that there would be no clash of vital interests, which was the best possible basis for cooperation between London and Washington.

With its victory over China some years before, the new Japan was a Far Eastern nation whose full potential was hard to measure. It had acquired substantial interests in Manchuria, was ready to exploit the Liaotung peninsula and the Island of Sakhalin, and most pointedly wanted to have control of Korea, by conquest if need be. All this added up to a set of unsettling ambitions and an open challenge to the Russians, who already had staked out some of these areas for takeover. China, the geographical expression, became a geopolitician's nightmare. All the industrial nations, including the United States, wanted some part of the China trade. By reason of its possession of the Philippines, the Americans had an approach point to the Asian mainland. The struggle between Russia and Japan that Spring Rice divined was in the cards could have the effect of redressing the balance of power across the world. Great Britain, not unnaturally, would favor a Japanese victory, perhaps a sweeping one.

France and Germany would incline to Russia. More germane was the attitude of the United States. With Roosevelt acting largely as his own secretary of state, his personal preference would be the centerpiece of the American response to any war and, as it turned out, how that war would end in terms of a peace treaty.

Roosevelt determined his assessments of Russia and Japan after a great deal of study, advice, and thought. Among those influencing him were Mahan, Brooks Adams, Lodge, and Spring Rice. At first Roosevelt looked upon Russia as a traditional American friend because national interests did not conflict, a fact well illustrated by the sale of Alaska to the United States in 1867. By 1896 Spring Rice had begun a campaign to warn Roosevelt of the menace of the Slav and thereafter missed no opportunity to remind his friend of the Slavic threat to the Anglo-American world position and as an enemy of liberalism.[1] Roosevelt was led to accept this view after 1900 because of Russia's expansionist intentions in the Far East. Once the president had been converted, Spring Rice continued to preach the salvation of a firm line against the Russians. He wrote Roosevelt in 1905; "We have read the manifesto of the Czar in which he tells us he is determined to maintain the contrary principle to free government and to take his stand on that. The manifesto is his own heart-felt expression of conviction."[2] To Teddy Roosevelt the czar was "a preposterous figure at the head of one hundred million Russians." Spring Rice pressed on, telling the president that Russia had only contempt for the United States. America was a "standing reproach" to its system of government. "You deny their first principle and have the impertinence to exist, even to prosper."[3] As he came to respect Spring Rice's global thinking more and more, Roosevelt was sure to be disposed less and less favorably toward Russia.

The president required no encouragement in his friendly manner toward Japan and heard no dissent from Spring Rice. He told Spring Rice of the visit in June 1904 with Ambassador Takahira and Baron Kaneko at Sagamore Hill, the private Roosevelt residence in New York. There had been a meeting of the minds respecting China and the Far East generally. He liked the Japanese, and they greatly interested him, as he explained to his English friend.[4] In so saying he assumed that what lay behind a workable balance of power was a workable balance of vital national interests. In pursuit of that fundamental balance

Roosevelt watched the Russo-Japanese War with a mixture of horror at the slaughter of so many men and distress over the possible impact on world politics.

Once the war had begun Roosevelt received a steady supply of unofficial intelligence from Spring Rice. By no means was the secretary of the British Embassy the sole source of information and impression, especially after George von L. Meyer, an astute diplomat in his own right, became the American ambassador at St. Petersburg. But Spring Rice was his intimate who could report both fact and rumor, the effects of the war upon the czar, the czardom, and the Russian people, and, in as far as discretion permitted, the views of his own government. With England and Japan in formal alliance, London's commitment to a favorable outcome of the war was hardly in doubt, nor could it be ignored by Washington. And there was some danger that the conflict might ignite Europe. The implications of the Russo-Japanese War were spread that wide.

At first Spring Rice told Roosevelt the war had been "a real case of drift . . . with both ships gradually drawing together until the collision."[5] This nonpartisan judgment quickly gave way to a rancorous and perhaps overdrawn interpretation. "That Japan could have dared to resist is inconceivable [to the Russians]; that she attacked Russia was monstrous. The explanation is England and America. These friends of Japan incited her against holy and just Russia. Since America could hardly be made to pay, it must be England who suffers, whether in India or Persia or elsewhere." Spring Rice also yielded his judgment to an unreasonable dread of Russia by continuing to insist that Germany and Russia were to bring about a piecemeal dismemberment of the British empire. "This sounds all fancy, but I really don't believe it is. It is possible—almost probable."[6] Considering the serious tone of the president's response, TR did not find such charges far fetched; he simply expressed doubts that such a coalition existed and let it go at that. There had been a time when he would have resisted such a notion vigorously.

Roosevelt was more concerned about the extent of a Japanese victory. "If Japan seriously starts to reorganize China and makes headway, this will result in a real shift of the center of equilibrium in so far as the white races are concerned."[7] This consideration Spring Rice did not allude to, but whatever the menace to England, he counted always on the sympathy of the Roosevelt administration, which would have another four years in office.

At one and the same time he insisted on the need of England to prepare defenses of its own.[8]

Preoccupation with the international ramifications of the war did not prevent Spring Rice from reporting on other matters from St. Petersburg. He was constantly aware of the place of tyranny in the Russian homeland as dramatized in the capital, the city of the czars. "Tyranny made the empire and maintains it, and its prestige is enormous."[9] "The mass of the people, ill-treated, over-taxed, over-worked have an enormous strength of patience and passive endurance, and perfect faith in the mission of the empire and the authority of their Czar."[10] Although assassinations were multiplying—Bolrikoff, the governor of Finland, and Plehve, minister of interior, were victims—czardom was safe; there appeared to be no change in this autocratic government in the offing.[11] Spring Rice's most scathing description of the situation he included in a letter to John Hay, the American secretary of state.

> It is a curious state of things. There is the Emperor, a religious madman almost—without a statesman, or even a council—surrounded by a legion of Grand Dukes—thirty-five of them and not one of them at the war at this moment, with a few priests and priestly women behind them. No middle class; an aristocracy ruined and absolutely without influence, an underpaid bureaucracy living, of necessity, on corruption. Beneath this, about 100 million of people absolutely devoted to their Emperor, absolutely ignorant, kept ignorant for fear of the consequences of knowledge (by an elaborate conspiracy between Church and State), gradually becoming poorer and poorer as they bear all the burden of taxation; drafted into the Army in thousands—which they enjoy, as they fare far better than they do at home. This army, devoted, brave, enduring, religious, will do everything which their Czar tells them.

Spring Rice concluded this letter: "Well, here is a tirade against absolute monarchy. I used to laugh when I heard it talked of in America as a danger and a crime, and really I don't wonder now. I wish I were in a Republican country again with all my heart."[12] Quite unexpectedly, within six months, that would happen, all in the working of the cycles of diplomacy.

Cecil Spring Rice stepped into the foreground of Anglo-American affairs when he went to Washington in March 1905, an unofficial representative of the British government in matters relating to the Russo-Japanese War and its settlement. He himself may have been responsible for inspiring the move. He had writ-

ten to Ronald Ferguson: "It is most important that we should
have some cordial cooperation between persons—if not governments—in the Far Eastern Question. It is a curious fact that
the U.S. embassy in London does not seem to be consulted
by Lansdowne and our embassy in Washington reports nothing
from Roosevelt. Yet I know that both Roosevelt and Hay would
like—not joint but parallel action—and would be ready to coop-
erate in spirit if not in deed. The Pacific Coast which once
divided us is now a great bond of union. Our interests are
identical and we should pursue them side by side."[13] He urged
that Sir Edward Grey be sent, or Ferguson himself. His proposal
was bolstered by Roosevelt's election to the presidency in November 1904. "This is the very best news I have had for ages,"
he wrote TR in congratulation. "Now you are safe for the four
years at least."[14] Would it be reading too much into Spring Rice's
mind to suggest that he believed England was also safe "for
the four years at least?"

What Spring Rice thought about the need for "some cordial
cooperation between persons—if not governments—in the Far
Eastern Question," Theodore Roosevelt echoed at almost the
same time, that is, toward the end of 1904. In a lengthy, confidential letter, the president was direct. Lamenting that there was
"no one in your Embassy here that I can speak to with even
reasonable fulness," he went on: "I do wish to heavens you
would come over, if only for a week or two, and I think it
would be very important for your Government that you should
come over."[15] This was a no-nonsense communication with the
president, because of the limits of his time in office, declaring
himself "something of an opportunist." He contended further
that the United States could not fully depend on Great Britain
as an ally in his pursuit of American advantage because England,
like his own country, experienced changes in administrations
due to the vagaries of the electoral process. Roosevelt also had
praise for the Japanese in their war with Russia but warned
that a totally victorious Japan might be hard for both the United
States and Britain to deal with once a treaty had been signed.[16]

The problem at the British embassy that Roosevelt referred
to was confirmed by Ferguson after a visit to Washington; he
declared the English handicapped when compared with the
French, the Germans, even the Austrians. These embassies were
headed up by professional diplomats who had standing with
the president.[17] Ferguson concluded that Durand badly needed
assistance, and by mid-January 1905, he had communicated this

to the Foreign Office. In the wake of his recommendation, Lord Lansdowne agreed to send out Spring Rice on a mission to have discussions with the president regarding the war and especially the delicate position in which Britain found itself as a result of the treaty with Japan. Spring Rice, technically on leave from his Russian post, came to Washington on a personal visit to Theodore Roosevelt. He stayed neither at the White House nor the British embassy but was the guest of his long time friend, Henry Adams. His assignment was simple: reassure Roosevelt that the views of the Foreign Office accorded with the American position, at least in broad outline; at the same time the United States must understand that His Majesty's government must respect its treaty obligations to Japan.

Not too much should be claimed for this ad hoc diplomacy. Roosevelt gained some insight into Foreign Office thinking along with useful information. Lansdowne in turn would know the mind of the president, who had already indicated he hoped to have a hand in bringing about an end to the war by means of his good offices. Anglo-American efforts were intended to parallel each other. Even Sir Mortimer Durand profited. Spring Rice affirmed his confidence in him when consulting with TR. The embassy staff was to be reorganized and strengthened and new personnel appointed. Not the least aspect of the affair was the heightened reputation of Spring Rice. Because of his unique entrée into the corridors of Washington power, he became the most prominent American expert in the diplomatic service. He was consulted by the foreign secretary, asked to advise Edward VII in establishing a personal relationship with Roosevelt, and had contributed in a tangible way to Anglo-American accord. Whether he would ever represent Great Britain as ambassador at Washington was, at this juncture, less a consideration than was his widely respected expertise on American affairs generally and on Theodore Roosevelt particularly.

After a stopover in London for consultation in the Foreign Office, Spring Rice returned to St. Petersburg to resume his duties as first secretary, there to witness the threat of disintegration of a nation wracked by war. He could not find within himself any sympathy for czardom in its hour of trial. He was unimpressed by the March Manifesto in which the czar, while urging that the war be fought until victory was achieved, also promised to draw upon the best men in the country, to be elected by the people, and to develop political reforms. "It is generally understood that nothing will be done for months,"

Spring Rice predicted correctly.[18] The dilemma that daunted both Czar Nicholas and the nation was plain enough. Military disasters revealed the gross inefficiency and ineptitude of the leadership, both political and military, which could only stimulate demands for reform. But as long as the war continued, reform was unlikely because all energies had to be concentrated on achieving military success. If reforms were pushed at the expense of victory, reformers would be blameworthy. If reforms were not initiated, however, Russia could not expect to win the war. And if, by some strange alchemy of arms, Russia should prevail over Japan, reform would lose its urgency, with Russian autocracy vindicated. It was a logical dead end from which there was no way out. Spring Rice reduced the future within Russia to a frightening formula: the assassins versus the autocrats.

He also kept his eye on the condition of the mass of people. In reporting on Bloody Sunday (January 1905), he told how Father Gapon had led people to the Winter Palace to petition the holy czar to be mindful of the sufferings of his subjects. "The crowd was permitted to assemble. They believed they could see the Czar. . . . The firing may have been necessary but the Government had no right to allow the people to collect. It looked so much as though they intended 'to show them a lesson'. There is absolutely no proof that the people were armed, and why did so many bring their wives and children?"[19] From what he could tell, Bloody Sunday was symptomatic of repression throughout the country. In March he noted: "In the spring the misery of the people will be at its height because they have had to sell all their foodstuffs to pay taxes and the new crop will not be gathered. There are thousands of women and children without support. The men are at war. No news comes as to whether they are alive or dead. . . . Every one has frightful stories of peculation."[20] When disorders did not occur spontaneously, they were organized by the police to discredit and intimidate the reformers. Government agents circulated among the peasants telling them that the liberals were really traitors to mother Russia and the holy czar. "In every town blackguards are organized and paid by the police to persecute the 'intelligence' that is students, doctors and other sorts of reformers. . . . The Government is with the people against the traitors, i.e., reformers."[21] As the weeks went by, Spring Rice felt that everywhere anarchy was about to reign.

The Foreign Office had not expected a revolution,[22] but at all events Sir Edward Grey wrote to Spring Rice about it. "I suppose you have no idea what the outcome of the Revolution will be; the laws of the course of revolutions are not capable of scientific analysis. A general rule is what was at the top at the beginning is at the bottom at the end."[23] Not himself versed in the dynamics of revolution, Spring Rice was able, nonetheless, to identify the classic elements of a pending breakdown in a fashion considerably more sophisticated than Grey. Taking a long view of things, he predicted the outcome. "First, the schools and universities are shut up. Then the mill hands refuse to work. Police are used to break up demonstrations. The people resist. An autocracy that rules by fear is now attacked by fear. The breakdown of law and order is frightening." It promised a return to the primitive. At the time only the army and the police remained loyal and reliable. "The center of government and the source of power was hidden in the palace and surrounded by his [the czar's] soldiers and spies, and no one can get to him and tell him the truth."[24] It is hard to say whether Spring Rice was describing 1905–6, or 1916–17, as he continued his analysis. The old autocracy would issue forth into a new autocracy as czarists gave way to comrades and comrades made way for commissars. In the midst of such dire circumstances occurred the massive destruction of the Russian fleet in May, at the battle of Tsushima. Demands for an end to the war were now more incessant, and a determined voice took up the cry. It was that of Spring Rice's American friend Theodore Roosevelt.

The quest for an end to the Russo-Japanese War was almost exclusively the work of the American president, and the Nobel Peace Prize was a fully deserved recognition of his efforts. Spring Rice, although peripheral to the negotiations, had access to both the foreign secretary and the president and was therefore in a position to contribute to mutual trust and understanding, both of which were in rather short supply in London. Roosevelt was pleased that Spring Rice and Meyer were able to communicate freely with one another once the United States, having responded to the Japanese initiative, sought to get Russian agreement to come to the conference table. On the Japanese side, TR proceeded independently, but as England and Japan were allies, and Spring Rice was in London for several weeks for consultation, his services were useful there as well. Yet the point deserves to be stressed that Roosevelt, either as a matter of style or as a piece of savoir faire—if not both—played a lone hand, neither consulting with Lansdowne nor informing Spring Rice until each party had agreed to sit down and talk. Once the agreement became public, Roosevelt wrote to Spring Rice at some length, disclosing his thoughts about Japan and the future of East Asia. He believed it proper to reveal to the British government both his hopes and his fears, and to this end he remarked: "I earnestly hope that your people will not permit any feeling that they would like to see both combatants exhausted, to prevent them from doing all they can to bring about peace. . . ."[25] Spring Rice's reply, that Roosevelt's words reflected the views exactly of the king, the cabinet and the foreign secretary, was a qualified one: "The question arises—how to bring it about?"[26] In plain words, England would not overlook its treaty obligations to Japan, simply to promote a quick finish to the war. The British would only exert pressure on Japan to settle when, in their judgment, the Japanese were making impossible demands. Spring Rice labored to make this condition clear, that it could not, "in honour" go back on an ally.[27] Roosevelt chided him on his "needless heroics" on the matter of honor. "I wholly fail to understand the difference in the position which makes it proper for France, the ally of Russia to urge it to make peace, and yet makes it improper for England, an ally of Japan, to urge Japan to make peace." The fact is, the president was critical of British foot dragging. He believed that the Japanese would strive to make the best possible deal, irrespective of London's attitude and independent of its advice.[28] At this juncture the two friends were not in accord. If, as Spring Rice insisted to Lansdowne, Roosevelt failed to "grasp the point of view that our alliance is a specific one relating to the Far East,"[29] Spring Rice failed to grasp the proposition that Roosevelt was a truly honest broker with peace his prime objective. He had no hidden agenda. Nor had he ceased to be "opportunist" as he practiced the art of real politik. When Lansdowne continued to play a waiting game, allowing the Japanese considerable latitude, Roosevelt pushed for peace then and there. He did not mistrust the British position; he thought it unwise. Certainly he retained his deep respect for Spring Rice, sharing with him correspondence with Baron Kaneko that had been a potent factor in bringing the Japanese to see the folly of insisting on an indemnity at the risk of having to resume the war with its heavy burdens.

The postmortems on the Treaty of Portsmouth, whereby Japan received the southern half of Sakhalin, the Liaotung Peninsula, and Port Arthur, as well as a dominant position in Korea—but no indemnity—suggest that not only Spring Rice but the Foreign Office was prepared to follow the American lead. "Japan had acted for the best," in Spring Rice's words. He was effusive in writing to Edith Roosevelt: "It is a fact beyond any question that the President single handed effected the peace, against the wishes of the Japanese people and the Russian Government," and, he might have added, despite some misgivings in Whitehall.[30]

In the world of diplomacy things are never really settled. The Peace of Portsmouth meant that the old concerns about German actions and Russian reaction returned to occupy Foreign Office minds and to all but haunt Spring Rice's thoughts. It was late in 1905, and the competing alliances were not finally in place for the showdown that all along Spring Rice argued would be the tragic result. Would England become the target of continental coalition with the renewal, in 1906, of the Anglo-Japanese Treaty? If so, there was gratification from the Taft-Katsura Agreement in August, which was being termed a virtual if unwritten accord between London, Tokyo, and Washington to guarantee stability in the Far East. The empire was safe on that side of the world, thanks in part to Roosevelt's *weltpolitik*. And what of Russia? Could it survive domestic unrest? Would unrest lead to upheaval? And what would be the meaning of the power vacuum should Russia become a nonplayer in the game of international politics? For that matter, would United States policy remain on course any longer than Roosevelt's tenure as president? There was, no doubt, plenty for a British diplomat to think about, whatever his post. If he were at St. Petersburg, domestic uncertainties seemed to outweigh diplomatic possibilities in importance, or so it was for Spring Rice, who was in Russia for the Revolution of 1905.

While serving as chargé (from October 1905 to late May 1906), Spring Rice was engaged in four separate but closely connected affairs of state. First and most expectedly, he had responsibility for the safety of British subjects living in and around the capital, where most of his countrymen and -women were concentrated. In discharging this duty he was cool and confident and by his demeanor undoubtedly muted the voice of panic whenever it was raised. He was particularly disgusted with the actions of Wickham Steed of *The Times*, who, upon receiving a threatening telegram, bolted the country without informing the embassy. Such defections aside, the Foreign Office cabled him: "All your arrangements regarding British subjects seem excellent."[31] Spring Rice saw to it that Steed's cut-and-run tactics were not contagious. When there was talk of sending a British cruiser to stand by for the purpose of evacuating Britons, Spring Rice strongly opposed it as both unnecessary and likely to provoke the Russian government to a hostile act. To dispatch the cruiser was "just plain folly."[32] No warship was sent. Whatever doubts lingered about his ability to act boldly or to handle delicate situations with courage and honor were completely dissipated.

His responsibilities now took on an added feature. Through Lord Knollys, private secretary to King Edward, Spring Rice became a special source of intelligence to the monarch. Beginning in November he sent a series of reports that the king read with much appreciation. Throughout, Spring Rice urged caution and skepticism regarding the rumors coming out of Russia in these fateful months. Yet he felt justified in giving his own opinions, which were anything but cheerful. In December he described the struggle going on between the government and the reformers "as almost civil war."[33] A number of the czarist aristocracy had already fled the country, taking their wealth with them. Of course Spring Rice hoped the reformers would succeed in bringing into being a constitutional monarchy without the shedding of blood. "Pure repression" was ever present on the part of the authorities, he told the king. Financial conditions were bad, and the inability of the government to obtain further foreign loans would destabilize the country. The flow of money out of Russia only complicated matters. The swing back and forth between reason and repression made Spring Rice optimistic at times, and all this he communicated through Lord Knollys. "What is needed is a Lord Melbourne to give advice of a constitutional character to the Sovereign. If . . . the Emperor knows how to reconcile constitutional ideas to the intense feeling of loyalty which still exists all through the Empire, the result may be a very workable form of Government."[34] But there was no Lord Melbourne to advance methods of compromise, and the czar and the reformers stood at an impasse. No one could predict the outcome of the events of 1906, and Spring Rice wisely hedged his bets. In a letter to Knollys in March, he spoke of two tendencies, "the one . . . rather radical" and the other "extremely reactionary." He went on to characterize the leadership of the rival factions. The reactionary minister of interior, Durnovo, was a "frank savage." It was an "awkward position to have to choose between a gentleman like Mirski—

which would mean universal anarchy—and a known savage like Durnovo who can keep order only by the most violent and unscrupulous methods."[35] In any event, without financial assistance the reform movement could not succeed. With elections to the Duma—the legislative body the czar had promised—in April, the results greatly favored serious but responsible reform. Liberalism, the centerpiece of Spring Rice's public philosophy, had apparently triumphed. He deemed this good news for England and thought he detected among the liberal leaders a desire for a friendly understanding in international matters with London. At the same time he cautioned that any definite agreement along such lines was out of the question "unless it was negotiated directly between the Emperor and the King."[36] Spring Rice admitted that this was unlikely to happen easily.

Another episode in his time as chargé, and one that involved a sensitive issue, had to do with the efforts of the Anglo-Jewish Association to come to the aid of Russian Jews who had been dispossessed and who lived in fear of their lives. During these months of disorder, a committee of the association raised funds and proposed to work through the embassy in St. Petersburg to manage a distribution of the available money. In the implementation of this enterprise, Spring Rice was helpful but cautious. Oswald Simon, the son of Sir John Simon who had served in Parliament and had been one of the founders of the Anglo-Jewish Association, visited St. Petersburg in order to get some firsthand awareness of the plight of his fellow Jews and what, of a practical nature, might be done to help them. Oswald Simon had been a contemporary of Spring Rice at Balliol and was fully at ease in his dealings with him; in turn, Spring Rice spoke to him cordially but candidly when it came to the role of the embassy in the distribution of the money raised. He had to point out to Simon the government's suspicion of Jews, who had, by a goodly measure, favored the ideas of the reformers. He added that the Russian people had a defensive attitude toward the Jews that was reinforced by the church and the state. Jews, in consequence, were victims of both popular and official anti-Semitism and suffered terribly. In granting all that, Spring Rice thought it entirely unacceptable to allow British officials to appear in any way to help in the distribution of relief funds. But he was "perfectly ready to do everything to assist in the distribution by recommending good persons for that purpose." He opposed "from the first the employment of Consuls for that purpose" because he "could not consent to them being exposed to the risk of being accused of subsidizing men who were said to be enemies of the Government."[37] He did not leave the matter there, however, and informed the Russian authorities of the purpose of the association and the suggestion of Lord Lansdowne, who advised them to work through private citizens who were trustworthy. In this way the monies would serve humanitarian purposes and not be used to purchase weapons under the guise of charity. In keeping official British skirts clean, he took it upon himself to advise Simon, and by inference, the Anglo-Jewish Association, of what he believed was the best way for the Jews to respond to their environment.

My advice would be to remember that the past must have its effects, but that the present may be utilized in order gradually to redeem the errors of the past. But you must not act as if the past had never existed. Your friends here are numerous. But in trying to befriend you, they very often advocate a course which would be more fatal to you than the advice of your worst enemies. Like many Russians they believe that a new world can suddenly be created out of chaos and that the old world will die without leaving a wrack behind. That is quite wrong. As I said, until the Russian nation is educated and able to compete in the struggle for existence, it will defend itself against the competition of its superiors by disabling them from competing at all. And if they try, as is natural, to remedy the disabilities under which they suffer by calling in the sympathy and assistance of the civilized world, they will suffer for it, for they will be looked on as having once and for all given up the hope and expectation of sharing in the fortunes of the country and people among whom they live. And this would be fatal. They are here and they intend to stay here. They must help, as many of them are helping, the people of this country to find some means of attaining to that degree of culture which is at present almost the monopoly of a section of the population. They must help the Government to attain this end, and they must show that they are as much and more the real friends of this unfortunate people as those who profess their friendship so loudly. I am as you see the *advocatus diaboli*, but the view which I explain to you is, I believe, the view of some of your own people here, and a view which has some important backers.—This is a long letter and is a very ungrateful recompense to you for your kind remembrance of me. Besides, to whom am I preaching that they should be *ipsis Christianis Christianiores*?[38]

It could well have struck Simon as gratuitous advice, the wisdom of which he might question, but he could not doubt its sincerity, for it derived from deep within Spring Rice's liberal conscience. If he had underestimated the hatred the Jews had experienced under the czars, counseling patience where it was not reciprocated, he did so out of the conviction that unless liberalism triumphed over czardom, the fate of both Russia and the Jews would be tragic.

The special demands placed on the chargé by tumultuous conditions did not deflect Spring Rice's attention from more conventional diplomatic concerns. Immediately after the Treaty of Portsmouth, the Russians put out the story that Roosevelt had been pro-Russian during the negotiations and had been especially grateful to France for bringing pressure on St. Petersburg to accept peace terms; the story was embellished by an assertion that the president was hostile to a renewal of the Anglo-Japanese Treaty. England's roadblocking of the peace was thrown in for good measure. Spring Rice made all this known to the White House by writing to Mrs. Roosevelt. In direct response to his request, TR called in Ambassador Jusserand and directed him to convey to the Quai d'Orsay that all elements of the story going the rounds were untrue, while at the same time his admiration for France was reaffirmed. He then instructed Secretary of State Elihu Root, who had succeeded to office with the death of John Hay, to inform the British ambassador, Durand, indirectly and apparently subsequently. Roosevelt's method of procedure was all too obvious: Durand remained outside the presidential privileged circle. At times diplomacy can be concerned with bagatelle.

Of genuine significance, however, was the Foreign Office decision—and really that of the new foreign secretary, Sir Edward Grey—to move ahead to a rapprochement with Russia. Spring Rice was alarmed by this development, but as a mere chargé could expect to have small influence in the shaping of such high level diplomacy. He merely followed the lead set down by Grey. Grey told him that he wanted to see "Russia reestablished in the councils of Europe and . . . on better terms with us than she has yet been."[39] This marked the beginning of a working relationship between Spring Rice and Grey, both official and personal, that was to have real impact on early World War I British foreign policy. It was a close and confidential combination of like-minded men who did not always see eye to eye on how best to gain their common objective, the security and well being of England and the empire. Their diverging ap-

proach was especially evident at the time of the Anglo-Russian
entente in 1907, which Grey earnestly and successfully sought
and Spring Rice persistently criticized. But Sir Edward was
the foreign secretary and Spring Rice the loyal subordinate, giving advice and opinion but never obstructing the path leading
to the agreement. Grey understood conditions in Russia as well
as he did in large part because Spring Rice supplied him with
information ranging from financial reports to the latest rumors,
the latter duly salted with skepticism. At first his advice was
that little should be attempted in the way of an international
agreement until the domestic unrest had subsided. Once that
came about, Grey intended to proceed speedily.

What in particular did Spring Rice bring to Grey's attention?
He reported that Count Witte as premier had become persuaded
that "the friendship and sympathy of England was now of the
greatest value to him and to Russia, that what Russia needed
was the support of a great liberal and commercial power."[40]
Of course there was mention of a loan, which made Spring
Rice offer this caution. In concert with the French ambassador
he recommended against advancing any credit until the Duma
had met, and no loan without the approval of that body. To
do otherwise would be a totally wrong step. Further, he frankly
doubted that Czar Nicholas had the will or the desire to bring
liberalism to the Russian system of government, and failing
that, any understanding with St. Petersburg would be a tenuous
affair. Because of his experience in Persia, and supported by
the Persian ambassador to Russia, Spring Rice informed Grey
that no concessions could be expected from Russia regarding
the future of Persia. Meanwhile he could only say that the domestic situation continued jittery and that czarist ministers did
not want to discuss foreign policy matters. "You can't talk geom-
etry to a man on a tight rope," as he explained it to Grey.[41]
As a bedrock liberal, he was invincibly convinced that Russian
liberalism would founder on the rocks of Russian absolutism.
British accommodations with Russia were as unwise as they
were unworkable. It made no difference whether Grey was to
deal with Count Witte or the czar.

Dealings with Russia, as it developed, had to await the outcome of the Algeciras Conference, as well as a reordering of
Russian governance. The 1906 conference arose from the kaiser's
effort to gain ascendancy in Morocco, a move that the French
and Spanish, along with the British, resisted. When it was clear
that a German wedge could not be driven between France and

England over spheres of influence in North Africa, these international winds calmed. Simultaneously, the confirmation of the Anglo-French entente of 1904, when read in conjunction with the long standing Russo-French understanding that went back to 1894, put matters in order for the creation of the Triple Entente in 1907, bringing Britain, France, and Russia together. Grey became the man the Russians would trust despite his position as the spokesman of an elected government who was subject to being turned out of power. Spring Rice was consistently skeptical. To him the Russians were devious in their methods and in their promises, and the liberal ministry of Count Witte was unconvincing.

In contrast, Grey believed that time was working in favor of the liberals, who would prevail eventually; in this proposition, his wish appeared to persuade his judgment. In the diplomatic actualities, Grey was more occupied with the place of Persia in effecting improved relations with Russia than with internal politics. "If Persia breaks up we must protect lives and property of British subjects but we shall not lend money to the Persian government to strengthen our hold."[42] Put another way, Britain was preparing to yield in Persia to help cement the entente. Spring Rice was reduced to pious expectancy that Grey was right and he was wrong.[43]

Having lost the war—Grey was determined to have a Russian understanding—Spring Rice continued to advise him on how to fight the battles involved in the negotiations. He warned the foreign secretary not to count on the Russian army based on commitments by the foreign minister, for the two bureaus were usually at odds. Indeed, no authority below that of czar or Duma was worth his trust. He urged cooperation with the Russians in the extension of the railroad to Baghdad, otherwise the Germans would involve themselves in the enterprise. He also told Grey that the proposed visit by King Edward to St. Petersburg——a kind of *beau geste royal*—might be useful if it could be arranged. But it was an opinion given without much enthusiasm as "it was like visiting a man just declared bankrupt."[44] The Foreign Office took the hint and no royal visit ensued. Spring Rice was getting some of his views across and having his advice taken seriously, if not always acted upon, which must be the common fate of diplomacy from the field.[45] In April he was informed by Grey that he was "trying to re-open the Baghdad railways question so as to get the Russians to come in," and he promised to be guided by Spring Rice's advice should there be a political crisis in Persia. He insisted to Grey that unless Great Britain acted in concert with Russia, enabling it to keep an eye on Russian activities, the whole of Persia would fall into their hands. Meanwhile he was informed that the king was an avid reader of his dispatches.[46]

Regarding his efforts to keep his king and government informed about Russia, Spring Rice once remarked: "I repeat what I hear."[47] He was tireless in keeping up his many contacts and made it a point to get to know as many of the diplomatic corps in St. Petersburg as he could. Once the Duma began to convene, he attended its sessions regularly. No doubt he committed errors of judgment; for example, he believed the British and French embassies were at risk of destruction should loans not be offered by London and Paris. But on larger questions, he was more often right. Commenting on the struggle between the czar and the Duma in 1906, he underlined how isolated St. Petersburg was from the remainder of the country. Because the emperor had a pile of telegrams on his desk, sent by officials from all over the nation and protesting devotion to the holy czar, Nicholas believed that public opinion was with him. He rarely left the palace or showed himself to the people so that it was easy for him to misread official displays for signs of affection. Spring Rice put it well: "The capital is of all places where Russia is least known." History was to bear out his judgment.[48]

Time in Russia utterly convinced Spring Rice of the wrongness of political absolutism and, with the same stroke, of the rightness of liberalism. Liberalism now became the dominant concern; he wanted to see it spread around the world. It was not a Western phenomenon and should not be confined to Western peoples. It was the last best hope for mankind in Persia and Japan no less than in England and America. Conversely, the more liberalism was compromised, the weaker it grew. This was the root cause of his doubts about the Anglo-Russian agreement in the making: was there a spoon long enough to sup at the table of autocracy? Privately he thought not, and as he assumed the minister's post at Teheran, he was full of misgivings. He talked of "sticking it out" until retirement. Further disillusionment awaited him in Persia.

Spring Rice left St. Petersburg in mid-1906, before the Russian entente was formalized. He traveled to England where he saw his new daughter for the first time, and he was quite overcome with emotion. The formal investiture of the Knight Commandership of the Order of St. Michael and St. George took place, and he was able to spend time with Sir Edward Grey at his home in Northumberland. There he was fully versed regarding his upcoming tasks in Persia. Despite such pleasantries and the sort of rejuvenation that only Old Church on Ullswater afforded him, the Levant was much on his mind. At the end of the summer, Spring Rice arrived in Teheran—minister, wife, and little one together. Chirol spoke of the post as "a very good one and you ought to find it congenial,"[49] a prediction that was to be less than accurate.

He was quickly at his duties. He was present at the first meeting of the Mejlis, a body representing the various classes and interest groups authorized by the Shah just a few weeks before. One look at the business of that day impressed Spring Rice with how illusory the outward forms of representative government could be. Without a constitution to guide it, the assembly was shadow without substance. Neither the classes nor the Persian people had any concept of the realities of self-rule or even the operation of its machinery. Yet only a total cynic—which Spring Rice was far from being—could fail to find a glimmer of promise from the existence alone of the Mejlis. There seemed to be a "new spirit" at work that could not be discounted. "The popular movement here is national as well as religious and it is easily directed from race as well as religious motive. . . . Liberty is here!" he declared.[50] The patriots in the Mejlis were the Near Eastern champions of liberalism, and Spring Rice felt a special kinship with them. He wanted to do what he could for them, supporting their efforts to achieve freedom for the individual and independence for their nation. These constitutionalists should be encouraged by all liberal-thinking men to move in the direction of a ministry responsible to the Mejlis. But due to internal conditions, the Mejlis was probably doomed to failure from the start. And fail it did, and not without some help from the Russians. In June 1908, the Shah suppressed the assembly with the support of the cossacks, and a Russian general was named military governor. In a letter to Spring Rice, Professor Browne of Cambridge wrote out of sad frustration: "So brilliant and hopeful a movement quenched by fire and blood."[51] Having been on the spot, the minister was not surprised but was every bit as anguished as Browne over this turn of the tide.

The troubling events in Persia Spring Rice related directly to the large policy of Great Britain toward Russia. Grey had not relented in his attitude of indifference to the fate of that country and was not interested in building up British strength there, calling it "an extension of responsibility I do not desire."[52] Spring Rice was saddened by this hard-line policy. His first Persian tour of duty taught him to like the people and to respect their history. His "Persian experience" had moved him profoundly. Now he saw his own liberal nation and government coldly indifferent to the growth of liberalism in a far away country, of which England knew little. Concessions to the Russians in Persia were part of the price to be paid for a more secure empire. Spring Rice's suspicions about these moves were unabated.

One of the problems he had been advised he would have to deal with in Teheran was the use of the legation compound as a sanctuary for political opponents of the Shah, the so-called Bast. In particular this was a sensitive matter because many of the Bast were liberal reformers who sought a safe refuge under the protection of the British flag. He would have been loath to turn them out. It was fortunate for his conscience that his predecessor had managed to reduce the number of Bast to about two hundred; Spring Rice judged these men to be the most dedicated opponents of political repression and therefore bona fide refugees. But the Foreign Office pressed him to reduce the number to a couple of dozen, which put further stress on his liberal principles. In his instructions he was frequently reminded that his government was interested neither in liberalism nor independence for Persia. "Of course, we would want to keep out of the way of anything which would look like cooperation against the patriotic movement," but, added Grey significantly, "I deprecate interference in their internal affairs though I gather that the Russians on the spot are seeking to force their hand."[53] Grey's policy had placed Britain in an awkward position. Persia could not progress toward liberalism and independence without help from countries of like disposition. On the other hand, Britain would do little to encourage the growth of a modern Persia if Persia could not at first maintain itself as a liberal, independent state, showing that it was deserving of support. In consequence, Persian aspirations to become a Western-style nation would fall through the cracks made ever wider by the demands of the Anglo-Russian entente. It must be repeated, therefore, that Spring Rice distrusted the Russians because he found them devious, and they were devious because they were autocratic, hiding their true intentions behind the ample folds of czardom. England's collaboration with Russia in trampling down the seeds of liberty in Persia was a cruel thing for him to accept. The same instinct that would crush the Duma in St. Petersburg worked to destroy the Mejlis. Years later, in 1913, Spring Rice said that he had misjudged Grey's scheme because he could not see the wood for the trees when it came to Persia and the entente.[54] This admission only suggests that he himself was becoming adjusted to the methods of realpolitik in a world on the brink of disaster.

His distrust of Russian absolutism went very deep. "It was easy for two civilized and Liberal nations like France and England to come to terms and to act together," Spring Rice wrote Lord Cranley, alluding to the Anglo-French entente of 1904, but "common action between an English liberal and a Russian bureaucrat is a pretty difficult thing to manage. A wild ass and a commissary mule make a rum pair to drive."[55] In the same letter he sharpened the point of his objection. "The question is how far the Anglo-Russian Entente includes a joint campaign against Liberal principles here [Persia]. This was the real issue." As Spring Rice warmed to his subject he grew more outspoken. "You see it is not considered advisable to consult me and my *amour propre* is naturally rather wounded. . . . I can't say I find it in my bones to join our old friends, the Russian bureaucracy in treading down a people trying to reform its own bureaucracy." But to Whitehall, Persia was still "an unprofitable place," and Spring Rice's job was "to keep us out of rows on the spot and mark time until we see the results of the negotiations at St. Petersburg."[56] To a warmhearted liberal, this was cold comfort.

When Spring Rice raised his eyes to take in the outline of developing British foreign policy, he was further disturbed. To him it was an erroneous assumption that one autocratic nation would be the enemy of another in a showdown. Russia and Germany simply would not go to war with one another. It was, he asserted, "absolutely out of the question."[57] He was incorrect in this assessment; the Triple Entente was actuated in 1914. The ineffectuality of czarist Russia during the war Spring Rice did not hesitate to assign to the corrupt, authoritative system of the Romanovs. He was surprisingly candid in reviewing the Triple Entente as soon as it was proclaimed, directing his remarks to Sir Edward Grey. "I need not remind you of what you said yourself, that the value of the agreement will depend on the manner in which it is carried out. It is possible that Russia will use the agreement with Japan about Korea, in order to carry out her old designs under a new cover. . . . The breach by treachery of a formal agreement is a far more serious matter than the open prosecution of a policy of undistinguished hostility." Then he reverted to his real sticking point. "We are worse off in Persia than the Russians because we are not feared as they are, and because we are regarded as having betrayed the Persian people."[58] It was strong medicine to be meted out to a superior, but Spring Rice was determined to have his say.

Cecil Spring Rice was not named British ambassador to the United States upon the retirement of the unfortunate Durand. The choice would have been a natural one and welcomed by many in the American capital. His American expertise was virtually unique. No appointment would have pleased the American president more, a fact well known in Whitehall. Yet Lord Bryce was given the post. Not a professional diplomat, his credentials for that particular embassy were impressive, and he proved to be a hugely successful figure in Washington and around the country. The naming of Bryce—or the passing over of Spring Rice—undercuts the contention that Sir Cecil was destined to be Britain's ambassador to the United States. Nineteen seven, not 1913, was the prime time for such a promotion. Whether Theodore Roosevelt would seek another term, and should he win such an election, were matters still to be determined. But Spring Rice's appointment could well have meant that the London government had a direct and influential presence virtually in the White House. After all, 1907 was the year Grey was circling the wagons. To look at the situation from another angle: had Bryce chosen to stay in Washington for another year or more, he could well have been the wartime ambassador. His presence in America would have added greatly to Britain's advantage, and Spring Rice might well have gone into retirement. His health was not good, and thoughts of retirement persisted. The best explanation of why he continued in the diplomatic service and accepted the American assignment in 1913 is that, in spite of discouragement, poor health, and fatigue, he was the completely devoted servant of his country and was determined to serve it and its principles so long as he was wanted.

The nearly twelve months Spring Rice had in England during 1907 and 1908, there recouping some of his physical strength, afforded him the occasion to examine closely conditions in the mother country from which he had been absent for years at a time. Prior resentment at what he considered a faltering of the liberal spirit in diplomacy he came to identify with the government as a whole. He told the Roosevelts that his country "was in the hands of a sort of family trust which exploits the Empire for its own benefit." His indictment was sweeping. "The press almost without exception was in its [the government's] favour. If the liberal movement had been organized and led by one man he would be the object of a steady persecution which would do for him in the end as it did for Gladstone."[59] He had few qualms about condemning England to the president because he trusted his liberalism and felt that TR shared his concerns about England's future. "For England as a nation the serious aspect is . . . no one is willing to submit to the self-sacrifice of all for the common defence and this must lead to serious consequences."[60] His English confidants, especially Ferguson, were aware of his deep pessimism, which he learned was being treated as alarmist. The fact is, Spring Rice was alarmed and did not disguise his feelings. The same lack of coordination between the Foreign Office and the forces that he believed worked to Britain's disadvantage in Persia he attributed to general administrative practices in Whitehall. "If we persist in our present policy as regards the army and the navy, we shall have to sing very small in our foreign relations; the F.O. must not bark if the W.O. can't bite."[61] Disarray in government he traced back to a want of leadership, most obviously registered in the defenselessness of the realm. "If we have a row in any part of the world which withdraws our ships from the N. Sea then the danger is very real." He had in mind of course the growing German fleet. The unpredictability of the electorate was a further concern; "As Asquith says, you can not brigade public opinion."[62] The kaiser's army, as well as navy, was another factor in the unbalanced equation tilting dangerously against England. He wrote contemptuously: "Our philanthropists have again appealed to the kaiser to stop arming."[63] It is well that the Foreign Office found new employment for him in Stockholm. The longer Spring Rice stayed at home the more he fulminated, and to no good effect.

Foreign Secretary Grey thought Stockholm "a comfortable place" for Spring Rice and Spring Rice himself commented that it "just suits me."[64] Neither judgment was correct. The post carried with it a certain amount of prestige. Sweden was one of the old, established northern nations, and Stockholm was an attractive city. It was not an assignment that would be very taxing, probably one of the reasons Grey made the appointment. As a legation it was a step above Teheran and without the tensions of the Levant. The chief significance attached to the appointment was Grey's intention of keeping Spring Rice in the ranks of active diplomats. Someone of his wide experience could be moved quickly to a more sensitive station should circumstances require it. While it was not an emergency that brought Spring Rice in as a replacement for Bryce in Washington, the move was accomplished without leaving a key embassy uncovered. For Grey the 1908 assignment of Spring Rice to Stockholm was a case of sound personnel management.

Spring Rice was glad to be back in harness, his interview with King Edward the month before he departed for Sweden having given him a tremendous lift. As he recorded the royal conversation, it is evident the king placed great confidence in him and his ability to handle affairs with the Swedish government and the royal family. They also discussed events in Persia, for the Russian-inspired dismissal of the Mejlis had just taken place. Royal interest aside, Spring Rice knew that the real diplomatic action was elsewhere than in Stockholm. Austria-Hungary had recently annexed Bosnia and Herzegovina in contravention of the Treaty of Berlin, and Russia was likely to seek compensation by having the Dardanelles open to Russian ships of war. These and other events were churning the diplomatic waters from which Spring Rice was far removed. "It is so strange, being completely out of it," he complained to his wife.[65]

While the world was "getting painfully interesting," Sweden was dull but in some ways instructive. Englishmen, for example, had much to learn from the Swedish passion for a healthy citizenry, capable of quick mobilization to defend the country from attack. He discovered that in many ways the Swedes exhibited a Germanic cast to their thinking: the civil service was modeled on Germany's, the army was Prussianized, and the conservative government was decidedly prokaiser.[66] As Spring Rice wrote Lord Cranley, who was now in Berlin, "I suppose you realize that Sweden is in effect a province of Prussia, not in will but in necessity. But the Swedes simply hate it being said or thought that they are dependent on the Germans, and personally Germans are very unpopular here. But in case of war I think we should have to regard Swedes as German in effect—out of necessity and contra-coeur."[67] He discovered the German menace everywhere. To offset this, Spring Rice favored consideration of a military convention between Russia, the new ally, Britain, and Sweden, and reducing German influence all around. To the Swedes neither a German nor a Russian alliance was attractive, and had it been known what the British minister favored, he would have been much less popular in Stockholm than he was.[68]

There was no denying, however, that geography if nothing else pointed Sweden in the direction of Germany, should war come. For this reason, Spring Rice made specific studies of Swedish industry that might supply Germany with military requirements. He gave quite detailed information, for example, on the new steel mill at Trollhattan, including the capacity of the three electric furnaces, costs of production of finished steel per ton, sources of raw materials, and the like. He also reported that "there is no prospect of the Swedes limiting the export of ore; on the contrary, they will probably increase it."[69] Expeditions into various Swedish cities and the useful data collected appear to be no more than distractions from Spring Rice's German phobia, however. He wrote Roosevelt that thanks to the Germans, Europe had returned to a "primeval reign of force."[70] This was a bad situation for a country like England, which he described to Sir William Tyrrell at the Foreign Office as "an artificial creation made by the character of Englishmen, and it will last as long as the character remains, but it will not last longer."[71] Would English character be successful in resisting German force? That was the question to be faced. In Sweden the mood, talk, and expectation were widespread that the climactic struggle was soon to come, or as Spring Rice pessimistically put it: "The time was drawing near when Germany would assert its superiority."[72] In such a war he hoped Sweden could be neutral. The Swedes "still had the gait and manner of free men," he told Ferguson," and perhaps a little of their swagger. But it is better than a slouch."[73] Neutrality might be difficult for the Swedes to manage nonetheless; trade in arms was likely to influence them. Sweden had already sold Germany designs for machinery to manufacture a new torpedo, and other deals were pending. Spring Rice was downcast. What kind of a world would his children grow up to live in? he wondered, but he had no answer as he prepared for his assignment in Washington.

No official representative of Great Britain to the United States, including James Bryce, had better preparation for the position than did Sir Cecil Spring Rice. Whether by virtue of his knowledge of the country, sympathy for its ideals, understanding of its governmental machinery, awareness of its weaknesses and divisions, or a determination to have the two nations work together for common, high-minded principles, Spring Rice was without peer. The prospects for a successful embassy were accordingly bright. Judged by pre–world war standards, the three major issues on the table—the Panama Canal tolls, the revolution in Mexico, and the arbitration treaty—were all manageable, although the Mexican revolution was an ongoing source of friction between London and Washington. Spring Rice's immediate responsibility was to take up these three matters.

The new ambassador was fortunate to have a talented staff to assist him, and they served him loyally throughout his time in office. Colville Barclay was the counselor; Lord Eustace Percy and Ivor Campbell were secretaries. On financial matters Richard Crawford proved to be very able; and the ambassador relied on John Broderick, acting consul-general in New York as well, especially on matters relating to Irish-American public opinion. It was a team that gladly pulled together, with Spring Rice supplying the leadership. Arthur Willert, Washington correspondent for The Times, has left a memorable impression of him: "I can see him now, sitting at his desk, dispensing wisdom seasoned with sardonic wit, a neat, compact figure, grey suit, rimmed spectacles, a dispatch box or two before him."[74] Constantin Dumba, the Austro-Hungarian ambassador, recalled him in another way. "An Irishman of positively scintillating wit, a classical scholar, Sir Cecil was in every sense of the word a 'character.' He laid less stress on externals—clothes, ceremonial, and so forth—than is becoming a diplomat. Moreover he was so absent-minded that his charming wife . . . had to remind him of invitations . . . and make sure he did not forget his tie or anything else of that sort. . . . He was a gracious personality and in every way a gentleman, a most affectionate father and the kindest of men."[75] These two word portraits, when brought together, convey much of the human side of Spring Rice, a consideration too easily submerged and forgotten in the welter of diplomatic activity that was common to his time as ambassador.

There were certain considerations that would trouble Spring Rice in doing his work. The most disconcerting of these was his health. He had led a sober life, balanced in habit, was active, and took exercise regularly and enjoyably. Yet he had had several major illnesses, one of which was life threatening, only to recover and be able to return to routine and even strenuous duty. In August 1913, only a few months after his arrival in Washington, he fell ill again, confiding to Roosevelt what he referred to as "summer complaint."[76] His ailment was diagnosed as Graves disease, a disorder of the thyroid that can manifest itself in irritability and verbal outbursts, especially when the person is under stress; the disease also can produce heart complications. Grey rejected Spring Rice's offer to resign, advising him instead to spend some months away from Washington. He and his family passed the autumn and early winter in Dublin, New Hampshire. Strength returned sufficiently to permit the ambassador to take up partial duty in December, and after the new year he was back in full swing; the doctors assured him he was "practically cured."[77] Had his tenure in Washington been taken up with affairs no more strenuous than canal tolls and arbitration treaties—these would have occasioned small difficulty. The burdens of wartime diplomacy were, in contrast, beyond calculation. An individual in the most robust of health would have been staggered by the demands of office, a drain on both physical and mental states. That Spring Rice maintained himself through the most trying months of the "special relationship" is a tribute to his stamina and his devotion to duty.

In his early days as a diplomat, Spring Rice had made his American friends largely among Republican party members or those sympathetic with Republican principles. There was some thought that as ambassador he might be resented by the new Democratic administration of Woodrow Wilson, but neither the outgoing Republican President Taft, who was decidedly anti-Roosevelt, or Wilson offered any serious reservations—no reservations at all insofar as the record shows. Spring Rice was soon on excellent terms with Secretary of State William Jennings Bryan, with Franklin Lane of the Interior Department, and David Houston, secretary of agriculture. He made it a point to get to know (and found it easy to like) Robert Lansing, the counselor at the State Department who would follow Bryan as secretary, Frank Polk, who took Lansing's place as counselor, and the international lawyer John Bassett Moore. No one was to appreciate Spring Rice's work as much as Moore. Such was his prestige that the ambassador was accepted generally, even by those who did not know him well. In short, Spring Rice established the necessary rapport with Wilson's official family, whose members could be expected to speak well of him if consulted by the

president. At the State Department his friendly contacts were
critical to keeping a working relationship with officials there,
especially in the tense days brought on by an ever tighter British
blockade.

In contrast the ambassador had little success when he sought
a close association with Wilson. Looking ahead, this may be
cited as one of his failures, but the fault was not entirely his.
The president preferred to keep his own counsel, passing over
his secretary of state in favor of Colonel Edward M. House.
House had no official position; he liked being an *eminence
grise*. He wanted to be Wilson's full confidant and proved to
be so. House emerged as one of Spring Rice's chief critics,
who downgraded the ambassador's importance in dealing with
Wilson. It is also possible that Wilson, aware of Spring Rice's
intimate association with leading Republicans, may have unconsciously inclined to keep him at a distance. Wilson's personal style, that of self-containment, remains, however, the more
probable explanation of his attitude toward Spring Rice.

Although Lord Bryce had expressed the desire to stay on
in Washington until the Panama tolls issue was resolved, that
topic was still on the table when Spring Rice arrived in April
1913. It became his responsibility to keep up the pressure on
the Wilson administration to agree to maintain the provision
of the Hay-Pauncefote Treaty that all nations could use the canal
on a basis of rates equal to United States registered ships. By
1912, with the canal almost ready to open, many Americans,
including the Congress and President Taft, were taking a different view. Since the United States had borne the total cost of
building the canal, American vessels ought to have some concessions in the matter of tolls. Congress passed a bill to that effect,
and President Taft signed it into law in June 1912. Wilson,
however, insisted that the United Staes must stand by the original agreement, which made the task of the British ambassador
an easier one. He relied on the president's good faith and political mastery to see the affair through.[78] It was much better to
allow the American president to fight the American Congress
in a way that would be a great boon to England, whose merchant
marine was then the world's largest, than to be involved in
the fight himself. For domestic political reasons, namely, the
need to keep the Democratic party unified while major pieces
of reform legislation were before Congress, Wilson held back
from addressing the tolls issue. At the same time he promised
that the United States would live up to "the spirit and the

letter" of the treaty. By June 1914, the exemption of American ships from paying equal tolls had been nullified by Congress.

The illness that forced Spring Rice to the sidelines from August to December was unfortunate in several respects. Not only was he frustrated at being out of action, but his sickness occasioned him to miss early crucial meetings with President Wilson. To act in his stead, Grey dispatched his personal secretary, Sir William Tyrrell. His explicit charge was to meet with the president, concentrating on the problems regarding British interests in Mexico as these were being affected by the revolution there. Spring Rice had no cause to worry about Tyrrell preempting him as ambassador, for Grey was determined that Sir Cecil was the man he wanted in Washington. But the seed of an idea may have been planted, a bad seed at that. In dealings between the Wilson administration and the British government, the president would use his man, House, to work directly with Sir Edward Grey or his personal agent. In 1913 it was Tyrrell; in 1916 it was Sir Horace Plunkett; in 1917 it was Sir William Wiseman. The American secretaries of state, Bryan and Lansing, and the British ambassador were sidestepped. For Spring Rice, Tyrrell's coming was an ill omen.

In Mexico in 1913 the situation was this: elimination from office of the aged President Diaz had created a political vacuum at the center of Mexican public life, and a struggle ensued to fill the void with a new president. The first successor to Diaz was Francisco Madero; he introduced democratic reforms so sweeping that a conservative backlash was predictable. Madero was murdered by a new military strong man, Victoriano Huerta. The Taft administration withheld formal recognition of the Huerta regime, but it was willing to treat him as the de facto ruler. Wilson agreed to continue this arrangement in March 1913. In the meantime Great Britain had formally recognized Huerta in the belief that he was the leader most likely to maintain law and order, conditions essential for the protection of the large British investments in Mexico. Then Wilson, after a careful review of the facts, decided against United States recognition on the grounds that Huerta's involvement in the murder of Madero made his government morally repugnant. When Tyrrell asked the president what his policy objective was, he replied that he wanted to teach the Mexican people to elect honest men. Whereupon American support was thrown to Venustiano Carranza, another ambitious Mexican politician who called his party the Constitutionalists. Great Britain, for its own reasons, supported one claimant, and the United States, for its own reasons, supported another. These policies were bound to work at cross purposes, and by the autumn of 1913 it was clear that consultation between the two governments was imperative. Tyrrell came to Washington carrying assurances from Sir Edward Grey that England would stand aside out of respect for North America as a U.S. sphere of influence but not before guarantees were given protecting British interests in Mexico. Grey made no secret of his motivation in taking this position—his desired friendship with the United States.

Unlike some senior staff at the Foreign Office who had strong reservations about the need of Anglo-American cooperation, Grey was willing to protect and indeed to promote cordiality between London and Washington. As he grew more apprehensive about the outbreak of a general war in Europe, he feared a fallout with the United States would only complicate matters for Great Britain. This was a fixed position for the Foreign Secretary, which implied that there would have been every opportunity for the new ambassador to work constructively with President Wilson on problems arising from the Mexican revolution had he not been ill. A close, practical relationship with the president regarding issues brought on by World War I could have followed naturally. And with Grey and Spring Rice on intimate terms, the success of the Spring Rice ambassadorship would have been further enhanced. But history has a different story to tell.

Once back at his post, Spring Rice began to supply Grey with information and advice. In reporting the decision to allow the Constitutionalists to import guns from the United States, he pointed out that behind the facade of Carranza's government stood the figure of Pancho Villa, "who had spent his whole life burning, killing and raping."[79] The hypocrisy of having Villa, or anyone like him, as a champion of American political principles was peculiarly offensive. The ambassador protested sharply the killing by Villa of a British subject, one Benton, arguing that while Britain would continue to allow the United States to take the lead respecting Mexican affairs, the Wilson administration should not lose sight of European interests south of the border.[80] In short, Spring Rice was an active, hard-working envoy who had missed the best of opportunities for dealing with the president. In early 1914 no one read it that way, and Tyrrell, who was back in London, was able to tell Spring Rice that "the Chief is simply revelling in your success. Each time he hears from you his face lights up and he says: 'Isn't Springey doing splendidly!'"[81] It was a fair judgment for the moment.

One of the objectives uppermost in the mind of the secretary of state was the conclusion of a series of arbitration treaties between the United States and the great powers. As some one strongly attached to English law and civilization, Bryan was especially anxious to gain the adherence to such a treaty by the London government. Bryan was a pacifist and recognized in Spring Rice a diplomat he could work with in pursuit of his aim of arbitration. The secretary's position within the Wilson administration was unfortunately ambiguous. He had been given the State Department as a matter of party politics and was not at all suited for the job. Spring Rice was alternately amazed and appalled at what he knew and did not know. "He is, I should think, unlike any Secretary of State or Minister of Foreign Affairs that has ever been known." His work was so full of errors that John Bassett Moore had to "correct" his mistakes and misimpressions.[82] With respect to the arbitration proposal, Spring Rice advised his government to allow things to take their own course in the United States, being willing to sign such an agreement but not to encourage it. He wanted to avoid any appearance of subservience to Britain, as Irish-American senators and voters might charge England with leading America. At one juncture, he referred to the treaty as "quite harmless."[83]

Spring Rice thought of Bryan as an interesting character study and a friendly man besides, and he was genuinely impressed by the secretary's determination to put the treaty into law. Bryan trusted the ambassador and confided in him so that he had no cause to complain that the secretary did not conduct business in an honest and straightforward manner. In later years Spring Rice remembered these qualities with appreciation. As for the Anglo-American Arbitration Treaty, delays in signing were inevitable because of the press of other, more critical matters. It was not until September 1914 that the two men affixed their signatures to the document. There was a real sense of irony, for by this time the general war in Europe was under way. What Spring Rice faced for the duration of his stay in Washington was a wartime embassy, one fraught with peril for Anglo-American friendship, and for England itself.

5
WARTIME AMBASSADOR: 1914–1916

The outbreak of a general European war in August 1914, an event that found Spring Rice in London for consultations, was the first great catastrophe of the twentieth century. The hopes of mankind, for nations as for peoples, that such massive conflicts belonged to history past were dashed utterly, the debris scattered across the breadth of the land and the length of the century. Americans, more than others perhaps, were stunned by the force of the conflict because they had been long and far removed from the European cockpit of power politics and the wars common to it. To Americans it appeared there was in place a finely tuned balance of power across the world that enabled the United States to keep the Monroe Doctrine intact, and at the same time it appeared that Great Britain ruled the oceans in a fashion beneficial to international order. The 1914 war brought a direct challenge to British naval supremacy and destroyed the reality if not the principle of balance of power. Americans saw their vision of a progressive world order suddenly and unexpectedly shattered. At the same time they took heart in their isolation from the fighting. With no perceived vital interests involved in the outcome, and safely removed from death and destruction, the immediate and continuing response of the people and, for that reason, the government, was a desire to stay neutral. This policy President Wilson proclaimed on 4 August 1914.

Two considerations bore adversely on this ideal of "strict neutrality." America was a free society with a fresh mix of people from the Old World. The country was susceptible to various appeals and entertained certain prejudices. It was eager to learn details of the fighting and ready to react openly to the tide of battle on land and sea. It was, in short, a nation inviting propaganda from both sides as to war aims and war claims. A second consideration was how the war might affect the United States. This would depend on the British use of the blockade and the employment by the Germans of the submarine when it involved American shipping. As the war intensified, the blockade and the submarine were to have an increasing impact on the American economy. For example, as early as November 1914, Spring Rice reported that copper shipped through the port of New York had increased in amount by 300 percent from the previous year; he spoke of Denmark as "Germany's backdoor."[1] The policy and the actuality of strict neutrality came more and more under pressure. The people were nonetheless resolved to maintain formal neutrality. However much the United States might become a nation trading in arms, it was adamantly opposed to taking up arms. For more than two years Americans were prepared to endure the loss of life and cargo arising from submarine warfare and the blockade without resort to military action to defend themselves. It was a prudent and a self-serving position. The Wilson administration, responding to public feeling, came to accept both British and German hostile measures as the unavoidable fallout from the war.

These circumstances as generally described would put great responsibility on the ambassadors of Great Britain and Germany who were then serving in Washington. The British envoy, for example, whoever he might be, would have to explain and defend interference with the rights of neutrals on the high seas, the British definition of contraband, and tampering with the mail—which were among the chief factors causing friction between London and Washington. He would also have to justify blacklisting United States firms thought to be dealing with the enemy. Great Britain was determined to win the war (or, at least, not to lose it) while the United States insisted on respect for certain neutral rights. The situation demanded an envoy well trained and widely respected, and one thoroughly knowledgeable in American affairs if Great Britain expected to keep a workable relationship with its largest potential supplier of food and arms. Problems were bound to arise and did arise— misunderstanding of policies, mistaken intentions, and miscalculation of the effects of actions once taken. The Americans were thus placed in a largely reactive position, defensive but demanding of fair treatment. This meant that the British ambassador might often find himself on the spot and sometimes on the hot seat. The office would inevitably become one of stress, especially if the ambassador was to play an important role in

Anglo-American diplomacy. Ambassadors are not foreign ministers, it must be remembered. They do not make policy ordinarily, and do not necessarily agree with the policy they are bound to represent. Yet they must deal with officials, usually higher in rank than themselves, and sometimes with a head of state, alongside whom they are inferior beings. They are consequently at considerable disadvantage.

During World War I the British ambassador had to deal routinely with the secretary of state and, ideally, with the president, once Wilson began to assert more control over the direction of foreign policy. The problems for an ambassador dealing with a head of state are complicated by the fact that as foreigners they are pressing objectives of a foreign government that can be at odds with the interests of the host country. The comparative pleasantries of peace time diplomacy can quickly give way to wartime abrasions. It is rarely otherwise, as the ambassadorship of Sir Cecil Spring Rice amply demonstrated.

In the discharge of his responsibilities Spring Rice brought to the task well-practiced powers of observation and analysis and considerable experience as a diplomat who possessed a degree of understanding of American affairs unmatched in the British diplomatic service. But he brought more—a profound awareness and pride of ancestry combined with a refined sensitivity to the obligations of duty to produce, under immense strains exerted by the war, a patriotism of uncompromising disposition. Further, he was possessed by a cause that featured a liberal public philosophy as part of his love of country. It was the interaction of these various elements, responding to the exigencies of the war, that explain Spring Rice's conduct of the Washington embassy.

As wartime ambassador, Spring Rice enjoyed a unique position, but all the factors did not work in his favor. He was a close friend and confidant of Foreign Secretary Sir Edward Grey. Grey himself was a highly regarded statesman, the strongest member of the Asquith government, which was in power from 1906 to 1916, the year both Asquith and Grey resigned. Furthermore, Grey believed wholeheartedly in the value of American friendship: "The surest way to lose the war would be to antagonize Washington."[2] As he phrased it in his memoirs, "The crucial mistake would have been to break with Washington."[3] Grey and Spring Rice were in complete accord. Yet the strength of their relationship developed into a weakness for Spring Rice once Grey left office. At the end of 1916, Anglo-American relations were clouded by the blockade and the blacklist, and the ambassador found himself not only without a like-minded chief but without a man who had been the constant defender of his conduct of the embassy. Grey's successor, Arthur James Balfour, was not ill disposed toward Spring Rice, but he was never his champion.

No less meaningful for assessing Spring Rice's record was his situation in America. As I have indicated, most of his good friends were influential men, associated with the Republican party, at a time of Democratic ascendancy. In itself this need have caused no trouble. But the ambassador's oldest American friend, Roosevelt, was a relentless critic of Wilson and his policies, especially on the subject of neutrality. At one point Roosevelt was moved to say the trouble with the president is that "he is plain yellow." It is true, Roosevelt and Spring Rice saw little of one another, each wanting the ambassador to escape guilt by association. But at the time Wilson could hardly have been sure of that. It could have been no secret in the White House that the ambassador talked with Henry Cabot Lodge on an almost daily basis. Although to Spring Rice he was a much-valued friend, he was also an outspoken Republican critic of Woodrow Wilson before and after the start of the war. Wilson would have been more than human had he not resented the Lodge attachment. Spring Rice's close association with the House of Morgan—one of the symbols of the pernicious influence of Wall Street and a red flag to the charging bull of progressivism—simply added to the image of a "Republican ambassador." As the ambassador was later to observe: "The Morgans have been of the greatest service, but there is always a danger because they are identified with the Money Trust," which was true enough.[4]

How warranted were suspicions about the partisanship of His Majesty's envoy? There is no evidence at all that Spring Rice was prepared to exploit his Republican contacts to undermine Wilsonian diplomacy. He was careful to remain entirely out of view in interparty quarrels. All indications are that he got on well with many members of the president's cabinet. He deplored, of course, what he saw as the anti-British attitudes of senators like O'Gorman and Stone, but he refrained from registering displeasure openly or in public. In such respects Spring Rice was a model of discretion, in marked contrast to his German counterpart. But here again his strength was also a weakness to those who believed he could have been a more active, vocal, freeswinging spokesman for the Allied cause. Von Bernstorff was a fervid propagandist who involved himself directly and boldly in internal American politics, imploring the German-Americans to show support for the fatherland by seeking to influence votes in Congress. There was a well-defined German-American vote (and an Irish-American vote, which the German Press Agency wooed persistently), but as Spring Rice observed, there was no British-American bloc in the electorate. He would not have pandered to it had it existed, convinced as he was that "instinctively" Americans "feel that our struggle is the same as their old one, for personal freedom."[5]

Critics of Spring Rice's ambassadorship have pointed to his ill health as a limiting factor in his effectiveness. That he was not a robust man is to be admitted, and I have mentioned his bout with Graves disease. The claim in early 1915 that he was "practically cured" may have been exaggerated, yet it is hardly believable that, had he been severely ill, he could have carried the heavy burden of responsibility for more than three years. It is best to play down the consequences of Graves disease as a negating factor in his work, or at least to get it in perspective.

Two high-ranking Americans in particular, Colonel House and Secretary of State Lansing, in their accounts of wartime diplomacy, accused Spring Rice of wild outbursts, which tended to shake confidence in him as a reliable envoy. As early as 1915 he was described by House as a "highly excitable invalid," and he suggested to the president that the United States request his recall as ambassador. House was prepared to state that "some one of the Bryce stripe" be sent over.[6] He changed his mind about the recall but thereafter tended to avoid conducting important business through the embassy. Robert Lansing has left a harrowing description of his meeting with Spring Rice in January 1917. The subject of their discussion was whether the United States would look upon the arming of merchantmen by the British as an unneutral act, something which London insisted was essential to reduce the menace of the submarine to its shipping. In his diary Lansing set down how Spring Rice grew "livid with rage, . . . his eyes wide with passion, . . . his faced twitched and his eyes blazed, . . . his hands clenched until his knuckles showed white." All in all it was the account of a man who was out of control. The climax of the encounter came when Spring Rice told Lansing that if any lives were lost as the result of the sinking of unarmed merchant ships he and the president would be "personally responsible." When Lansing asked him to sit down and think about what he had said, so the Lansing account runs, Spring Rice was contrite. "He apologized profusely in a voice that shook with emotion."[7]

Several considerations ought to be kept in mind respecting this episode, as it can be assumed to be an honest rendering of what took place. In January 1917, Spring Rice's England was in a state close to despair; if its spirit was still high, its supply of food and medicine was very low. Perhaps it could remain in the war only a few weeks longer. Spring Rice had been under unremitting strain since late 1914, as American friendship heated and cooled, heated and cooled. The future was anything but certain. Grey was gone from office, and the ambassador missed him in mind and spirit. He was fully aware of the attacks on him in the Northcliffe press as a do-nothing ambassador, the more hurtful because they were untrue. It was this distortion of his record that so deeply troubled him. In May 1916, he suffered a severe personal blow when his younger brother Gerald, who had come from Canada as a volunteer, had been killed in action in France at the age of fifty-two. Soon thereafter he had news that Ivor Campbell, one of his former embassy staff and a favorite of his, had also died in battle. Spring Rice's sensitive nature was sore distressed. He appeared to be a man coming to the end of his endurance, yet invariably he regained his composure and carried on with his work. If, as he once told Colonel House, he intended to write an account of his ambassadorial years,—incidentally Doubleday Page had offered to publish his story in the United States—there would have been painful memories to recall.[8] His outbursts were attributable mostly to his temperament, whatever the effects of his chronic sickness. The further proposition, that irrespective of the source of his behavior, he was not suitable for his post, can be addressed only by looking at how he discharged his office.

Spring Rice's dealings with President Wilson were almost entirely a matter of formality. The president had a limited confidence in professional diplomats and less so in amateurs like Secretary Bryan. He shed no tears when Bryan resigned from office in protest at the stiff note Wilson sent Berlin after the sinking of the Lusitania. The ambassador's influence on Wilson's thinking was negligible; perhaps James Bryce would have been treated with a greater show of courtesy, but probably no more than that. Wilson was impenetrable.

In offering an estimate of Wilson to Sir Edward Grey, Spring Rice at first was guided by the opinions of those who knew him well: "His friends say he is honest, of high principles, and lofty intentions, but obstinate and stubborn."[9] Upon closer examination he was able to add to the profile: "A humanitarian, responsive to the will of the people, politically adroit, ambitious, mysterious and messianic."[10] In dealing with Wilson as with other leading Americans, including Roosevelt, Spring Rice learned anew that a common cultural tie with England was largely sentimentality that had, and was to have, little bearing on national policy. England's peril did not translate into United States vital interest. "The President will be with us by birth and upbringing," he told the foreign secretary in August 1914, but "he will have to be rather conspicuously neutral," a judgment he repeated to Robert Cecil as the war went on. In any event, "Britain must not count on American sympathy as assured to us."[11] But the reverse side of the coin was to Britain's advantage. The ambassador was certain that the United States would never go to war against England, that were it ever to come in, it would be on the side of the Allies, but for distinctly American reasons.

At the very start of the war, Spring Rice was able to establish, briefly as it turned out, a personal and professional relationship with the president. He acted quickly and surely to squelch the story being circulated by the Germans in September that they were ready for peace but England was unwilling to consider their proposals. In fact neither London, Berlin, nor Paris was much interested in ending the war at this early date. The Germans were also hinting at American mediation, which was likely to sit well with Wilson and Bryan. In a September interview, the president and the ambassador discussed a variety of matters, including the bad effects America's participation in the war would have on its system of government and its political ideals. They also talked about Wordsworth's poetry, especially some of the sonnets written at the time of another great war. Spring Rice intimated that the president and the foreign secretary "were fed on the same food, and I think you understand."[12] In recounting all this to Grey, he spoke of "tears in his [Wilson's] eyes, and I am sure we can at the right moment depend on an understanding of the heart here." Spring Rice was encouraged to go directly to the president, providing him with the text of Grey's telegram explicitly denying that England stood in the way of peace. "There is no evidence whatever that the suggestions which appear to emanate from the German ambassador [in Washington] are authorized by his government or really meant."[13]

The effect was to show that either German pronouncements were not coordinated, with the ambassador saying one thing and Berlin another, or the German Press Agency was already at the job of disinformation. Spring Rice took the Wilson administration's response to his counterstroke as a harbinger of his acceptance by Wilson and a good omen for Anglo-American relations. Americans appeared to be as dubious about the German peace offer as the British.

At this time Spring Rice came face to face with Colonel House, who spoke and acted in behalf of the president. Writing Grey, he quoted the colonel to the effect that the "President's intervention was really the best hope for the eventual restoration of peace." He also pointed out that House had been in contact with the kaiser because he "did not want the President to lose touch with the warring nations."[14] The general outline of American policy was therefore discerned by Spring Rice as early as September 1914, and it remained in place until the nation entered the war in 1917. The United States would remain neutral, but was more favorably disposed to England and France than to Germany and its allies. Peace could only be achieved and made permanent by Wilson's mediation. Meantime, Colonel House would be responsible for this policy in detail whenever mediation appeared likely to be asked for by either set of enemies. Particulars in this scenario would have to be filled in, but Spring Rice had, with his accustomed acuity, laid out the American position to his chief, just as the war got under way.

The potential for serious, ongoing disagreement between London and Washington became evident in 1914 with the refusal of the British to agree to abide by the Declaration of London of 1909. This set of rules proposed to distinguish between the rights of a blockading nation and those of neutral trading countries in time of war. Contraband was defined by categories (absolute, conditional, free) in a way that tended to favor the neutrals at the expense of the blockade. Neither Great Britain nor the United States had signed the declaration but it appealed to the Wilson administration as an expedient guideline. The Foreign Office rejected the proposal. Spring Rice was conscious of the possible bad effects outright rejection might have on important segments of American public opinion. "It happens to be just the sort of question that takes the popular fancy and also entails the monied people as well," he warned Grey. It was a key issue because Britain's refusal to hew to the guidelines of the declaration might easily be interpreted as an effort to "cripple all trade except ours."[15] With Bryan as secretary of state it almost necessarily fell to Lansing, then the department counselor, to draft a statement of the American position. He did so in a manner that Spring Rice found harsh and that if delivered could damage good relations between the two nations. He predicted fallout worse than that which followed Cleveland's Venezuelan message of 1895.[16] Lansing insisted that the declaration was the "only common basis on which action could be taken," to which Spring Rice replied: "Parliament which speaks for the British people has never accepted it."[17] In a tactic that was soon to be characteristic, the ambassador urged conciliation on both sides. Thus he hoped Lansing would soften the rhetoric and advised Grey: "A little forbearance on both sides may make matters all right."[18]

Spring Rice also communicated directly with the president several times over the issue. These were soothing letters, in keeping with his conviction that conciliation was always the better course to pursue, and that the essence of successful diplomacy is to give way on minor points in order to preserve a friendly atmosphere, while holding fast in the main. He confided in Wilson by making a telegram from Grey available for discussion, a message that while moderately stated, yielded nothing. Spring Rice correctly predicted to the president a troubling future: "I fear that many difficulties will be in store for us but I am sure the American people will not forget that in 1861 and 1862 the whole labouring population in Lancashire was thrown out of work; but because they believed the struggle here to be one of liberty and justice, the very men upon whom starvation fell were the most steadfast in repudiating the demand that the British government should interfere."[19] Wilson was susceptible to that sort of appeal. Although he was born a Southerner who as a child had lived through the Civil War, he rejoiced in a Union victory as being best for all sections of the country and all people in the nation. Grey rejected the second revised but no less firm note devised by Lansing and expedited by Spring Rice's conciliatory moves. The foreign secretary's argument was that Britain was doing only what was "absolutely essential to our very existence."[20] Faced with this intransigence, the United States backed off, effectively accepting the methods of the blockade as announced by Orders in Council. Not a few Americans saw in this a reminder of a similar disagreement of one hundred years before that had helped start a war. But too much had happened to sweeten Anglo-American relations since 1898 to allow this piece of history to repeat itself.

In some ways Grey was playing a dangerous game with his own principle; that is, the ill will of the United States would be fatal to England in the war. Although full-scale military operations between the English-speaking nations was altogether unlikely, there were degrees of tension that, if taken far enough, might do real harm to the Allied war effort. But all things considered Grey had handled the affair well, and his interlocutor in Washington must share in the credit. Wilson was of this mind when he wrote Spring Rice that the accommodation of the United States to the blockade was due in part "to your fair spirit in these trying days."[21]

American acquiescence to the British position on the blockade hardly meant that the issue was thereby disposed of. The implementation of the principles of blockade—how it was to be enforced in practice, and against what producers and what products—were recurring pressure points. "The fact remains," Spring Rice told Chirol, "there is and must be very real conflict of interest. . . . The Americans seem to have a sort of idea that their ships are or ought to be sacroscant. This we can not admit."[22] Versed in the ways of American politics, he knew about special interests, as in copper, oil, cotton, and meatpacking, that would insist on their right to sell on the world market, war or no war. The war in fact was likely to increase the dollar value of such trading items, with profits enhanced. These special interests had power in Congress and could be expected to exert it. How all this would play depended on events. Spring Rice advised Grey that without a formal agreement regarding neutral rights—something he was adverse to because it would arouse public opinion—each American protest of search and seizure could be handled on its own merits. Great Britain must always try to appear to be working out arrangements to reduce friction with the United States.[23]

The London government became expressly concerned by the ease with which false manifests were obtained as ships departed United States ports. It took the position that the State Department must be prepared to tighten procedures, with Spring Rice making the strongest kind of representations to Secretary Bryan. The ambassador was active in other ways. He suggested that private agreements be made between the British government and large American suppliers. Great Britain would undertake to buy all a company's output destined for sale on the world market. This was a spin-off from conventional economic warfare. As the United States government was not involved, technical neutrality would be preserved.[24] The fact is Spring Rice was ready to bend over backwards to keep American suppliers and shipping companies happy. Of course London did not want to make the export of contraband materials illegal. Therefore what trickled through the blockade had to be tolerated so that growing amounts of arms and ammunition would continue to be available to the armies of France and England. Various issues raised by the blockade continued to vex Anglo-American relations for the coming two years with Spring Rice endeavoring to keep the atmosphere free of bitterness and recrimination. This was to him a practical approach to a set of thorny problems. "American sympathy is a good thing to have but it does not affect American policy where the American pocketbook is concerned."[25] Spring Rice had come to be a realist as warranted by the situation.

If Grey was able to appreciate the need to conciliate the United States, his ambassador in Washington should be given some of the credit; a steady stream of advice to the Foreign Office not to count much on American good will in practical results was a constant reminder. A case in point was the president's idea to buy German merchant ships stranded in American ports at the start of the war. Wilson viewed it as a way to enlarge the U.S. merchant fleet. Grey saw it as a windfall for Germany resulting from the money to be paid out. Spring Rice was quick to offer advice in the matter. He argued strongly against the purchase of the ships by anyone save the American government, because only the government could guarantee that they would not be employed to Germany's advantage. But as a matter of tactics, such a British position should be conveyed on the following condition. "We should I think make it very clear that we are making a concession. In return for the concession he [Wilson] should show a real desire to prevent the unneutral use of the ships and we should I think make a written statement of the conditions. . . ."[26]

The Ships Purchase Bill failed to pass in Congress, but there were other worries, well illustrated by the *Dacia* affair. A private United States citizen, Edward N. Breitung, had purchased the *Dacia* from the Hamburg-American Line, reflagged it as American, loaded it at Galveston with eleven thousand bales of cotton, and requested the State Department to obtain clearance for it to sail to Rotterdam, a neutral port. In taking up the matter with the secretary of state, Spring Rice insisted that "the British

Government feel that if they recognize the transfer of the *Dacia* it will clearly be followed by the wholesale transfer of German ships to neutral flags to the enormous relief of Germany and the general prejudice of British interests." The ambassador was strongly supported by Grey; indeed, he was acting in pursuance of the foreign secretary's prior instruction in a situation that Sir Edward had described as ominous.[27] The *Dacia* sailed, was intercepted by the French, and, according to their practice, was confiscated and later sunk in a German submarine attack. The failure of the Ships Purchase Bill and the fate of the *Dacia* severely limited the transfer of interned German vessels.

Not many weeks had passed after August 1914, when Spring Rice realized that his main contribution to British diplomacy would be to advise the Foreign Office and to represent the views of His Majesty's government to the Wilson administration. Unlike the American ambassador in London, Walter Hines Page, he would enjoy no persona grata position at the State Department, nor would he have special access to the president. Ambassadors, however prestigious, are rarely able to influence decisively the thinking of their home government; but what is less rare, perhaps, is the ability to redirect the thinking of their host government, especially if the latter faces a crossroads of policy formulation. In the case of Anglo-American relations after 1914, this would presume frequent, regular, and confidential contact with President Wilson. But that was not to be. No later than November of that year, Spring Rice began to complain that he was required to deal with lower echelon officials, men quite without authority. "And even if I could see the President," he wrote, "he is notoriously difficult to move when he has made up his mind."[28] As the months gave way to years, this predicament would worsen. Not that Spring Rice left off attempting to meet with Wilson, but the president had put Colonel House in charge of handling all important matters relating to American diplomacy and the European war. Within a year's time House confided in his diary: "I know of no official anywhere who is serving his country so badly" as Spring Rice.[29] Despite such harsh and gratuitous a judgment—and it is naive to think Spring Rice was innocent of House's attitude—he sought to maintain a friendly connection with America's surrogate secretary of state.

Limited to the role Wilson and House would permit him, Spring Rice was a trustworthy analyst of American public opinion, a critical element as Britain sought to fine tune its foreign policy and keep the United States friendly. On the subject of embassy-directed propaganda, for example, his 1914 judgment stood the test of time. "On the whole it seemed wisest to do nothing against German propaganda which is conducted by hired agents with large sums of money. This seems to be more than met by the willing and unorganized correspondents who answer their articles in the newspapers."[30] This conviction he elaborated in urging Lord Newton to forego a speaking tour of the United States. "Public speaking would be fatal, because people here don't like to be preached to; they like to think they are able to make up their own minds. . . . If you come out and talk to people I am sure you would have an effect on them if you did it in the ordinary way of conversation. But if they thought you were here to preach to them, they would immediately suspect you of imposing your opinions on their free and unbiased minds."[31] He wrote along the same line to Chirol, saying that he was "fully aware of the frantic efforts" of the Germans to force American public opinion, by giving a rather full description of the efforts directed by the German ambassador, Von Bernstorff. "Every one who has had the slightest connection with Germany either in business, science, or literature, or whose name is known, or who is in an official position here receives special copies of pamphlets and personal appeals signed by distinguished men of letters and scientists. The place swarms with special agents. There is Dernburg for the Jews, a purveyor of movies for the populace, princes for the ladies, even a professor of Celtic (Kump Meyer) for the Irish societies. There is Bernstorff for everyone and he is unfortunately always with us."[32] Bernstorff acted less like a professional diplomat and more like a clever and aggressive business man, not the least reluctant to use hard sell on the American public, the main purpose being to keep the United States neutral. Voices were raised in England urging Spring Rice to follow the lead of the German ambassador in assaulting public opinion, but he was willing to go only as far as a press bureau on an experimental basis. In defense of his policy he made sense. "At the moment the larger part of the American people are with us, or rather are against our enemies, not from our merits but owing to the demerits of our antagonists. Their deeds are mightier than their words. Would it be worthwhile to try to alter the situation which is on the whole favourable?"[33] All in all it was a cautious, even a smug, attitude, and one he could really luxuriate in because British propaganda, directed from London, was already in full swing. There, efforts to shape American public opinion had both a negative and a positive character. By exercising censorship through a press bureau, the British sought to insure that only news favorable to the Allied cause was reported, and control of the trans-Atlantic cable aided them greatly in these efforts. But mere negative control was accompanied by a massive propaganda campaign, expertly orchestrated from Wellington House. This operation remained semi-secret until the United States entered the war, and Spring Rice may have been generally unaware of its scope. Sir Gilbert Parker was in charge of the dissemination of information in the United States. Well over 250,000 names of prominent and influential Americans figured in Parker's list of people to be wooed and won to the Allied side. Numerous well-known Britons, including Arthur Conan Doyle and James Bryce, were mobilized to help win the war of words. Volunteer groups were eager to help, and hundreds of speakers came to the United States "on their own," determined to convince Americans of the rightness of their cause. Much of this was done with the same heavy hand that Spring Rice had scorned in the German campaign, and President Wilson for one thought some of these British activities "abominable and inexcusable." The striking difference between the German and British was that Spring Rice would have nothing to do with propaganda, which he regarded as distinctly unworthy of an accredited diplomat. It is significant that in Horace Peterson's blistering indictment of British propaganda he failed to identify any activity of Spring Rice.[34] This should be taken into account in evaluating the ambassador's boast that the embassy refrained from active propaganda because "Americans like to do their thinking for themselves and the less we try to help them, the better."[35] Yet even this policy had its limits, and Spring Rice always contended that no effort should be spared in exposing the false impressions of events emanating from the German embassy.

No doubt Spring Rice had taken a controversial view of the place of embassy-sponsored propaganda in a war where to engage the mind of the masses was a key element in an overall strategy for victory. The Germans had lost no time in commencing their efforts, hoping that the prestige attaching to an embassy would tend to legitimize their claims. Could Great Britain do less? Judged in retrospect the Spring Rice rationale is defensible, at least to a point. Blatant British propaganda coming from the embassy in particular might have offended a number of interest groups that were neutal or friendly to the Allies. It might well have encouraged people to appreciate more the advantages of neutrality rather than having to prefer one or the other of two snarling adversaries. Embassy propaganda could easily have galvanized the Irish-Americans, pushing them into the hands of the Germans with possible dire political results. Such a combination could have forced an arms embargo, to the acute distress of France and England. German appeals to American prejudices were deemed counterproductive; would the British embassy be able to manage things differently? Finally, the very silence of Spring Rice, contrasting sharply with the noisy von Bernstorff had by 1917 helped to convince Americans of the underlying rightness of Anglo-French war aims. As the senior British representative in Washington, it was the ambassador's responsibility to justify a strategy that could be fully proved only at the end of American neutrality. Meanwhile, a "silent Ambassador" may appear to be slack, unimaginative, or wrongheaded, especially by press lords like Alfred Harmsworth, the proprietor of The Times and The Daily Mail (the so-called Northcliffe Press).

Harmsworth had brought the penny press to England and then moved up-market by gaining control of The Times. Fleet Street was by definition in the propaganda business, and with the war it smelled blood and wanted to fire propaganda salvos at will. Because of his friendship with Lloyd George, Harmsworth's fortunes rose as the Welsh Wizard became prime minister, and Spring Rice's stock dropped accordingly. Yet Grey actively supported the policy of embassy restraint in the war of words over the use of words in war, and wrote the ambassador in March 1916 to say as much. After referring to the Northcliffe criticism, he continued: "However, one result of the attacks had been that most gratifying letters come from persons of knowledge and good repute in America, praising you exceedingly and contrasting you most favourably with Bernstorff. I delight in reading them. I think you have done most wisely and well."[36] Spring Rice had other encouragement from the English side. Lord Newton wrote that "the Harmsworth press is so full of the most appalling balderdash about our failure in American propaganda. We are taking steps to teach those idiots, whose only tangible suggestion so far has been to send Winston Churchill on a tub thumping tour of the States. There seem to be quite a lot of people who honestly believe that if we had dumped enough Nurse Cavell pamphlets upon Wilson that the whole attitude of Americans would have changed."[37] Perhaps home-based Britons like Lord Newton were unaware of the work of Wellington House, which would show Spring Rice's ignorance of it as more probable. Whatever the case, Spring Rice was not alone in thinking embassy propaganda unwise. As Grey left office at the end of 1916, he gave a summary appraisal. "I never had time," he told the ambassador, "to say how much I sympathised with the exceeding difficulty of your position in Washington. It has been a special field for militant German propaganda, and it is a real triumph that the Germans have never got their knife into you or the British embassy. If the war ends well, this will be recognized even by the Press in time."[38] Of the several false steps Spring Rice managed to avoid, misconceived embassy propaganda was one of them.

When Balfour succeeded Grey as foreign secretary, Spring Rice deemed it useful to restate his position. "A good many people think we should undertake more active propaganda," he wrote Balfour. "The safest course would seem to be some sort of clearing house of information, with an American adviser and a competent specialist with a library or reference." This hardly matched the German tactics or Wellington House for that matter, but as Spring Rice wryly observed: "It is doubtful that we can change the weather by rigging the barometer."[39] He later restated his views on the subject to Balfour so that the foreign secretary could better understand his reasoning. "If Americans do not share our views, we do not propose to persuade them when they can only be persuaded effectively by themselves. I have always said that I would have nothing to do with any propaganda directed against the President to whom I am accredited. The President is rather apt to resent this and we suffer accordingly."[40] By 1916 Spring Rice had several occasions when he disapproved of the Wilsonian style and substance. It was simply that his sense of propriety forbade him such a breach of diplomatic discipline as to attack, even in a veiled way, the president of the United States. Restraint, patience, conciliation—these were habits out of keeping with the primordial urge to war. They made him appear out of step. But as Grey had said: Spring Rice had done "most wisely and well." He was seconded by E. L. Godkin, the British-born editor of The Nation, who wrote: "The quiet way is more effective."[41] But the argument that inaction was the better tack to take is hard to prove until the results of the total of Spring Rice's diplomacy have been judged.

The sinking of the Lusitania on 7 May 1915 by a German

submarine, with a loss of 128 Americans among the more than 1200 fatalities, was ready-made for a propaganda blast from British quarters. Spring Rice argued that the deed spoke louder than mere words and held that to capitalize on such a disaster would have been ghoulish as well as counterproductive. There was widespread belief in England that the sinking of the *Lusitania* could in itself catapult the United States into the war. To Colonel House, war with Germany was a certainty unless iron-clad guarantees were forthcoming from Berlin that such an attack would never again be authorized. From England Lord Crewe wrote to Spring Rice: "It would be very greatly to our advantage should the U.S. decide on hostilities." He had sound reasons: the moral effect on the neutral nations, the financial aid it would mean for Britain and France, and the unassailability of the United States by German military forces. "This view," he added, "is shared by a majority in the Cabinet."[42] In Whitehall generally, the presumption grew that the United States could not now avoid a rupture with Germany and that this would lead to open warfare. This was especially so because Allied-American relations were running smoothly. But Spring Rice was skeptical. As he told Grey, "I believe the predominant feeling is 'let us keep out of it—let us defend our just rights but remain neutral and only come in at the end as peacemakers.'" In the same dispatch, the ambassador reminded the Foreign Office of the long-standing Anglophobia in the United States and the honored tradition of nonentanglement with the nations of Europe, stemming from George Washington's advice to his countrymen as he left the presidency in 1797. Spring Rice insisted that this attitude was so ingrained that no single incident, however monstrous, would jar it loose.[43] In a private letter to Grey he was no less insistent. "Nothing is more certain than that the people of the United States are ready to accept any reasonable excuse for Germany's contention, and all Germany has to do in order to preserve peace is to afford some reasonable excuse [for the destruction of the *Lusitania*]." In fact he feared the Bryan resignation over Wilson's protest note was "giving a visible head to the 'long haired men and the short haired women' who are agitating the country for peace, prohibition and against the export of arms."[44] This last issue was a great worry, Spring Rice calling it "the most serious question of all." Again wanting to play down the likelihood of American entry into the war, he reiterated: "The prevailing sentiment is undoubtedly for peace. Not perhaps peace at any price, but at a very considerable price. . . . It will take more than the *Lusitania* to change this."[45]

Although ammunition accumulated for an embassy propaganda campaign, the ambassador continued to speak against it. "Some of your friends," he told the foreign secretary, "seem to think there is now a need for an energetic propaganda on our side. A distinctive English propaganda would be a mistake. Without it on the whole American public opinion is becoming more favourable to the Allies partly because the German danger is ever near and looming larger." He did concede that it "might be useful if some one could be found who could persuade the Irish that the English Government are not, as they say here, going back on their promise as to Home Rule. . . ."[46] But to some critics Spring Rice's resistance to running a well-oiled propaganda machine seemed a question of drift over mastery. His long experience in assessing Americans and their outlook and his respect for them as a free people told him again and again, to use Wilson's phrase, that "free men need no guardians." He wrote movingly to Theodore Roosevelt: "There is more real community of feeling between men who think the same according to their own free will and judgment, than between men who act together in obedience to another man, be he who he may. Our kingdom is within us."[47] This was in essence the liberalism that Spring Rice so much valued in public affairs.

In the summer of 1915 Sir Cecil was nearly the victim of what looked like a spontaneous plot to do him physical harm. Emotions were running high at the time. American agitation over the *Lusitania* and the German response to Wilson's stand on the submarine issue were still strong. There were allegations that the German government had paid agents to destroy American factories by bombings and sabotage. The temper of the country was ugly. Against this background the story unfolds. Spring Rice had maintained a close contact with J. P. Morgan, Jr. The House of Morgan was in effect an Anglo-American financial institution so that the ambassador's attitude was natural enough, and he had been influential in arranging that Morgan handle most of the money transactions between the British government and private American investors. J. P. Morgan, Jr.—Jack Morgan, as he was known—had been a spokesman for Wall Street when the decision was taken on 31 July 1914 to stop all trading on the stock exchange when panic selling of American securities in London threatened. He had also been an informal messenger from the British cabinet when it wanted to warn Wilson that any recently purchased German ships flying the United States flag would be intercepted. Spring Rice had every reason to cultivate an American so friendly to his own country. As it hap-

pened, the ambassador was a house guest of the Morgans at
their place at Glen Cove, Long Island. As Morgan, his wife,
and their British guest were breakfasting one morning, an in-
truder was discovered in the house, a man brandishing a gun
who clearly had set out to kill Morgan. He leveled his gun
at him, once he determined who Morgan was. Morgan acted
quickly and courageously, managing to disarm his assailant and
suffering only two flesh wounds. Spring Rice helped get the
weapon as the struggle was going on. In recounting the episode
to Grey he said the would-be assassin, Erich Muenter by name,
probably had confederates and was supplied by outside money.
Muenter was arrested but died in prison the next day, listed
officially as a suicide. Spring Rice believed, "It is most likely
that he was shot on order as he had promised a full confession
the day before he died."[48] The incident was widely reported
in the New York papers, which mentioned that the British ambassador had been a witness to the affair. Thus his whereabouts
was public knowledge. Two days later, as he was being driven
from the Morgan home, a car with five men in it pulled past
the chauffeur-driven automobile carrying Spring Rice and
stopped ahead of it. The five men stood across the road as
though to block passage, but the chauffeur drove directly through
them, hardly slowing down. The police treated the incident
as a robbery that was foiled, but it could have been more sinister.
No connection between the attack on Morgan and the Spring
Rice threat could be demonstrated, but speculation was rife
for a time. Federal authorities took the matter seriously, and
from then on the environs of the British embassy in Washington
were policed by agents of the American secret service.[49]

War, even on the home front, wears many faces, and occasionally the face of humanity. A German-American youth, by the
name of Triest, had gone aboard a British ship in England with
the intention of stealing the wireless code book to turn it over
to German agents. Upon his arrest by the police, his parents
appealed to Theodore Roosevelt, asking the ex-president to try
to secure his release. He contacted Spring Rice, who sent his
appeal on to the Foreign Office. Spring Rice wrote Grey: "As
to Triest, Theodore Roosevelt who has done a lot for the Allies,
is worth consideration and you might take his advice and tell
him you have taken it. His suggestion is a plea for insanity
and confinement until the end of the war."[50] After some weeks
Spring Rice advised Roosevelt: "Sir Edward Grey informs me
that Balfour and he have carefully gone over your letter about

Triest. Not insane but possibly unbalanced. The Government will give him full benefit if his father comes to England and takes him home under his charge. He will be handed over without trial. If he were to be tried on the evidence available he would be found guilty and executed."[51] The contrast between the British action in this instance and the execution of Edith Cavell was not lost upon people in England and America, although again Spring Rice refused to propagandize it. At least one life had been spared however, and one individual tragedy averted by good will in England and America. It was about this time that Spring Rice was mourning the death of Nanny Lodge; thoughts of friend and strangers alike mingled.

It is now appropriate to follow the ups and downs of pro-Allied sentiment in the United States. As Spring Rice noted, these fluctuations were never very far from President Wilson's mind as he pondered various strategies toward the war and the arrangements for peace to follow. In Spring Rice's judgment, America's part in the war, whether as a belligerent or a mediator, hinged on the swing of public opinion. The president was no doubt a man of high principles, and his administration, especially the State Department when headed by either Bryan or Lansing, influenced by either John Bassett Moore or Frank Polk, was animated by a spirit of justice under law. Wilson was also a politician who had to look to electoral trends and, more precisely, to his reelection chances in 1916. He could not forget that it was a split in the majority Republican party that had given him the office in 1912, and that he must be sensitive to the will of the people in the matter of neutrality if he wanted to continue in office. Spring Rice made the point frequently that, like Asquith in England, Wilson had to march to the tune of public confidence. It is somewhat strange then—paradoxical rather than contradictory—that the ambassador opposed embassy participation in propaganda designed to sway opinion in favor of Anglo-French liberalism and the simultaneous rejection of German militarism. The explanation continues to be his professed faith in the basic liberalism of the American people, which meant support for the Allies and perhaps eventually armed intervention. It was not a promissory note to be called in at a definite date but a matter of American history and conscience. It was incumbent on Spring Rice to keep his government apprised of meaningful alterations in American opinion as it responded to the increasingly desperate actions undertaken by both sides as the war dragged on. Not a few men in the Foreign Office came "not to give a damn" about American opinion, and when he came to full power, Lloyd George could be counted as one of them. So long as Sir Edward Grey presided at the Foreign Office, however, calculations respecting American good will were carefully shaped, with Spring Rice often feathering the arrow.

Initially, as has been suggested, Americans favored the Allied side largely because of the brutality of the German attack on "poor, little Belgium." Like all knee-jerk reactions, it did not of necessity indicate a fixed position, given the overwhelming American preference for neutrality once the western front was established. Spring Rice estimated that as of October 1914, "about ninety per cent of the English-speaking people and half the Irish are on the side of the Allies." And he added sardonically, "In the glorious annals of German propaganda nothing is so remarkable as the fact that Germany has made England almost popular in America."[52] Later Spring Rice would read the Bryce report, but even on the evidence submitted there he did not believe the American people would contemplate coming into the war.[53] The next year he confessed himself worried about the mid-term elections because of the uncertainty of the mercantile interests in responding to the British blockade. With the elections over he concluded that public opinion had not much altered if one looked at the voting patterns, and that "on the whole the public takes the blockade in a calm and reasonable way and fully understands that we must take some defensive measures."[54] At the same time he reported serious divisions in American political life and attributed it to "the violently pro-German elements in the German-American population who have rejected the principles of the revolution of 1848."[55] "Twelve million Germans in one's belly is a rather severe weight for a nation . . . and that is the situation here." Repeating the 90 percent figure, Spring Rice argued that "the German-American is very often but not always a very strong and violent advocate of German kultur." He concluded that Wilson thought German methods of exerting political pressure had an "extremely exasperating effect" on American public opinion and that this government was in danger of having to face a violent racial division."[56] The Foreign Office took some comfort that the mass of Irishmen were not following the Sinn Fein leadership, but the ambassador believed that most Jews, particularly bankers and newspapermen, were pro-emperor. Their influence consequently needed to be guarded against. He specified Paul Warburg, the chairman of the Federal Reserve Board, as fanatically pro-German.[57] Oscar Straus, a prominent Jewish leader who had once been a member of Roosevelt's cabinet, disputed this. He wrote Spring Rice in April 1915 that he was "quite confident fully 80% of the Jews of this country are in sympathy with Great Britain and France. Russia is a rather hard pill to swallow and it is only swallowed because of Britain and France."[58] On balance, Spring Rice had some reason to be optimistic that "the popular mind is made up and German propaganda has no results," and had no reason to think a change would come about.[59]

There was trouble brewing, nonetheless. By early 1915 it was increasingly clear the conflict in Europe would have no quick resolution, and a war of attrition would be the result. In the United States a German-American political faction came into existence. Nonpartisan in outlook—neither of the two major parties welcomed the development—it was ready to throw its considerable weight into Congressional elections and to argue issues in the press. Spring Rice reported the situation at length. "The German faction was organized for un-American and purely German purposes to put pressure on all candidates for office, irrespective of party and to seek to carry out their purposes by the intimidation of Congressmen and Presidents, either actual or would-be. . . . The present object of these people is to put pressure in order to stop the exportation of arms to the Allies. . . . In the Senate and the House of Representatives the pressure they exert is very strongly felt. . . . The President once spoke of the danger of civil commotion and the spread to America of the national antipathies of Europe. . . . There is the strong probability that if the country went to war with Germany, there would be something like a civil war here. . . ." He promised to warn Grey if "there are signs of active discontent" and once again expressed the view as to the wrong-headedness of German propaganda: "The Americans whom it threatens most are the best qualified to defend themselves."[60] As far as Spring Rice was concerned the Germans were "indefatigible in their attempts to influence public opinion to obtain the prohibition of the export of arms," to the point of direct interference in internal American politics. He worried about the effects of all this but was able to report at the end of April that public opinion was still in the Allied corner while German exertions to capture the Irish vote were not working out. He questioned the attitude of the Catholic church, however, and targeted the Jesuits as

being Prussian without explaining this strange association of
Junkers and the pope's shock troops.[61] He seems to have overlooked the lasting negative impact on German Catholic minds
of the *Kulturkampf*, no doubt some Jesuits among them. Some
Catholics were pro-German, or pro-Austrian, but the American
hierarchy was neutral for the most part if not pro-Ally. The
American primate, Cardinal Gibbons, was outspoken in support
of the liberal cause, and Spring Rice probably misjudged Cardinal O'Connell of Boston, who was merely pro-Irish. An amusing
incident occurred in this connection. The ambassador protested
the appointment of George Mundelein as Roman Catholic bishop
of Buffalo, New York. A man with so German a name should
not be in charge of a diocese close to British Canada. Soon
thereafter—although there is no evidence that the protest was
instrumental in bringing this about—Mundelein was named
archbishop of Chicago, later became cardinal, and was one of
the Catholic advisers to Franklin Roosevelt in the late 1930s.
God does indeed move in mysterious ways! More seriously,
Spring Rice was somewhat justified in his fear of civil disturbances in the United States provoked by radical segments in
the German-American population, and latter-day historians have
concurred in his judgment.[62]

The loss of the *Lusitania* had stunned Americans but it was
not decisive. One reason was that the German-Americans "almost without exception have gone underground or acclaimed
their devotion to the American flag," the ambassador told the
Foreign Office, "but the strong impression is it is temporary
and will not last."[63] The horrified reaction of Americans was
ascribed to sentiment, and sentiment is notoriously subject to
change, and in unpredictable directions. Spring Rice secretly
hoped that the response of the German government to the presidential protest would work to England's good. He cited the
papers of Dr. Dumba, the Austro-Hungarian ambassador to Washington, which had fallen into the hands of British intelligence
and which indicated plans to blow up United States arms works,
as the sort of public disclosure that was far more persuasive
than routine propaganda in getting the right results. Again, actions spoke louder than words.

Try as he might, Spring Rice could not purge the German
internal menace from his thinking, nor from his dispatches
and letters. He wrote privately and extensively about it to his
nephew, Dominik. ". . . Owing to emigration and still more to
the conscious development of national feeling among the citi-

zens of German origin, the country has become divided into entirely separate and distinct sections which do not speak the same language and think the same thoughts. . . . Thus when the war broke out the government found itself confronted with a fact. The old view was that the U.S. was a united nation formed with a view to certain fundamental ideas of liberty and so on. . . . They found that the old view ceased to be true."[64] Was he exaggerating or even distorting the situation because of his well-honed German obsession?

According to Colonel House, it was Spring Rice who early in the war had given the impression that President Wilson was pro-German. House told Grey personally that "Sir Cecil was very nervous and constantly seeing spooks and that he told me we would all be pro-German before the end of the war."[65] The colonel's purpose in confiding this to Grey is hard to fathom. He may have wanted to undercut the ambassador's influence by questioning his reliability, thereby clearing the ground for his personal diplomacy. He may well have remembered with particular vividness how agitated Spring Rice became whenever the subject of Germany arose; should Grey be advised that Spring Rice did not have an altogether level head? House did not go through with his original desire to see to the recall of Spring Rice, however. Whatever the one thought were the other's limitations, the colonel and the ambassador had much in common when it came to international affairs. Sir Horace Plunkett, who was a friend of both men and an advocate of Anglo-American cooperation, insisted to Spring Rice that House "has been throughout a very true friend to you in the extraordinarily difficult and critical times through which you have passed in the last couple of years."[66] Neither man favored the total destruction of Germany in the post-war settlement, for example. House wanted a reasonably strong and stable Germany as a bulwark against Russia. He warned Spring Rice: "If the Allies win and Germany is thoroughly crushed, there will be no holding back Russia."[67] Spring Rice said much the same thing to Roosevelt: "By finishing the job, I don't mean finishing Germany; putting an end to the fever does not mean putting an end to the patient."[68] Although he had not been explicit, his fears of czardom continued as strong as ever, and he may well have had in mind Germany as a counterweight to Russia. Had circumstances been different, House and Spring Rice could easily have been good friends in the manner of Grey or Lodge.

Spring Rice was well disposed toward the American government and its officers and remained so during his time in Washington. But as the war went on, relations between London and Washington grew more complex, and he tended to become disturbed by the drift in Anglo-American relations. The trend was away from rapport and toward misunderstanding, which could easily slip into confrontation. Oddly enough, this change in attitude from mutual respect to mutual suspicion was in part a consequence of events following the *Lusitania* disaster. Wilson's stern warning had prompted Germany to promise to refrain from attacks on large passenger ships; it appeared further that the president had wrung this concession from a reluctant German government. This apparently successful move to protect at least some neutral rights must be read in conjunction with Wilson's testament, also pronounced in the wake of the *Lusitania*'s loss, that "there is such a thing as a nation being too proud to fight." As justifiable as this proposition may have been from an American perspective, it was sure to have a deflating effect on the British spirit. The German concession, furthermore, caused the United States to expect that Britain would make its own concessions to American neutral rights. Spring Rice kept the Foreign Office informed on this new wrinkle in administrative thinking.[68] The Congress could also be expected to make demands. Although the ambassador sometimes got letters praising him for his determination to stay out of the limelight, he was skittish toward the legislature and its weather-vane behavior. Because many Americans, officials and others, expected Britain to back down from some of its blockade tactics, Spring Rice urged conciliation as before. But in London conciliation was looked upon more and more as a failed policy, something he did not want to admit. By the end of the summer of 1916, he began to see matters as "tit for tat" as he reported conversations with Colonel House. "For everything that is said against Germany, a newspaper thinks it must say something against England," which he deemed unfair.[70]

Spring Rice persisted in his conviction that in diplomacy, if not in the press, conciliation could produce desired results. He and Grey were perturbed by the Wilson administration's demand in 1915 that cotton not be placed on the list of absolute contraband. Pressure for citing cotton as contraband was coming from within the Asquith cabinet. That convinced him that hardliners in London would simply make more hardliners in Washington, thereby jeopardizing Britain's best interest. He recognized that the president was under heavy assault from cotton senators and congressmen to allow cotton to sell freely on the world market, and he warned that if cotton were not so listed, the Congress could retaliate with a law prohibiting the export of arms. It was evident that a fair amount of American cotton was getting past the blockade by moving through neutral ports, and there was a hard core in the cabinet determined to stop it. Working closely with Sir Richard Crawford, the economic counselor, Spring Rice suggested that his country agree to buy the entire American cotton crop destined for export at ten cents a pound as the clamor for an arms embargo grew louder and louder.

The idea of purchasing the American cotton crop was common property; the Germans were apparently ready to bid up the price to as high as thirty cents a pound. Spring Rice made his proposal to Colonel House in a prearranged meeting in Manchester, Massachusetts, on 2 August 1915, the same day he sent a long dispatch to Grey outlining his exchange with the colonel. If he was extravagant in proposing purchase of the whole crop, he was correct in supposing that for the Southern states the cotton issue was an economic matter entirely. Grey, who had first broached the proposal in cabinet, thought Spring Rice had made the right impression on Wilson via his talks with House as it would be up to the president to give approval. Should London agree to such an offer cotton could be declared absolute contraband and at the same time the price of cotton agreed to in advance could be maintained. Political pressure on the president would be eased in the bargain. Spring Rice was convinced that the situation was "largely psychological and any action taken should be regarded as a form of political insurance as well as from its economic aspect."[71] Conscious of public opinion, he urged Grey in handling all this to speak of the Allied blockade rather than tying it solely to the British. "The question for us is the opinion of the mass, not of the Government which fully understands the situation, and like yourself must follow not lead."[72] The purchase proposal was adopted in principle. The cabinet was persuaded to agree to buy enough cotton to keep up the price, and as an analogue, cotton was declared absolute contraband. Wilson's political fortunes improved and the noose was tightened around the Germany economy.

As the real crunch and its accompanying confrontation did not occur until 1916, Spring Rice continued his sober optimism, streaked at times by his sardonic wit. In mid-November he wrote Grey about feelings in the United States. The truth was, and the danger as well, "if eighty per cent [of the people] are in favour of the Allies, they are in favour of them as we are of going to church; the remaining twenty per cent are in favour of Germany as we are of eating our dinners."[73] The ambassador was under no illusions, nor did he conjure any to share with his chief in London.

One of Spring Rice's serious concerns was the growing Allied dependence on American credit. Ordinarily he was not thought of as expert in financial affairs, but he had shown himself quite perceptive regarding the first Anglo-French war loan, which was initiated in the late summer of 1915. When the subject of a loan was first raised, with a target of $1 billion dollars, he was cautious to the point of doubting if such a sum was realistic. His reasons were simple and sound. Americans were unused to lending money to foreign governments and could not be readily persuaded to do so. Second, the outcome of the war was undecided, and Americans would hesitate to invest in case the defeated nation or nations were unable to pay off the loan. Finally, a great many American bankers were sympathetic to Germany and would advise their customers not to invest in Anglo-French bonds. "Any attempt," he cautioned, "to float a large loan would be an immense disaster" as it was likely to fail by falling short of its goal.[74] Contrary to his advice, an Anglo-French team, headed by Lord Reading, the English lord chief justice, arrived in New York in September and immediately huddled with a banking consortium organized by Jack Morgan. As Reading was later to admit, the obstacles were "stupendous." A $500 million loan was agreed to, at an attractive rate of 6 per cent interest. This represented only half of the original sum talked about as Reading and his colleagues took the advice of the American bankers in scaling it down. After two months $130 million was still unsubscribed and had to be absorbed by Morgan. Furthermore, only $33 million had been taken up by private investors, even at a high rate of interest. Reporting all this to Grey, Spring Rice said that Lord Reading "got on to everything and everybody. I think he will be a most useful adviser." At the same time, wanting to keep his own man in the fore, he suggested that Crawford "should advise from here on all finances. He is very able and very conciliatory."[75] Spring Rice took no comfort in being correct in his forecast of the perils facing an Anglo-French loan, but he might well have hoped that his future advice would receive an earnest and respectful hearing. There had been one reassuring development regarding the loan; that is, Wilson favored it because it would supply the credits needed to buy American goods. The economic ties that bind had begun to be fastened in place.[76]

Thereafter Spring Rice often reminded the Foreign Office of a growing dependence on American goods and credit and on American good will, although he did not advocate an abject attitude. The American economy had been pulled out of a depression by Allied war orders, and the fact that Britain and her colonies took about 40 per cent of the American export trade was a psychological bargaining chip in keeping America friendly to the Allied side. "We have therefore," Spring Rice pointed out to Grey, "the claim of their best customer and at the present moment our orders are absolutely essential to their commercial prosperity." Yet there was no blinking the reality: Britain was dependent and conciliation could preserve good relations. Colonel House, whose opinion counted for much with President Wilson, appreciated the ambassador's role "in accommodating our shipping problem."[77] Being on the right side of the colonel could only help the cause, which was what the war was all about. Spring Rice could be remarkably clear sighted about such matters even though he was knee deep in the effort to see Great Britain victorious. He objected to the battering that Wilson was undergoing in 1916 from the German press, the British press, and some jingo American newspapers. As he saw it, all the president was doing was looking out for the interests of the United States, which was his sworn duty to do.[78]

Lord Eustace Percy, who was a staff member of the embassy, analyzed Spring Rice's conduct of affairs down to the year 1916 in this way. The ambassador chose to give the impression to London that he was treating the Americans with kid gloves because he wished to emphasize to Foreign Office officials—men like Arthur Nicolson and Eyre Crowe who doubted the wisdom of being beholden to the United States—that it was foolish to disregard the American position on the blockade or blacklisting. In contrast he sought to convey to Washington that he was taking a tough line with the Wilson administration, lest Americans come to believe that British good will could be presumed upon indefinitely. According to Percy this was a deliberate tactic. If so, it was one fraught with danger, namely, dissatisfaction with the ambassador's performance by his own government and his host government as well. Percy was a shrewd judge of people perhaps, with the advantage of working on a daily basis with Spring Rice. His interpretation would be more plausible, however, if he had called Sir Cecil's methods less than deliberate efforts to play a hazardous diplomatic game. It would have been more in keeping with Spring Rice's character, which was largely innocent of guile, and it would have been in line with the evaluations of Grey, House, and Lansing.[79]

The fact is, the ambassador might be faulted by some for being too conciliatory in pursuit of American good will and by others for being too firm. There was no text book formula for him to follow. Diplomacy, like politics, is the art of the possible, and Spring Rice's judgment as to what could and could not be managed was conceived with the possible in mind. But in diplomacy, as in politics, the players are fair game for critics within the government and from newspapers on the outside. He could not hope to be spared cudgeling. Too much can be made of his disagreements with United States officialdom; too little attention can be given to the attacks on Asquith and Grey for their direction of the British war effort. Such attacks unavoidably and in some respects unfairly included their agent in Washington. When in 1916 dissatisfaction with the liberal government began to build, one of its policies that came under fire was Grey's soft line on America. Spring Rice had been a willing and indeed an enthusiastic partner in pursuing it, but a junior partner surely. If politicians, the press, and the public became more and more exasperated with United States neutrality and its claims against the force of the blockade, Spring Rice was bound to suffer and with considerably less defensive power than a foreign secretary. It was easy to gang up on the ambassador as it was known he did not rate very high with Wilson or House. Interestingly enough, when Grey bailed out of the government, Spring Rice stayed on. There were sufficient reasons if not numerous precedents why he might have exited arm in arm with Sir Edward. His health was uncertain; his often-expressed desire to retire indicated part of his thinking; the presence of opponents to the Grey pro-American policy was ominous; and his detractors in Fleet Street were vocal. Yet Spring Rice did not cut and run; he stayed and worked for the new foreign secretary as assiduously as he had for the old. Some part of the explanation of why he soldiered on is already evident; further reasons may be read, between the lines, as the account of his ambassadorship continues to unfold.

6
WARTIME AMBASSADOR: 1916–1918

Three distinct but related matters preoccupied Anglo-American officials at the start of 1916. One was the response the United States would make to any renewal of unrestricted submarine warfare, in light of the stern American condemnation of the destruction of life and property wrought by the U-boats. A second was whether the United States would tolerate a British blockade that was becoming tighter and more restrictive of neutral trading rights. The forthcoming American presidential election was the third of these common issues. The reelection or the defeat of Wilson was bound to have repercussions for the American response to the wartime actions of both sides. On the other hand, should a new man come into power, what would his policy be? If the cabinet or the Foreign Office felt the need to comprehend the political/presidential situation, they had only to turn to the dispatches and reports of the ambassador. A more thorough or expert canvass of the scene could hardly have been forthcoming. What Spring Rice produced was a model of informed accounting. What made his communications valuable was that he was able to present the American perspective and the Wilsonian perspective in a cool and detached way. His grasp of American politics was sure; he pulled no punches but called no names. His sense of satisfaction that the president would not go along with the German arguments in support of open submarine warfare was balanced by the awareness that the Allies themselves would be an object of severe pressure in the form of diplomatic notes that would take issue with the blockade and related matters. In his analysis of Wilson's chances for reelection, there was no trace of Spring Rice's alleged Republican bias, nor can any be found in his correspondence. If anything, he equated the Republicans with Wilson, who seemed both to have made up their minds that they would not accept German votes at the sacrifice of American patriotism.[1] In one letter he bracketed the president and his chief critic, Roosevelt. "Both Mr. Wilson and Mr. Roosevelt have made the most earnest endeavors to arouse the country to a sense of its obligations."[2] Whatever his personal likes and dislikes, when Spring Rice spoke even semiofficially, he played his cards fairly. His one great undisguised bias was in favor of a victory for liberal England.

There were corelatives to Spring Rice's American notes, to be found in the accuracy of his forecasts of United States policy moves. Depth of knowledge produced a peculiar gift of insight. The first of these was his prediction that America would not enter the war until its vital interests were threatened drastically and directly. Second, he was convinced early on that in Wilson's mind he, as president, was the only mediator who could end the fighting by proposing his good offices, the one leader who was able to speak openly of peace without victory. A final example of the ambassador's accurate forecasting was his insistence that the president could not be counted on to bring the United States into a permanent arrangement to secure the peace once the war ended. The president did, in fact, fail to persuade the Senate to approve the Versailles Treaty, which had incorporated in it the Covenant of the League of Nations, the presumed guarantor of peace and security. From the Allied view, every one of these corelatives was a negative, and the ambassador's frequent iteration of them added to his reputation as an invincible pessimist, a man "who saw spooks." What he saw, of course, was reality, unpleasant, off-putting reality. But some read it as a lack of verve, or worse, a loss of nerve. Once again a genuine strength was to appear as a weakness.

Of the three issues that promised to dominate Anglo-American relations in 1916, the first, renewed submarine warfare, flared to a climax with the sinking of the cross-channel passenger steamer Sussex in March. Wilson's note of protest, although it was something less than an ultimatum, was effective nonetheless. For whatever reason or calculation, the Germans in May gave the "Sussex pledge," which, were it to be fully implemented, would shift advantage to armed merchantmen because they would not be attacked without warning. Wilson had won a stunning diplomatic victory and a powerful slogan for his upcoming presidential campaign: "He kept us out of war." Spring Rice's report to Grey on the Sussex crisis was exceptionally matter of fact. "It can not be said that the United States has been set on fire, and it can be said with certainty that if there is any sign of a conflagration every effort will be made to extinguish the flames," he wrote as a reference no doubt to Wilson's extreme caution in drafting his note of protest.[3]

The second issue, the blockade, persisted all through 1916 and at times was about to rupture Anglo-American cordiality. At least Spring Rice interpreted the signs in that way. The stepped-up blockade was due to the ability of the Royal Navy, for the first time, to apply maximum force, and the determination of the new men in the cabinet to use this weapon to the limit, best summed up by Lloyd George's announced intention of "a fight to the finish, a knockout." The United States had accepted the fact of the blockade almost as soon as the war broke out, although it protested the principle. But a tighter blockade with new items on the absolute contraband list and the resort to the blacklist and the white list and interference with the mails caused outcries throughout the United States. The British government rejected all formal protests and Spring Rice warned of a growing hostility. "We are certainly invoking on our heads a great deal of indignation from a great many powerful people."[4] Henry Hall of the *New York World* advised him of a "marked anti-British feeling"; even Secretary Lane, who was British born, complained to Hall that the British government "does not take what we say seriously."[5] Joe Tumulty, who was the president's secretary, said much the same thing. Lane and Tumulty were typical of the "powerful people" Spring Rice had alluded to. It fell to him to try to make plain his government's policy in a manner as soothing as possible. He appealed to the precedent of the blockade used by the Union during the Civil War. Although he argued the case with conviction, he was hardly able to dispel the misgivings Americans had toward his country. He predicted a "new phase in our relations."[6] "There is a strong sense our sea power is exercised in a way not so much to injure American trade and commerce but to hurt American pride and dignity."[7] He favored minor concessions and advised the Foreign Office to proceed along such lines. It would calm the atmosphere and relax the tensions.

The Irish rebellion, its suppression, and the execution of one of its leaders, Sir Roger Casement, were events intruding themselves unexpectedly into wartime diplomacy. While the whole affair was internal to British politics, it was bound to have some impact on the special relationship. Much American opinion was hostile to the English handling of the rebellion, whether justified or not. To many the issue was liberal England, a blot

on the British image in America. There were other considerations. Spring Rice regularly warned of the danger should the
Irish-Americans join the German-Americans to turn sympathy
away from the Allied side.[8] With the 1916 presidential election,
such a combination might even affect the outcome of the vote.
The ambassador was all for caution. When the uprising in Ireland was put down, American attention focused on the fate
of Casement. He was a German agent and an Irish nationalist,
but it was in his latter guise that he was cheered by Irish-
Americans. Spring Rice once remarked to the foreign secretary
that "my duty is to represent to you what is the point of view
here."[9] He was mindful of his own admonition as he proceeded
to advise Grey in the matter of the trial, guilt, and condemnation
of Casement. "A great bulk of the American people, while they
may excuse executions in hot blood, could very greatly regret
an execution sometime after the event. This is the view of impar-
tial friends of ours who have nothing to do with the Irish movement."[10] He noted further that some Irish-American leaders,
highly respected men like Cardinal Gibbons, favored clemency
for Casement.[11] In keeping with such sentiment, the Senate
passed a resolution seeking clemency, but Casement was executed before it arrived in London. Casement had become the
martyr the ambassador feared he would. English liberalism was
given a black eye. Spirited protests laced with anger broke out
in most Irish-American districts, but the nation as such was
not greatly moved, and Spring Rice reported that press reaction
was "singularly reserved." He did not presume to assess the
long term damage.[12]

The ever stricter Allied (i.e., British) blockade also took a
toll over the summer of 1916. No aspect of British tactics was
more fiercely resented than the blacklisting of U.S. firms suspected of dealing with Germany via neutral ports. In July acting
Secretary of State Polk told Colonel House: "This blacklisting
order of the English is causing tremendous irritation and we
will have to do something."[13] President Wilson was totally exasperated. "This blacklist business is the last straw," the president
advised House. "I have told Spring Rice and he sees my reasons
very clearly. Both he and Jusserand think it is a stupid blunder.
I am seriously considering asking Congress to authorize me to
restrict or prohibit exportation to the Allies."[14] Spring Rice cabled Grey, recounting Wilson's extreme displeasure: "Blacklisting is causing the most violent propaganda" because "of the
bulldozing policy of Britain."[15] In seeking to moderate presiden-

tial anger, the ambassador took a soft line by suggesting to Grey that each blacklisting case be treated on its own merits. Firms might also be allowed to request removal from the list, and this should be done if the facts warranted it. The foreign secretary was willing to be reasonable in the face of official American indignation, but he was opposed by a number of ranking Foreign Office staff. In this instance Spring Rice's advice prevailed, a good example of how much Sir Edward respected his opinion, at least in matters of detail. Yet it was the big picture that had motivated the advice. By October 1916, the ambassador was fearful that England and France could not carry on the war much longer without significant additions of United States credit. As minister of munitions, Lloyd George had made British virtually self-sufficient in arms and ammunition, but where was the money to come from to purchase the raw materials required in their manufacture? There was only one source as far as Spring Rice was able to tell: the United States. In his message to Grey urging a relaxation of the blacklist, he put it bluntly: "If you are independent of the United States you can take what you like but if you have proclaimed your dependence, and that being so, you must pay the price."[16] He had given unpopular guidance to his chief and was happy to report back that Grey's concessions "gave great satisfaction" to Wilson and the State Department.[17]

The degree of the president's anger over the blacklist may be measured by his decision to ask Congress to authorize him to ban exports and to deny port clearance to merchant ships, legislation that the Congress enacted in August. Alarm bells sounded in both the embassy and in Whitehall. The law was aimed directly at those nations that refused to trade with companies on the blacklist. Its underlying purpose could not be mistaken. As a standby authority it was a menacing one. Why Wilson had acted in this fashion Spring Rice explained with his accustomed analysis. The administration would have the power to act quickly should a need arise; it feared Germany would renew its all-out submarine war unless the United States did not appear to take action against the blockade; the president needed more diplomatic victories in an election year; the enactment provided a sound legal basis for any use of force. As an addendum he pointed out that Secretary Lansing's language in discussing the matter had been conciliatory, wanting to avert any collisions with Britain in the weeks running up to the election.[18] In consequence Spring Rice felt comfortable in urging his country to remain calm while he went about his task of soothing American distemper. The Foreign Office should not, he believed, respond in writing to this American move, but it would be well to realize that there were limits to American willingness to acquiesce to blockade practices.[19] At the same time he advised Wilson of London's distress. Although he had denounced aspects of the blockade, the president made no effort to recommit Germany to honoring the Sussex pledge. The Germans had continued to use their U-boats to roam the ocean and sink ships. Figures were released to the American press showing that from June 1 to September 30, 251 ships had gone down, of which 68 were neutral—an average of one in four. Wilson was apparently unmoved by these statistics. London and Paris consulted on other steps to be taken to defuse administration anger; a note of protest and explanation was discussed but never formulated. Spring Rice's prescription for calm was not lost on the policy makers at home.

The third matter of concern to the British ambassador in 1916 was the presidential election, or to be more exact, the policies, current and projected, of Woodrow Wilson. Among these policies was Wilson's determination to be the mediator between the two sides at war. That added another complication for British statesmen. Spring Rice felt himself responsible for evaluating the president's peace feelers; but in his capacity as the ranking British official in Washington, he was in no way involved in such proposals. Colonel House rather than any of the key envoys—Jusserand, Von Bernstorff, Spring Rice—would be the conduit through which Wilson would float his ideas about ending the war without victory. House had first gone to Europe in January of 1915 to sound out both sides on an early cessation of hostilities, but he had no success. The face of war had grown so horrible and the fate of Europe, and possibly the world, was in such precarious balance in the intervening months, that in October Wilson sent the colonel on a second mission. In this more studied effort, the Americans offered to act as mediators and indicated a willingness to become associated with other great powers to maintain the peace. House consulted with Sir Edward Grey, striving to find some basis for the war's end. He did not want Germany dismembered, it will be recalled. Grey showed some interest in the scheme, provided the United States would be one of the guarantors of the postwar settlement. On the strength of this encouragement, the colonel went on to Paris and Berlin but got no concrete support from those quarters while even England's commitment softened once the colonel had left Grey's presence. The House-Grey Memorandum—a plan to be implemented at a later day and with Allied cooperation—was a tangible result of this peace initiative only to those who insisted on such an interpretation. To Spring Rice it appeared based on irreconcilable points of view.[20]

At the same time House was touring European capitals in search of peace, Wilson and Lansing were attempting, with some success, to finalize a settlement with Germany over claims arising from the loss of the *Lusitania*. Reflecting what was the mood of the moment, Lansing proposed to notify the Allies that the United States could make no distinction between merchantmen armed for defensive purposes as opposed to armaments for offensive action. The reason he gave was British ships themselves never kept the distinction in mind in operating against the U-boats. There was an intimation by Lansing that merchantmen might be treated as cruisers. That would have dealt a crippling blow to British naval tactics and undermined its commerce. House and Lansing were working at cross purposes: House's scheme presumed Allied good will; Lansing was provoking Allied ill will. American face was saved when the German government announced that from 29 February 1916, all merchantmen would be sunk on sight, thus dismissing any nice distinction about defensive and offensive armaments. Grey in particular was shaken by this ambiguity in United States diplomacy. Then in March the *Sussex* went down, followed in May by the *Sussex* pledge, Wilson's triumph of pen over sword. Spring Rice had no part in the House-Grey undertaking, having been deliberately shut out by the president. But his reports to Grey over these weeks when House was working one side of the street and Lansing the other were as useful to the foreign secretary as they were pointed in their judgments.

From May onwards Spring Rice bore down hard on Wilson. "It is quite plain from the president's language that he has no intention whatsoever of entering the European arena as a belligerent and that he has every intention of entering it as a mediator. His stand point seems to be that the world is mad and that it can only be saved by a few sane men who are left in it. As one of the mad men you will form your own opinion, presumably a mad one as to the claims of our sane saviour."[21] In a follow-up letter to Grey he added, "The President desires what we all desire, that is a general and effective sanction by the common consent of all the powers backed by a readiness to enforce that sanction. This is a pious wish in which we share."[22]

More sobering were the ambassador's expressed doubts that the United States would become part of the sanction applying force. His line of argument was sound. "How can the President give us the desired pledge? He can not pledge the action of Congress in advance and the execution of the pledge must depend on the action of Congress which, as recent events have shown, can not be depended on. If Congress had supported the President Germany would have long ago been forced to give satisfaction on the question of the *Lusitania*. Congress was not ready to take action. We have no security that Congress would act otherwise where the question at issue is not American but European. Therefore in giving this promise, the President gives a promise the fulfillment of which does not depend on him."[23] This cautionary he stated in May. By September he had returned to the subject. ". . . The American tradition is against any sort of intervention in outside affairs and the present disposition of the country is absolutely opposed to the employment of force. I do not see how any international arrangement likely to be accepted by us as a guarantee of peace would be accepted by the Senate if it implied a definite armed intervention on the part of the United States."[24] The next month he reported that Senator Stone "has rather unkindly warned the public that the Senate would not pass any treaty which required the United States to act in the name of an internationl organization for the forceful maintenance of peace.[25] Spring Rice had been making such statements since early 1915, very probably reflecting the views of Senator Lodge, one of the future leaders of the fight against the Versailles Treaty in 1918–19.[26] But whatever the input of Lodge, Spring Rice understood perfectly well the theory of the Constitution and the ways of American diplomacy. As Wilson stepped up his plans to mediate, presidential pledges to secure the peace took on increasing significance. To continue to pursue these ambitions he would have to await the results of the November elections.

Spring Rice was consistent in his efforts to keep his superiors in London abreast of political happenings in the United States with the elections drawing near. Of course he was scrupulous in favoring neither side. Charles Evans Hughes, who had been the progressive governor of New York state, won the Republican nomination. He inclined toward the Allies but promised to follow a policy of "straight and honest neutrality."[27] Wilson's nomination was hardly in doubt but the overwhelming sentiment of the Democratic convention was for peace not preparedness.

With the presidency in the balance, Wilson had very little desire but to conform to the sense of his party so that the slogan "He kept us out of war" became the main theme of his limited campaign. Spring Rice reported that Hughes was the choice of German-American Republicans because his chief rival, Roosevelt, had been a bitter critic of "hyphenated-Americans," whose loyalty to the nation he openly doubted.[28] The German-Americans had little to choose from between Hughes and Wilson. Correctly understanding the Constitution, they placed their hopes on their ability to influence Congress rather than the chief executive; only Congress can declare war. As for calling the election, the ambassador saw Hughes as "a very good campaign speaker and his chances are thought to be good."[29] In any event, Wilson would be president until March 1917, and as he was likely to be reelected, his "peace programmes" deserved careful study. Of its many features Spring Rice was especially struck by the demand for freedom of the seas. The British "would probably look with some suspicion on a peace programme that would cripple our sea power," for example.[30] Irrespective of the outcome of the elections, he trusted that "no confidence would be placed on American intervention in our behalf."[31] Nothing in the way of benefit to England or France could be expected from Hughes or Wilson. Again his analysis was simple but sound: aid to the Allies, apart from making money by supplying them with war material, was not smart politics. And he gave an unqualified, outright warning to his government: "It would be a very dangerous thing to trust this government in any peace settlement."[32] Such was his remarkable ability to balance views that he could at the same time contend: "If you are to look at it from the American point of view there are many reasons why America should form common cause with neutral countries" in defense of its rights.[33]

The political heat of the day found Spring Rice in Canada to spend the preelection weeks there, on the advice of Sir Edward Grey. Or, as the ambassador put it, he was "to lie as quietly as possible and to occupy as little attention as we can."[34] There were two advantages. He would avoid personal involvement in the campaign, always a sensitive point with him. The other was that he would have some respite from the continual badgering by the State Department over blacklisting. Back in Washington just prior to election day, he observed that both Democrats and Republicans accused Great Britain of playing favorites in the race for the White House. To Spring Rice, this simply meant American public opinion was unsettled on all the issues except one: the people did not want to enter the war.[35]

On the strength of reelection, President Wilson was to have one last attempt at peace making, he informed Colonel House and Secretary Lansing. Spring Rice interpreted the move this way. The president "is bent on peace. He is determined to give Germany her chance; his great ambition is to be the mediator of peace without victory which would give the world permanent international law and mutual confidence."[36] He sensed in Wilson a commitment to see the peace process through, but once he was brought to realize that a mediated peace was not going forward, Wilson would no longer be willing to pay any price to avoid the menace of the submarine. It was not that Spring Rice failed to predict United States entry into the war—and it would have been foolhardy to make such a comment lacking hard evidence—but he preferred to wait and see as he advised his government, much as Wilson was to wait and see. His caution should not be mistaken for pessimism. He explained to Grey, for example, that as a result of the election the Republicans would have a majority in the House of Representatives when the new Congress convened in December 1917. The chairman of the House Ways and Means Committee was likely to favor neutrality. "As far as we are concerned Congress will be hostile."[37] These were facts; Spring Rice did not indulge in wishful thinking in the face of them.

Wilson's new peace initiative centered in a request for the Allies and the Central Powers to state their war aims and their terms for ending hostilities. Spring Rice hoped that the British press would fall silent; he advised the Foreign Office to make no quick response. The seriousness of Wilson's intention may be judged by the action of the Federal Reserve Board, which now began to warn Americans against further foreign investments. Spring Rice knew that this directive came from the president himself.[38] In London the cabinet considered Wilson's request carefully, held back a reply for the purpose of study, and eventually supplied a sufficiently detailed statement of aims and terms to be encouraging. But Britain did not acutally commit itself to mediation. Wilson had worse luck in Berlin, with the Germans holding aloof. Nonetheless, with the Federal Reserve Board cautionary in mind, Balfour asked Jack Morgan to consult with Spring Rice and Crawford if in his judgment further credits

were to be a problem. Simultaneously, Spring Rice was reempha-
sizing the strain on Allied finances.[39]

By this time Balfour had taken charge of the Foreign Office.
His ambassador in Washington felt the need to indoctrinate him
in aspects of American government and history, a short course
in modern America as he understood it. He wanted Balfour
to know "exactly the way business is conducted here. The President rarely sees anybody. He practically never sees ambassadors
and when he does, exchanges no ideas with them. Mr. Lansing
is treated as a clerk and receives orders which he must obey
at once and without question. The real business of foreign policy
is transacted by the President."[40] Balfour was told that Wilson
did not intend to give up on his efforts to bring about a mediated
peace; it "is a compelling reason, the natural ambition of the
President and the people of the United States to play a part
in the crisis. If the Allies give any reason to hope that peace
negotiations of some sort may be opened the President will
no doubt take full advantage of it. . . . It is almost inconceivable
that this country would take sides with Germany against the
Allies." All this was a straightforward recitation of views. He
ended the communication on a different note. "Here we regard
the White House rather as Vesuvius is regarded in Naples, that
is, a mysterious source of unexpected explosions."[41]

Throughout these uneasy weeks, realism continued to dominate both Spring Rice's thinking and his advice to the Foreign
Office. He could neither overcome his belief that Americans
were smug in an economic prosperity built on the death of
men, nor hide his contempt. Under the strain he sometimes
grew vindictive. "As some one said to me the other day, the
Statue of Liberty is an image of gilded bronze, hollow inside,
with its back turned on Europe."[42] But he was candid when
reporting to Balfour so that when things were looking up he
was happy to share the news. A letter of 19 January 1917 began:
"In so far as diplomacy is concerned, things are going well
for the Allies. It was expected that we would refuse to reply
to the President's inquiry as to our terms in the same way as
the Germans had refused. Now that we have accepted we hold
first place in popular respect. In spite of a strong temptation
to return an abrupt answer, we have given a full and courteous
one. The effect on the President's mind is highly satisfactory."[43]
But Washington and America together were a sea of turbulent
water, and to trace the rise and fall of every new wave, which

Spring Rice presumed his duty, conveyed the instable mood of the public and the government. To expect any observer to say with a degree of confidence what the United States would do was to invite a hazardous forecast. And so, as with other concerned parties, Sir Cecil watched and waited and reported what he saw.

The difficulty was that what Spring Rice saw was perceived only from a particular angle of vision in a line of sight not always unobstructed. He continued to be hard on Wilson, perhaps because the president consulted him hardly at all. He deeply resented Wilson's assertion that there was no difference in degree of guilt between the Allies and the Central Powers for starting the war, that there was enough blame to go around.[44] This greatly agitated the ambassador, who thought differently of the facts. For him, the evidence of events from 1900 to 1914 gave overwhelming proof of German perfidy. Spring Rice was ready to challenge presidential morality with moral judgments of his own. There remains the question of who may have shaped Spring Rice's estimate of Wilson and his diplomacy, of how susceptible he might have been to the prejudices of others like Roosevelt and Lodge. Yet in his hardness of heart toward Wilson, he pleaded for understanding. The president "is very different from Lincoln," he told Balfour. Lincoln "was brought up splitting rails, and not hairs. Lincoln had no doubt whatever as to right and wrong. But Lincoln was at war. Our own attitude then was the attitude which we now complain of in Mr. Wilson. If we remember this we will find it easier to understand."[45] It was good advice at a time when the outcome of the war was still undecided.

In the two months between the resumption of unrestricted submarine warfare and the convening of a special session of Congress, that is, from February 1 to April 2, events directed Anglo-American diplomacy. Slowly but certainly the United States moved toward war with Germany. Spring Rice had much to say as happenings turned the wheel of fortune in a way favorable to his country. His reports were matter of fact, despite the tension. The German decision to unleash the U-boats, was a bitter pill for Wilson, and "he no doubt suffered extremely. He has done everything possible to put a stop to the war," the ambassador continued, "in order to prevent the war from reaching this country; despite all his sacrifices he has now to choose between an ignominious surrender or rupture of relations with Germany."[46] Two weeks later he indicated that "feeling in the country is gradually increasing in intensity owing to the effect of the German declaration of ruthless warfare," but "the temper of Congress is pacific." By the next week "the spirit of the country was rising . . . the sense that something must be done to unify the nation and the people for war was growing."[47]

Many neutralists in the South and West were furious when the Zimmermann Note was made public in March. The German proposal that Mexico join her in a war against the United States with the prospect of regaining the American southwest dramatized the German threat to the North American mainland. Spring Rice told of the almost panic reaction sweeping the country. It "is feared there will be outrages without number as a result of the German plots."[48] Within a matter of days Wilson delivered his second inaugural address. "The essence of the President's address is that the United States government can not remain much longer indifferent to Europe. Apart from becoming involved in the struggle in defense of their rights, the Americans must take part in the settlement."[49] Sir Cecil had put a fair construction on the president's words. Almost immediately thereafter several American ships were torpedoed. "Opinion was considerably shocked by the sinking of the *Algonquin* and the public was prepared to consider it an 'overt act.'" It required the loss of three more U.S. flagged ships, news of which came in at about the same time, to arouse the public and the administration."[50] So went Spring Rice's running account of events. The president, addressing a joint session of Congress on April 2, asked for a declaration of war. Before the month was out the United States was fully committed to naval and military action. Sir Cecil, who had doubted and doubted, had not hoped and hoped in vain. That he deserved some credit for American involvement is hardly open to question. When Luxmoore wrote that "the entry of America justifies a letter of congratulations; it really must be the crowning achievement of your mission and I am clear that the main credit is yours," he surely oversimplified and exaggerated.[51] Yet he was not entirely wide of the mark. Spring Rice's pronounced judgments on public opinion, congressional attitudes, and Wilsonian intentions were usually valid, right down to particulars. He realized what were the limits of his power as only a self-effacing person could have done, and conducted his mission accordingly. He was not the perfect envoy; such a creature does not exist. But he was an effective representative of the policies and views of his government, both a spokesman and a symbol. If Luxmoore and others of his admirers overrated his accomplishments out of good will, those who decried his work appear to have done so not out of ill will but from a failure to understand the American temper with quite the touch displayed by Sir Cecil.

United States entry into the war marked a change in relations between London and Washington, and with that came a change in the work of the embassy. In the ordinary course of things, it would not follow that this required a change of envoys. The embassy could now be expected to become the nerve center of a combined Allied-American efforts on the financial and industrial as well as the military front. Perhaps the special skills required by all this were such that Spring Rice would find them foreign to his taste. Were the situation that simple, the embassy could be greatly strengthened with an expanded corps of experts coming under the authority of the ambassador, the specialists and their work harmoniously orchestrated by their chief. In that event the great knowledge and sympathy Sir Cecil had for the country could continue to advise British American policy. The Spring Rice embassy had not followed the ordinary course of things, however; its future after April 1917 was very much in doubt. The ambassador remained in office until January 1918, with his powers and prestige steadily reduced. Why and how this came about is itself an intriguing episode in the annals of the diplomatic service.

Personalities rather than heroes or villains featured in this *affaire,* and there were powerful personalities in abundance. Spring Rice must be ranked as one of them. He had been, after all, a controversial ambassador in his own mind, relentless in his hostility toward Germany, resisting demands for the embassy to be a propaganda mill, a possible target for German duplicity. And he had been something of a conversation piece in Washington because of his well-known and highly quotable acerbity. In this latter connection he could be indiscreet; rather like Clemenceau, he spared neither friend nor foe in using the verbal rapier. For example, during a sticky moment in Anglo-American financial dealings involving William Gibbs McAdoo (Wilson's son-in-law), he referred to Wilson as the shepherd and the treasury secretary as his crook.[52] It was a jibe too clever not to be repeated by others, perhaps with attribution. But few denied his virtues as the totally dedicated, hard-working representative of Great Britain with a power to disarm his critics by his charm and brilliant conversation.

In the *affaire*, Spring Rice's relationship to House was pivotal, the Colonel as alter ego and supreme confidant of the president, one of the lobes of his diplomatic brain. Wilson was remote and uncommunicative, a high lama, as the ambassador often complained. Unfortunately for their future dealings, at their first arranged meeting House had to be entertained by Lady Spring Rice; her husband, "not well enough to appear had to send words of regret."[53] The notion that here was an unwell man who would find the wartime embassy beyond his capacity to manage would not be easily dispelled. Contacts necessarily increased between the two men with the start of hostilities in Europe. Differences of opinion and temperament began to transform a conventional friendship into antagonism. In this the temperament factor should not be lightly dismissed. House preferred to work with *persons* rather than with *officials*, as he had personalized his dealings with Sir Edward Grey from the start of the war and later on was to rely on Sir William Wiseman. It was important for House to "get on well personally" with the people he dealt with; rank counted less than personality. There were other irritants. House was infuriated at Spring Rice's remark that the president was pro-German and went out of his way, in denying it, to identify the British ambassador as the source of the remark.[54] Before long he decided to bypass Sir Cecil to deal directly with Grey, and a bypassed envoy was to him tantamount to no envoy at all. Spring Rice simply ceased to figure in his plans, except perhaps on occasion when he felt the need to castigate British behavior. Because of his intimacy with Grey and his wide acquaintanceship in Washington, Spring Rice was almost certainly aware of House's estimate of him, and he resented it. Some of the explanation of his suspicions about the peace plans of Wilson and House were traceable to his exclusion by them from the work ordinarily carried out by a senior ambassador.

Spring Rice had been careful not to associate with Theodore Roosevelt, but his closeness to Senator Lodge, if it did not aggravate the president, aroused hostility on the part of Wilson's advisers. If he really did fear that the administration would turn pro-German and the senator was priming him to say so, he made no effort to hide his friendship with Lodge; from this may it be assumed that the views expressed were largely his own? In the cold light of history the answer may be "yes," but in the heat of partisanship it deserves an equally plausible "no."

Colonel House's taste for personal diplomacy, having rejected the ranking British official in Washington, finally settled on a relatively obscure staff member of the embassy, Sir William Wiseman. Wiseman was an army captain who had seen action in France before being invalided out of front line duty. At the embassy he was second secretary intelligence officer. House and Wiseman first met in December 1916 when Wiseman was directed to deliver a sensitive letter to the colonel in New York. They became friends, very close friends, almost at once. House soon called the attention of the president to Wiseman, describing him as the "most sensible Englishman that has been connected with the embassy here since the war began." And in light of Spring Rice's Republican weakness, he added significantly that Wiseman had intelligence enough to go with friends of the administration rather than with their enemies.[55] Since House and Wiseman got on and House and the ambassador did not, Wiseman was able to persuade the Foreign Office—now that Grey had departed—of his personal value as a link between the White House and Whitehall. He soon was indispensable to Balfour and did in fact do substantial and useful work in helping to break the impasse over credit in June–July 1917. Wiseman's triumph was Spring Rice's defeat. The young captain was named an official liaison between the cabinet and any special representative the cabinet might send to the United States. Wiseman was ambitious no doubt, one of the purveyors of the idea that Spring Rice was a "Republican Ambassador." House was to use this assertion in his dealings with Wilson, justifying both his rejection of Spring Rice and his promotion of Wiseman. All of the ambassador's natural attributes, which House was not reluctant to praise, were as nothing once the alliance between the colonel and the captain was cemented.[56]

To worsen Spring Rice's prospects, he had formidable critics at home in England. A number of ranking Foreign Office staff faulted his style and objected to his pro-American stance; but they were honest in questioning his judgments, and his reputation as a man doing the best job he knew how went unchallenged. His conception of the tasks at hand was what worried his London colleagues. "I'm rather afraid Springey may overwork himself . . . he will stick to it and not spare himself in the slightest" was a concern widely shared.[57] More and more of the professionals sided with Lloyd George's view that the embassy in Washington was too tame—that Spring Rice was a "silent ambassador"—and that what was needed was a dynamic effort to persuade the Americans to join in the war. The conviction expressed in June 1915 that the cabinet believed it would be very much to Britain's advantage should the United States declare war, had grown apace, but there was the ambassador in Washington doing little to foster it.[58] Rather than being a "silent ambassador," Spring Rice was a "quiet ambassador." Apart from dealing with the State Department and other bureaus in the capital and making himself available to the administration, he went frequently to New York City to nourish contacts with the financial and industrial leaders there. There were really few important men in New York, Boston, Philadelphia, or Chicago that he had not met. He went out to meet these leaders; this was the old-fashioned diplomacy in which he had been schooled and which he executed so well. But times had changed. When Lloyd George formed his coalition government in late 1916, much that was "old fashioned" gave way. Grey had always been ready and willing to speak up for Spring Rice, but with Balfour the ambassador had little protection from the heavy criticism leveled at him. Furthermore, as Balfour conceded, Lloyd George would be his own foreign minister, after the manner of Woodrow Wilson.

The liberal ministry had fallen to the onslaught of Lloyd George and the Northcliffe press because of its ineffectual preparation for and conduct of the war. Spring Rice was guilty by association. Unlike the Asquith government, and for which failures press and politicians had been generous in their condemnation, Spring Rice had long advocated preparedness in general and military conscription in particular. In 1909, for example, he voiced support for the creation of a British general staff, inspired by if not modeled along German lines—a most un-English proposal but one that showed that he was not unaware of changing times.[59] The ambassador's difficulties with the Northcliffe press stemmed from a personal not a policy matter, what he saw as an attack on his conduct. The Times had published a letter to the editor that complained of Spring Rice's prolonged absence from his embassy post and went on to scold him for returning to the United States on a German-owned ship (incidentally, he and the French ambassador Jusserand traveled together incognito). Spring Rice was convinced that Northcliffe had inspired the letter or at least given his explicit permission that the letter be published. Both contentions appear unlikely, but the ambassador could not dissuade himself from this interpretation. Northcliffe perforce was his enemy, and a powerful one, as his hand in the downfall of the Asquith ministry showed. Lloyd George had become prime minister for a host of reasons, but he had been abetted in his quest by a press hostile to the liberals and their war effort, on the battle front and the diplomatic front. David Lloyd George was one of the hardest-driving prime ministers in the history of the office; those who stood in his way were usually pushed aside. Spring Rice had been appointed to the most sensitive of all diplomatic posts by a liberal government. This was reason enough for his replacement.

Lloyd George's lack of confidence in Spring Rice mirrored the mind of Lord Northcliffe. For his part, Northcliffe was probably encouraged in his view by H. G. Wells, who once told the owner of The Times that Spring Rice was "a miscellaneous diplomat—Tokio, Cairo, Persia, an all covered with orders kind of person. We might just as well have a messenger boy in Washington."[60] It is hard to imagine a harsher and less informed characterization. Some element of Wells's indictment stuck in Northcliffe's mind and was subsequently transmitted to the prime minister. Willing to abide Spring Rice as long as the United States was neutral, Lloyd George was determined to remove him after April 1917.

From the start Spring Rice's ambassadorship was uncertain. His 1913 illness made him consider resigning. In 1915, with Wilson's approval, Colonel House contemplated seeking his recall but could not bring himself to do so. At the end of 1916 rumors were current that the Coalition Cabinet would soon send him away. Among others, Senator Lodge came to his defense, writing Balfour to urge him to keep Spring Rice on. He has done "extremely well" under "the trying circumstances created by the war," Lodge argued. He praised his "attention, thought and tact" as these traits were brought to bear on various issues and concluded his letter by saying, "I can not think of any one who could replace him with advantage in the midst of the war."[61] Others who worked in his behalf were P. F. Cunliffe-Owen, the English-born editor of the New York Tribune, and Shane Leslie. Sidney Brooks wrote a glowing account of Spring Rice's ambassadorship in an article widely syndicated in the American press. To Sir Charles Hardinge, his only faults were "his innate pessimism and his dislike of going into society."[62] These were flaws perhaps, but not sufficient to justify the sack. Semiofficial assurances came Spring Rice's way from Sir Eric Drummond, Balfour's private secretary. "I hope you entirely disregard all these rumors about your withdrawal, etc., they are based on nothing and I can't make out at present from what quarter they emanate (but I suspect Boche)."[63]

Drummond's assurances aside, one of the problems in replacing Spring Rice was the difficulty of finding the right man to succeed him. Bryce was not approached, and Grey, who was offered the assignment, gave a flat refusal. Either of them would have been welcomed as suitable by the Wilson administration and by the president personally. Yet both believed that Spring Rice had been doing a solid job, Bryce writing him in March 1917 that "your interesting letter gives the best possible logical analysis of the leading figures that I have ever seen."[64] Such were the methods of Lloyd George's government that at the time of Drummond's letter the prime minister was about to name Lord Northcliffe. The Foreign Office, led by Balfour, objected strenuously not only because of the individual but for the reasons behind the nomination, that the Americans would be flattered by the high-profile press lord. If this is accepted as valid, it is plain that Lloyd George little understood Woodrow Wilson—as dour a man as one might wish for. Lloyd George had one other thought in mind, however. By naming Northcliffe ambassador, he would be identifying the press lord with the ministry in power, and the prime minister would be less likely attacked by the jingoistic *Daily Mail* and the good gray *Times*. Facing determined opposition from the Foreign Office, Lloyd George dithered, and Spring Rice remained in Washington.

Fresh shadows fell across the ambassador's path after April 1917. Instead of replacing him, the cabinet sent out three successive "missions" to work closely with the United States government on various matters. First Balfour, despite his age, visited Washington in order to impress on the Americans the Allied need for ships, credit, and troops in that priority, if the war was to be sustained. He was well received by officials but felt that Spring Rice had wrongly advised him respecting the views of the Navy Department and the attitudes of Secretary of Navy Daniels and Admiral Benson. Spring Rice was not sure that things had gone smoothly and wrote to inquire if the embassy's work had been satisfactory. The foreign secretary thought this a strange query and wondered about Spring Rice's confidence in himself.[65]

In June Northcliffe arrived with ruffles and flourishes, but these were not supplied by the embassy. He was met in New York by a crowd of reporters, but no member of the embassy staff, much less the ambassador, was on hand to greet him. Spring Rice had made the decision not to attend him because he looked upon him as his personal enemy. Arthur Willert, Washington correspondent of The Times, had been instructed to tell Northcliffe that the ambassador looked forward to seeing him in Washington. Northcliffe was indignant and threatened to return home at once; Willert and Wiseman persuaded him to stay. Then came a note from Spring Rice explaining that he had not come to New York for security reasons, not wanting to attract attention to Northcliffe's arrival. The presence of a throng of reporters made the ambassador look foolish, as Northcliffe remarked. The cloth of propriety was torn further when the two encountered each other in Washington. It had been arranged that they would meet privately, just before a dinner to honor Harmsworth. According to one report, in predinner privacy Spring Rice accused his guest of libeling him, saying he was not welcome in his home. Taken back completely, Northcliffe proposed to leave the embassy at once, only to have the ambassador come forward quickly, take his hand, and say: "The war makes strange bed fellows and we must work together whatever our personal feelings."[66] In giving his account of the Northcliffe imbroglio, including the personal confrontation, the ambassador employed some very diplomatic language in a letter to Balfour, but it said essentially the same thing.[67] Balfour had hardly to read between the lines (and no doubt heard versions of the meeting from others) to realize there was to be a glaring lack of cooperation between the Northcliffe mission and the Spring Rice embassy on matters relating to the War Office, the Admiralty, and the Ministry of Munitions, which were the areas of Northcliffe's responsibility. He found it better to work mostly in New York City and stayed well clear of the embassy. At the end of his time in America, he sent a peace offering to the ambassador. "Please allow me to say that I am going across the seas without any feeling of irritation at your initial misunderstanding of my object in coming here. I am quite aware that the position is a difficult one."[68] But back in London there was added reason to question Spring Rice's competence.

In the months subsequent to the United States joining the war, finances were to become a major problem. Spring Rice was fortunate that he could still rely on the services of his economic counselor, Crawford. Both Britain and France looked to America to advance large sums of credit, which their new partner was willing to do, but not without some guarantees. Working out the procedures was the difficulty. At first London and Paris competed for financial attention. What was clearly required was coordination. A misunderstanding arose over payment of a $400 million loan to Morgan and Company out of funds advanced by the United States Treasury. The situation was exacerbated because Treasury Secretary McAdoo disliked dealing with Sir Hardman Lever, the British representative, whom he found presumptuous and lacking full authority. As Balfour was not prepared to trust these matters to the ambassador, the cabinet agreed that Lord Reading should again visit America to clear out the blockage. Within a matter of weeks after coming to Washington, Reading had regularized procedures to the satisfaction of all parties. He accomplished this as much by dint of his personality, being able to get men to sit down and talk together, as by reason of his quick intelligence. Again Spring Rice was put in the shade. He fought back his resentment by predicting that Reading's visit would be a success and in late November reported as much. "Several bankers told me that Reading's mission was most useful and that he was exceedingly adroit," he informed Balfour.[69] These successive missions left the ambassador under no illusions about his continuation in office. In late September he said this to Lord Robert Cecil and believed that Cecil himself would make an excellent replacement, as someone who could easily take charge once the special missions fulfilled their objectives.[70]

What do ambassadors do once they realize their days are numbered? For Spring Rice the answer was simple: work as usual. And with a new American ally, there was plenty of work to do. The excellent embassy staff, intensely loyal to their chief, was quickly on top of the myriad details growing out of the new relationship. Spring Rice explained it this way to Hardinge. "The general principles on which we conduct business here are to put all our knowledge and experience at the disposal of United States officials and to refrain as far as possible from offering advice. We tell of the holes we fell into and point out the mud on our breeches but we do not offer ourselves as guides. Crawford and Barclay and I not to mention other members of the Embassy are in constant contact with United States officials whom we see daily. They are accustomed to us and tell us quite frankly what they think of themselves, of us and of our country. The naval and military attachés are much in the same situation and are regarded I am sure with the utmost confidence. We are none of us remarkable or striking personalities but we are decidedly useful."[71]

As American public opinion crystallized in enthusiastic support of the war, Spring Rice filed salient reports. As late as 28 December 1917, he sent an eleven-page memorandum on a variety of matters ranging from the government takeover of the railroads to the decline of pacifism in the face of necessity. A five-page report was filed on 4 January 1918 after he had been removed from office.[72] He had kept up a running commentary on Wilson and his ideas for peace without victory, which to Spring Rice was always a sticking point. When Balfour's visit was pending, he had supplied lengthy and perceptive analyses of all prominent figures he was likely to deal with. He also explained President Wilson's dilemma on the Irish question. To a majority of American Irish, Irish freedom was the twin of Belgian freedom; as the Democratic party was heavily Irish, Wilson, an Orangeman by ancestry, had to tread warily. He implied that Balfour ought to do the same.[73] Later Spring Rice was to forward information about the Lever-McAdoo contretemps that had prompted the dispatch of Lord Reading.[74] Of special significance was his renewed warning that Wilson "is a co-belligerent but not an Ally. He has no end in common with other Allies but an ideal one. There was no practical bond of union and therefore there was no practical cooperation."[75] Such intelligence must have reverberated through the Foreign office, recalling to mind the ambassador's prior warnings that the United States could not be counted on to help make peace permanent. America might be a wayward ally with Wilson preferring to have an independent role for his country in the war and at the peace conference. But the end of the Spring Rice embassy was in sight. Shortly after Christmas he was ordered home, the implication being that he would not return as ambassador.

The standard for evaluating Spring Rice's performance as ambassador should be his own perception of what his responsibilities were and how well he fulfilled them, and what ultimate action the United States took regarding Britain in the war. Central to both propositions was his patriotism. His success or failure he himself would want to measure against love of country. In Washington, duty required a total honesty in dealing with Wilson and his administration, a realistic appraisal of America's

changing attitude toward the war, and a rigid adherence to proto-
col. He was no propagandist but a diplomat of the old school.
Nor was he a Pollyanna when it came to assessing the American
mood, for he early determined, and correctly so, that the United
States would only enter the conflict to protect its vital interests.
He would deceive neither himself nor his government because
deception was not part of his character, and it would be contrary
to Anglo-American friendship. His lack of flair in dealing with
the Wilson administration may be a valid point, but Spring
Rice did not perceive excessive display as having anything to
do with his work. Persistent pessimism about American entry
into the war may well have been overdrawn, but in light of
this he never raised false hopes in London (or in Paris) as to
when the Yanks were coming. The awkward position he put
himself in as a result of his close friendship with Senator
Lodge was a deliberately false step, but such was the value
he placed on genuine friendship that he was recklessly in
flagrante.

Admittedly, Spring Rice was less effective once the United
States came into the war. He took issue, for example, with the
American Navy's refusal to scrap its long-range capital ships
building program in favor of antisubmarine craft and merchant
ships, which did little to endear him to the Navy Department's
civilian officials or admirals. His position was seen as a bid
for British maritime supremacy in the postwar period, and it
was resented. But it would be excessive in the extreme to call
him paranoid at the prospect of the leadership of the English-
speaking peoples passing to the United States. He and his close
American associates had discussed this likelihood too often and
too candidly for that. Saddened to witness the pending eclipse
of his own country, he was able to face the stern realities of
power politics.

It was the common cause of Anglo-American solidarity that
he and his many friends, in England and the United States,
had labored to achieve that was the feature of his final talk
with Woodrow Wilson in January 1918. "I said [to the president]
that we could almost endure with equanimity all the horrors
of this terrible struggle if they led in the end to a close, sure
and permanent understanding between the English-speaking
peoples. If we stand together we are safe. If we do not stand
together, nothing is safe." And, he reported, "The conversation
ended with renewed and most cordial assurances from the President" on this hope for the future of the world.[76]

7

LAST DAYS, LAST WORDS

The last days of Sir Cecil Spring Rice were, on the surface, plain enough. At the end of 1917 a telegram was received from Foreign Secretary Balfour advising him that he was to be replaced. In Spring Rice's own words: "It was evident that some form of central control was required, and naturally the War Cabinet decided on sending someone to take control, including the Embassy. The decision was taken suddenly without warning as was to be expected under wartime conditions."[1] This chaste account, although it does great credit to Sir Cecil's sense of restraint, should not be allowed to disguise his chagrin at the peremptory way the Foreign Office chose to inform him of his removal from office. Many of his friends took umbrage at what appeared to be a cruel method of dealing with a highly sensitive, high-ranking diplomat. For some time he had known his head was on the block, but now the executioner offered him no solace as the deed was done. Little time was wasted in clearing out of Washington for his destination in Ottawa. Shane Leslie has left an indelible description of the departure in a diary entry for 13 January 1918. "Polk and myself at the station with the Embassy staff. Springey was utterly weary and broken. Owing to the intense cold the train was delayed and delayed. Every quarter of an hour his haggard face appeared at the window, beckoning his staff to return and be done with him. Sad and unhappy scene but we all stuck to it in spite of the freezing tears."[2] Plans called for the family to remain in Canada while Sir Cecil prepared to travel to England alone.

The stay at Government House, Ottawa, as guests of the governor general, the duke of Devonshire, who was a kinsman of Florence Spring Rice, promised to be pleasant, although with the war still raging it would be impossible to enjoy to the full the freedom Sir Cecil felt now that he had no official responsibilities. If he had pressing worries they were personal ones, and he wrote of his apprehensions to his old friend Chirol. Since in years past he had talked of retirement, the prospect was now attractive, provided he was to be on pension. Nearly fifty-nine at the time, he wanted to be certain "about the family and financial arrangements" as befit a husband and father of two young children.[3] Meanwhile, days were passed with the family, enjoying sports and games, and, of course, good conversation. He spoke with various Canadian officials on an informal basis, reiterating his view that Canada required a more distinctive representation of its views in Washington. And he studied military and diplomatic events closely. Sir Cecil was in fact retired and was under no illusions. He accepted the situation without affectation. At the first of February he wrote to Frank Polk, the one State Department member who had seen him off, "It is obvious that the U.S. being what is now in the world's drama requires some one to represent the belligerents who is more than a mere trained diplomat."[4] In so saying he was being both philosophical and sardonic, and typically Spring Rice.

His death in the early hours of February 14 was totally unexpected, although Lady Spring Rice later confided to Chirol, "He seemed well but I daily expected a reaction and he was very white the last week."[5] To those who loved him most, he had died of a broken heart. Henry Cabot Lodge believed that the abrupt deprivation of the embassy—"the sudden cessation of his work and responsibilities in which his heart was bound up"—caused him "the loss of the will to live."[6] The shock to his family was total, a void created never to be filled. Spring Rice was interred at Ottawa, like a soldier buried where he fell.

Every one who knew Cecil Spring Rice was necessarily aware of his subsurface spiritual nature, religious without being rigidly denominational, possessed of a touch of mysticism, an oddity in the diplomatic service. His poetry and translation from Persian folklore marked him as high-minded, intense, reflective. By the time he had arrived in Washington as ambassador, he had all but given up serious writing but retained a penchant for penning lines of doggerel to distract himself or amuse others. The poetic flame guttered, only to flare up again in one last burst of light in "I Vow To Thee My Country." A copy of the poem was on his desk the day he left Washington for the last time.

At Christmas time, 1917, his mind had turned very much in the direction of the message of hope that the birth of Christ had symbolized for Christians across the centuries. December 24 he sent a lengthy Christmas greeting to Cardinal Gibbons, the Roman Catholic prelate of Irish extraction who had supported the Allied side from the start of the war. Spring Rice wrote: "We are all followers of the Prince of Peace who fought and won the greatest battle ever fought on this earth. He fought against the kind of evil now cast in the form of German militarism."[7] What had fused in Spring Rice's thinking was Christianity and the cause. Some three weeks later, as he made formal good-byes to various leaders, he wrote to William Jennings Bryan, the former secretary of state, who had pushed hard for peace before and during the early stages of the war. Sir Cecil had often disagreed with Bryan's conduct of diplomacy, but he knew him as a sincere advocate of peace among nations. Enclosed with his farewell letter were the two stanzas of "I Vow To Thee My Country."

> I vow to thee, my country—all earthly things above
> Entire and whole and perfect, the service of my love,
> The love that asks no questions, the love that stands the test,
> That lays upon the altar the dearest and the best:
> The love that never falters, the love that pays the price,
> The love that makes undaunted the final sacrifice.
>
> And there's another country, I've heard of long ago—
> Most dear to them that love her, most great to them that know—
> We may not count her armies, we may not see her King,
> Her fortress is a faithful heart, her pride is suffering—
> And soul by soul and silently her shining bounds increase,
> And her ways are ways of gentleness and all her paths are peace.[8]

Some two weeks later in Ottawa, the ex-ambassador was invited to address the Canadian Club. He was pleased to accept because it would give him the opportunity to speak to a general audience about certain thoughts that had been occupying him for some days. The address he called "Two Ideals." There was sadness but no bitterness in his voice as he spoke of his regret in leaving Washington, and he recalled with great force the day President Wilson, in addressing a joint session of Congress, called for a declaration of war. "I shall never forget the cheer I heard at those words," he said, as he sought to capture for his listeners that rare historical moment. He welcomed America into the war because he insisted it represented a combination of the two great English-speaking nations, bound together in a cause that was righteous and just. He contrasted this cause with that of German militarism, an unmitigated evil. By drawing on examples from antiquity, he said it had always been thus, the struggle of good against bad, the contest between love and power. In fighting the good fight, England and America stood with the sign of the cross. Spring Rice spoke of one convinced of *in hoc signo vincit*. His peroration followed swiftly: "We are all subjects of the Prince of Peace who fought the greatest fight ever fought on the earth, who won the greatest victory ever won by his blood." As Spring Rice had written to Cardinal Gibbons, there was an evil afoot in the world and the war against Germany was against that evil. The last sentences of "Two Ideals" repeated this theme forcefully. "The Cross, that is the sign under which we fight against the hideous enemy. That is the sign under which we fight and by which we shall conquer."[9] It was the last phase in an ongoing catharsis.

Adding weight to the argument for catharsis is the fact that Spring Rice had written a different version of the first stanza of "I Vow To Thee My Country" while in Stockholm, probably in 1912. The original version tended to glorify war as it sang of girded swords and helmeted warriors, of "the noise of battle and the thunder of guns." It was a poem dedicated as much to the god of war as to the Prince of Peace. More than three years of carnage had altered his mood and inspired a call to loving sacrifice. Without quite realizing it, perhaps, Spring Rice had melded faith in God, belief in sacrifice, and love of country into a single creed for men and nations. Given the state of the world and the condition of mankind in 1918, it was a message drawn from the past but meant as hope for the future. If his judgment was to be proven naive, based on a view of life that itself had died on the barbed wire and in the fires of revolution, it remains a fitting epitaph for a poet as diplomat.

After his death numerous tributes were offered Spring Rice. Eton College memorialized him: "Vir animae cum poeticae tum Christianae, patriae, ruris, suorum amantissimus" (A man of the spirit, poetic, Christian, patriotic, a countryman, with a deep love of his own people) in the ancient tongue he knew so well.[10] In Washington a remembrance service was held in the National Cathedral with both President Wilson and the new ambassador, Lord Reading, in attendance. Soon thereafter American friends, "desirous to show their appreciation of the magnificent work done by him as British Ambassador in their country," collected money for a memorial fund. Jack Morgan was the organizer because he was aware of his friend's financial concerns as he left office. The income derived from the fund was paid to Lady Spring Rice, intended to help provide for the education of the children. The fund eventually reverted to Balliol College, there to be known as the Cecil Spring Rice Memorial Fund. The income was to be used by Balliol for "travelling scholarships for young men entering the diplomatic service who have to travel to acquire the necessary foreign languages for that career." Thus was established a permanent memorial to him and his work.[11]

Two contemporaries, Arthur James Balfour and Edward M. House, wrote what may be added to these last words on Sir Cecil. In a letter that was to be handed to him personally upon his return to England—the letter of honor and praise he was never to read—the foreign secretary, after reviewing the challenge of his tasks in Washington, went on to say: "With unfailing judgment and unwearied forebearance, you steered your course successfully through days of difficulty; and it is in no small measure due to your exertions that the suspicions that so easily embitter relations between the two great English-speaking peoples were dissipated—I trust forever. The decision of the President to advise his country to declare war on Germany was one of the turning points of history. You may well be proud to remember that at this great moment you were the ambassador in Washington, and that your conduct in that post largely contributed to prevent any trace of international friction which might have impeded or impaired the President's policy."[12] These words of benediction were made empty because they remained undelivered.

A second tribute was that of Spring Rice's old American nemesis, Colonel House. "What a ruthless and destructive fórce is war! Here was perhaps the ablest and best trained member of the British diplomatic service. There was no one who possessed to a greater degree the affection and confidence of his chiefs. With all his accomplishments he possessed a personal charm that made him a multitude of friends. But when the war broke loose he had a serious illness. Under ordinary circumstances he soon would have righted himself, but with the stress of disasters coming day by day, he could not regain his normal health. On he had to go, impelled by a high sense of patriotism and duty. He went as far and as hard as he could, but what he could not do he was willing to be done by others. He was one of the few men I have known who did not hesitate to yield his prerogatives in order that his country's best interests might not suffer. Even so, the task finally proved too great. He gave his life for his country just as surely as though he had been slain on the field of battle."[13] The pieties of Balfour yielded, in House's words, to stern realities.

Balfour and House had the Spring Rice ambassadorship in mind when they set down their thoughts. Some last words must now be written with respect to his diplomatic work from the beginning. What held his career together was, as it must be, the glue that bonded his two worlds. It was an ethereal substance, but it had verifiable results in diplomacy. The product was far from perfect. This was no ideal marriage, Spring Rice wedded to the diplomatic service. To assume this can only have disappointing results. Spring Rice, the person, needed to serve; England, the country, provided him the unique opportunity. An unexpected opening here, a chance meeting there—these are circumstances that can determine a life's work whether as an author, an academic, or a diplomat. Suppose that Spring Rice had prepared as earnestly for the competition for All Souls as he did for the Foreign Office examination. As a fellow, he might well have satisfied his need to serve while becoming an important literary figure.

For any man it is unrealistic to enter upon a career and for more than thirty-five years never seriously to doubt the correctness of the choice. For some one like Spring Rice, who occupied two worlds, it is simply unconceivable. But how is it that despite his frustrations he stayed the course? To answer that question it is not enough to look at Spring Rice standing apart. He must be placed in a cultural frame as well as historical time. The past is rehearsal for the present for the individual and the nation alike. His liberalism grew out of the Western tradition that placed the highest possible value on the worth of the person; his patriotism was completely congenial to service to the British empire at the height of its power. This devotion to liberalism and patriotism, while highly personalized, was by no means singular. Britain wore many different faces during the 1914 war. Love of country was one such face. Liberalism was less obviously so. Yet every class in British society, whether it was articulated or assumed, viewed the struggle as a defense of historic liberal principles against the assaults of autocracy. This ideological element must not be overlooked. Spring Rice's public philosophy was a rarefied version of what the British people came to understand in a tangible way—the horrendous wartime casualties. But for Spring Rice as well, this was no mere abstraction.

He left evidence of it throughout his life and work; it reached its ultimate expression in "I Vow To Thee My Country." Spring Rice had the last word after all.

Spring Rice liked to tell the following story. When he was at Balliol, a fire started accidentally in one of the halls, and it threatened real damage. He and another student fetched cans of water and were able to extinguish the blaze. Just then the master of Balliol came along and, surveying the scene, asked in a disagreeable tone of voice, "Who lit it?" "Just like the old boy," quipped Spring Rice. "He never asked who put it out." Jowett could be perverse in other ways. He once pleaded with Lady Sherborne, ". . . Do tell us his faults. Surely that is the most interesting thing about him." Whether Jowett's dictum is generally accepted or not, it was otherwise with Cecil Spring Rice. Whatever his faults, surely his virtues were the most interesting thing about him.

NOTES

Chapter 1. Families, Fortunes, Friends

1. Stephen Gwynn, *The Letters and Friendships of Sir Cecil Spring Rice*, 2 vols. (London: Constable and Company, 1929), 1:3–4; Cecil Spring Rice, *Poems* (London: Longmans, Green and Company, 1920), Bernard Holland, "Preface," vii–xxxi, vi–ix (hereafter cited as *Poems*).

2. Cecil Spring Rice papers, privately held (hereafter cited as SRPP).

3. Johnson to Mrs. Charles Spring Rice, 18 December 1871, Cecil Spring Rice Papers, Churchill College, Cambridge (hereafter cited as SRPC).

4. H. E. Luxmoore to Mrs. Charles Spring Rice, undated. SRPC.

5. Holland, "Preface," xix.

6. Gwynn, *Letters and Friendships*, 1:13.

7. Luxmoore to Mrs. Charles Spring Rice, undated, SRPC.

8. Ibid.

9. Spring Rice to Mrs. Charles Spring Rice, undated, SRPP.

10. SRPP.

11. Arthur Hardinge to Spring Rice, undated, SRPC.

12. Gwynn, *Letters and Friendships*, 1:45.

13. Ibid., 49.

14. Spring Rice to Ronald Ferguson, undated, SRPC.

15. Spring Rice to Stephen Spring Rice, 25 March 1887, SRPP.

16. Spring Rice to Ferguson, 23 May 1887, SRPC.

17. Ibid., 10 April 1887, SRPC.

18. Spring Rice to Stephen Spring Rice, 1 September 1887, SRPC.

19. Spring Rice to Ferguson, 22 January 1892, SRPC

20. Spring Rice to Mrs. Stephen Spring Rice, 23 August 1893, SRPP

21. SRPP.

22. Earl of Ronaldshay, *The Life of Lord Curzon*, 3 vols. (London: Ernest Benn, 1927), 1:191.

23. Spring Rice to Stephen Spring Rice, January 1893, SRPP.

24. Arthur Hardinge to Spring Rice, 1 June 1889, SRPC.

25. Spring Rice to Francis Villiers, 12 April 1895, F.O. 800/84.

26. Gwynn, *Letters and Friendships*, 1:245.

27. Spring Rice to Ferguson, undated, SRPC.

28. Spring Rice to Stephen Spring Rice, 9 January 1896, SRPC.

29. Spring Rice to Villiers, 18 January 1896, F.O. 800/84.

30. Ibid., 21 March 1896, SRPC.

31. Ibid., 21 March 1896, SRPC.

32. Gwynn, *Letters and Friendships*, 1:251.

33. Spring Rice to Ferguson, 15 October 1898, SRPC.

34. Spring Rice to Theodore Roosevelt, 15 November 1898, SRPP.
35. Gwynn, *Letters and Friendships*, 1:273.
36. Spring Rice to Mrs. Henry Cabot Lodge, 30 June 1899, SRPP.
37. Spring Rice to Luxmoore, 15 September 1899, SRPP.
38. Gwynn, *Letters and Friendships*, 1:280–81.
39. Lord Cromer to Spring Rice, undated, SRPC.
40. Spring Rice to Ferguson, 27 September 1902, SRPC.
41. F.O. 800/241.
42. Sir Edward Grey to Spring Rice, 28 June 1906, SRPP.
43. Sir Charles Hardinge to Spring Rice, undated, SRPP.
44. Spring Rice to Valentine Chirol, 21 June 1907, SRPC.
45. Spring Rice to Margaret Spring Rice, 7 December 1906, SRPP.
46. Spring Rice to Edith Roosevelt, 4 December 1907, SRPP.
47. Spring Rice to Ferguson, 7 July 1908, SRPP.
48. Grey to Spring Rice, 19 July 1908, SRPP.
49. Spring Rice to Ferguson, 18 November 1912, SRPC.
50. Gwynn, *Letters and Friendships*, 1:173–74.
51. Spring Rice to Stephen Spring Rice, 22 March 1887, SRPC.
52. Ibid., 20 December 1887, SRPC.
53. Ibid., 20 March 1890, SRPC.
54. Ibid., 1 January 1898, SRPC.
55. Ibid., 21 March 1901, SRPC.
56. Ibid., 18 August 1902, SRPC.
57. Spring Rice to Margaret Spring Rice, 8 September 1902, SRPC.
58. Spring Rice to Luxmoore, 24 September 1914, SRPP.
59. Luxmoore to Spring Rice, 31 December 1898, SRPP.
60. Spring Rice to Luxmoore, undated, SRPP.
61. Ibid., 3 October 1898, SRPP.
62. Luxmoore to Spring Rice, 17 March 1901, SRPP.
63. Ibid.
64. Luxmoore to Spring Rice, 7 July 1904, SRPC.
65. Gwynn, *Letters and Friendships*, 2:390.
66. Ferguson to Spring Rice, 10 December 1909, SRPP.
67. Ferguson to Florence Spring Rice, 28 February 1918, SRPP.
68. Spring Rice to Ferguson, 21 August 1886, SRPP.
69. Spring Rice to Stephen Spring Rice, 14 November 1899, SRPC.
70. Spring Rice to Ferguson, 10 November 1904, SRPC.
71. Spring Rice to Stephen Spring Rice, 20 September 1900, SRPC.
72. Spring Rice to Ferguson, 4 August 1911, SRPC.
73. Valentine Chirol, *Cecil Spring Rice In Memoriam* (London: John Murray, 1919).
74. Spring Rice to Chirol, 22 December 1898, SRPP.
75. Chirol, *In Memoriam*, 16.
76. Ibid., 19.
77. Frank Cobb to Spring Rice, 5 January 1918, SRPP.
78. Gwynn, *Letters and Friendships*, 1:191.
79. Ibid., E.g., 1:261, 264, 303; 2:75.
80. Spring Rice to Theodore Roosevelt, 1 November 1904, SRPC.
81. Ibid., 18 July 1896, SRPC.
82. Ibid.
83. *The Letters of Theodore Roosevelt*, ed. Elting E. Morison, 8 vols. (Cam-

bridge: Harvard University Press, 1951–54), 1:553 (hereafter cited as *Roosevelt Letters*).

84. Ibid.

85. Spring Rice to Edith Roosevelt, July 1898, SRPC.

86. Gwynn, *Letters and Friendships*, 1:270.

87. Roosevelt to Spring Rice, 9 November 1894, SRPP.

88. Ibid., 12 November 1912, *Roosevelt Letters*, 7:638.

89. Spring Rice to Chirol, quoted in David H. Burton, *Theodore Roosevelt and His English Correspondents* (Philadelphia, Pa.: American Philosophical Society, 1973), 9.

90. Lodge to Spring Rice, 12 August 1898, SRPC.

91. Gwynn, *Letters and Friendships*, 1:370.

92. Ibid., 2:141.

93. Spring Rice to Grey, 7 October 1915, SRPP.

94. Gwynn, *Letters and Friendships*, 2:293.

95. Ibid., 399.

96. Spring Rice to Agnes Spring Rice, 17 April 1888, SRPP.

97. Henry Adams to Spring Rice, 1 February 1900, SRPP.

98. Adams to Elizabeth Cameron, 8 April 1901, *Letters of Henry Adams, 1892–1918*, ed. Worthington C. Ford, 2 vols. (Boston: Houghton Mifflin, 1938), 2:326. C.C.A.: Conservative Christian Anarchists.

99. Gwynn, *Letters and Friendships*, 1:381.

100. Spring Rice to William J. Bryan, 12 January 1918, SRPC.

Chapter 2. The Literary Impulse

1. Spring Rice, *Poems*, xiv–xv.

2. Ibid., vii–xxxi.

3. Spring Rice to Luxmoore, 29 March 1900, SRPP.

4. Spring Rice to Edith Roosevelt, 29 November 1899, SRPP.

5. Ibid.

6. Spring Rice to Edith Roosevelt, 29 November 1900, SRPP

7. Spring Rice to Luxmoore, 29 March 1900, SRPP.

8. Ibid.

9. Spring Rice, *Poems*, xix–xx.

10. SRPP, 162. There are slight differences between the texts of the poems in manuscript and in the published form. For convenience sake, the page numbers from *Poems* are provided the reader for easy reference. Texts cited are from manuscripts.

11. SRPP, 143.

12. SRPP, 104.

13. SRPP, 100.

14. SRPP, 105.

15. SRPP, 59.

16. SRPP, 79.

17. SRPP, 16.

18. SRPP, 26.

19. SRPP, 37.

20. SRPP, 30.

21. SRPP, 15.

22. SRPP, 101.
23. SRPP, 2.
24. SRPP, 122.
25. SRPP, 169.
26. SRPP, 71.
27. SRPP, 7.
28. SRPP, 70.
29. SRPP, 75.
30. SRPP, 108.
31. SRPP, 50.
32. SRPP, 51.
33. SRPP, 58.
34. SRPP, 48.
35. SRPP, 96.
36. Spring Rice, *Poems*, xxiv.
37. SRPP, 116.
38. SRPP, 17.
39. SRPP, 23.
40. SRPP, 80.
41. Corinne Roosevelt Robinson, *Boston Evening Transcript*, 30 September 1915, p. 7.
42. SRPP, 124.
43. SRPP; 163.
44. SRPP, 163.
45. SRPP, 151.
46. SRPP, 170–71, 172–75.
47. SRPP.
48. *Times Literary Supplement* (1920), p. 664.
49. Edith Wharton, *A Backward Glance*, (New York: Appleton Century Company, 1934), 80–81. See also R. W. B. and Nancy Lewis, *Letters of Edith Wharton*, (New York: Scribners, 1988), 63–64; in a letter by Wharton to Margaret Terry Chanler, 17 November 1902, she recalls fondly her meeting with Spring Rice and expresses the wish to meet him again.
50. Cecil Spring Rice, *The Adventures of James* (privately printed).
51. Cecil Spring Rice, *Songs from the Book of Jaffir* (London: Macmillan, 1900).
52. Cecil Spring Rice, *The Story of Valeh and Hadijeh* (London: Duckworth, 1903).
53. Spring Rice, *Songs from the Book of Jaffir*, 57.
54. Ibid., 56.
55. Ibid., 67.
56. Spring Rice to Margaret Spring Rice, 12 November 1900, SRPC.
57. Ibid., 8 February 1900, SRPC.
58. Spring Rice to Stephen Spring Rice, 20 August 1900, SRPC.
59. Spring Rice to Luxmoore, 1 February 1903, SRPC.
60. Grey to Spring Rice, 19 July 1902, SRPC
61. Spring Rice, *The Story of Valeh and Hadijeh*, 5–6.
62. Edward Browne to Spring Rice, 2 February 1903, SRPC; see also Browne to Spring Rice, 5 November 1907, SRPC.

Chapter 3. Observer and Analyst Abroad

1. Chirol to Spring Rice, 24 February 1901, SRPC.
2. Bryce to Spring Rice, undated, SRPC.
3. Spring Rice to Ferguson, 18 March 1887, SRPC.
4. Ibid.
5. Spring Rice to Stephen Spring Rice, 22 March 1887, SRPC.
6. Spring Rice to Ferguson, 22 April 1887, SRPC.
7. Ibid., 2 June 1887, SRPC.
8. Ibid., 19 July 1887, SRPC.
9. Ibid., 6 June 1887, SRPC.
10. Ibid., 21 July 1887, SRPC.
11. Spring Rice to Stephen Spring Rice, 16 March 1888, SRPC.
12. Ibid.
13. Ibid.
14. Ibid., 30 March 1888, SRPC.
15. Ibid., 12 May 1888, SRPC.
16. Ibid.
17. Ibid., 24 January 1890, SRPC.
18. Gwynn, *Letters and Friendships*, 1:103.
19. Spring Rice to Stephen Spring Rice, 13 April 1891, SRPC.
20. Spring Rice to Ferguson, 10 July 1891, SRPC.
21. Gwynn, *Letters and Friendships*, 1:113.
22. Spring Rice to Ferguson, 25 April 1892, SRPC.
23. Gwynn, *Letters and Friendships*, 1:122.
24. Spring Rice to Stephen Spring Rice, 16 May 1892, SRPC.
25. Ibid., 27 June 1892, SRPC.
26. Spring Rice to Ferguson, 24 October 1892, SRPC.
27. Ibid.
28. Ibid., 28 May 1893, SRPC.
29. Ibid., 16 January 1893, SRPC.
30. Ibid., 28 May 1893, SRPC.
31. Spring Rice to Stephen Spring Rice, 27 December 1892, SRPC.
32. Ibid.
33. Spring Rice to Ferguson, 19 March 1894, SRPC.
34. Spring Rice to Stephen Spring Rice, 25 May 1894, SRPC.
35. Spring Rice to Ferguson, 7 October 1894, SRPP.
36. Ibid.
37. Ibid.
38. Spring Rice to Margaret and Agnes Spring Rice, 12 March 1895, SRPP.
39. Ibid.
40. Ibid.
41. Spring Rice to Stephen Spring Rice, 2 November 1895, SRPC.
42. Ibid.
43. Ibid.
44. Ibid.
45. Spring Rice to Villiers, 25 January 1896, SRPP.
46. Ibid., 22 February 1896, SRPP.
47. Gwynn, *Letters and Friendships*, 1:207, 204.
48. Spring Rice to Theodore Roosevelt, 14 September 1896, SRPC.
49. Ibid., 17 July 1896, SRPP.

50. Spring Rice to Edith Roosevelt, 20 December 1896, SRPP.
51. Spring Rice to Theodore Roosevelt, 16 May 1897, SRPP.
52. Spring Rice to Villiers, 24 July 1897, SRPC.
53. Ibid., 13 November 1897, SRPC.
54. Spring Rice to Stephen Spring Rice, 7 November 1897, SRPP.
55. Spring Rice to Villiers, 13 November 1897, SRPC.
56. Spring Rice to Stephen Spring Rice, 7 November 1897, SRPP.
57. Spring Rice to Villiers, 24 July 1897, SRPC.
58. Spring Rice to Stephen Spring Rice, 24 July 1897, SRPP.
59. Spring Rice to Theodore Roosevelt, 1 August 1897, SRPP.
60. Spring Rice to Henry Adams, 7 November 1897, SRPP.
61. Spring Rice to Villiers, 26 December 1897, SRPC.
62. Balfour to Spring Rice, 25 May 1915, SRPP.
63. Spring Rice to Henry Cabot Lodge, 8 July 1898, SRPP.
64. Spring Rice to Luxmoore, 13 October 1898, SRPP.
65. Spring Rice to Villiers, 3 October 1898, SRPC.
66. Spring Rice to Mrs. Lodge, 31 January 1899, SRPP.
67. Theodore Roosevelt to Spring Rice, 9 November 1903, *Roosevelt Letters*, 3:630.
68. Spring Rice to Ferguson, 15 October 1898, SRPC.
69. Spring Rice to Chirol, 3 October 1898, SRPC.
70. Ibid., 4 November 1898, SRPC.
71. Spring Rice to Theodore Roosevelt, 15 November 1898, SRPP.
72. Spring Rice to Luxmoore, 17 September 1899, SRPC.
73. Spring Rice to Theodore Roosevelt, 15 November 1898, SRPP.
74. Ibid.
75. Ibid.
76. Ibid.
77. Ibid.
78. Spring Rice to Thomas Farrer, 7 February 1901, SRPP.
79. Ibid.
80. Ibid.
81. Spring Rice to Chirol, 30 March 1901, SRPC.
82. Ibid.
83. Spring Rice to Henry Adams, 14 March 1901, SRPP.
84. Ibid.
85. Ibid., 1 April 1901, SRPP.
86. Ibid.
87. Louis Mallet to Spring Rice, 15 December 1903; Gwynn, *Letters and Friendships*, 1:374
88. Spring Rice to Margaret Spring Rice, Nov. 24, 1903, SRPP.
89. Spring Rice to Edith Roosevelt, 9 December 1903, SRPP.
90. Ibid.
91. Ibid., undated, SRPP.

Chapter 4. Veteran Diplomat

1. Gwynn, *Letters and Friendships*, 1:210.
2. Spring Rice to Edith Roosevelt, 13 March 1905, quoted in Burton, *Theodore Roosevelt*, 29.

3. Spring Rice to Lodge, 25 March 1904, SRPC.

4. Howard K. Beale, *Theodore Roosevelt and the Rise of America to World Power* (Baltimore: Johns Hopkins University Press, 1957), 267, 289.

5. Spring Rice to Edith Roosevelt, 11 February 1904, SRPC.

6. Spring Rice to Theodore Roosevelt, 10 February 1904, SRPC.

7. Theodore Roosevelt to Spring Rice, 19 March 1904, *Roosevelt Letters*, 4:760.

8. Gwynn, *Letters and Friendships*, 1:403.

9. Spring Rice to Margaret Spring Rice, 15 April 1904, SRPP.

10. Spring Rice to Luxmoore, 23 June 1904, SRPC.

11. Spring Rice to Daisy Spring Rice, 22 June 1904, SRPP.

12. Spring Rice to John Hay, 31 August 1904, SRPC.

13. Spring Rice to Ferguson, 10 November 1904, SRPC.

14. Spring Rice to Theodore Roosevelt, 15 November 1904, SRPP.

15. Theodore Roosevelt to Spring Rice, 9 November 1904, Gwynn, *Letters and Friendships*, 1:434.

16. Ibid.

17. Ferguson to Spring Rice, 7 January 1905, SRPC.

18. Spring Rice to Edith Roosevelt, 13 March 1905, SRPC.

19. Ibid.

20. Ibid.

21. Ibid.

22. 16 May 1905; 6 December 1905, F.O. 800/241.

23. Grey to Spring Rice, 12 December 1905, F.O. 800/241.

24. Spring Rice to Ferguson, 10 December 1905, SRPC.

25. Theodore Roosevelt to Spring Rice, 16 June 1905, *Roosevelt Letters*, 4:1234.

26. Spring Rice to Elihu Root, 10 July 1905, F.O. 800/241.

27. Ibid.

28. Theodore Roosevelt to Spring Rice, 24 July 1905, *Roosevelt Letters*, 4:1283–87.

29. Spring Rice to Lord Lansdowne, 29 July 1905, F.O. 800/241.

30. Spring Rice to Edith Roosevelt, 5 October 1905, SRPC.

31. Foreign Office to Spring Rice, 20 November 1905, F.O. 800/241.

32. Spring Rice to Foreign Office, 6 December 1905, F.O. 800/241.

33. Spring Rice to Ferguson, 3 December 1905, SRPC

34. Spring Rice to Lord Knollys, 16 January 1906, SRPC.

35. Spring Rice to Lord Knollys, 6 March 1906, SRPP.

36. Spring Rice to Ferguson, 3 January 1906, SRPC.

37. Spring Rice to Sir John Simon, 20 January 1906, SRPP.

38. Ibid.

39. Grey to Spring Rice, 19 February 1906, F.O. 800/241.

40. Grey to Spring Rice, 22 December 1905, F.O. 800/241.

41. Spring Rice to Grey, 16 January 1906, SRPC.

42. Grey to Spring Rice, 19 February 1906, F.O. 800/241.

43. Ibid., 8 August 1907, F.O. 800/241.

44. Gwynn, *Letters and Friendships*, 2:67.

45. Grey to Spring Rice, 18 April 1906, F.O. 800/241.

46. Gwynn, *Letters and Friendships*, 2:72.

47. Spring Rice to Chirol, 24 May 1906, SRPP.

48. Ibid.

49. Chirol to Spring Rice, undated, SRPC.
50. Spring Rice to Chirol, 27 April 1907, SRPC.
51. Edward Browne to Spring Rice, 1 July 1908, SRPP.
52. Grey to Spring Rice, 19 February 1906, F.O. 800/241.
53. Ibid., 17 April 1907, F.O. 800/241.
54. Spring Rice to Ferguson, 21 February 1907, SRPC.
55. Spring Rice to Lord Cranley, 28 March 1907, SRPC.
56. Ibid.
57. Spring Rice to Chirol, 27 April 1907, SRPP.
58. Spring Rice to Grey, 13 September 1907, F.O. 800/241.
59. Spring Rice to Edith Roosevelt, 4 December 1907, SRPC.
60. Ibid., 16 February 1908, SRPP.
61. Spring Rice to Ferguson, 21 June 1908, SRPC.
62. Ibid.
63. Ibid., 10 July 1908, SRPC.
64. Ibid.
65. Spring Rice to Florence Spring Rice, 8 October 1908, SRPP.
66. Spring Rice to Ferguson, 8 April 1909, SRPC.
67. Spring Rice to Lord Cranley, 12 May 1909, SRPC.
68. Spring Rice to Sir Arthur Nicolson, 6 November 1910, F.O.800/241.
69. Reports, September–October 1910, SRPC.
70. Spring Rice to Theodore Roosevelt, 2 April 1909, SRPC.
71. Spring Rice to Tyrrell, 7 September 1910, SRPP.
72. Spring Rice to Gerald Balfour, 1 December 1909, SRPP.
73. Spring Rice to Ferguson, 18 September 1910, SRPC.
74. Arthur Willert, *Washington and Other Memories* (Boston: Little Brown and Co., 1972), 83.
75. Constantin Dumba, *Memoirs of a Diplomat* (London: Allen and Unwin, 1933), 162.
76. Gwynn, *Letters and Friendships*, 2:194.
77. Spring Rice to Sir William Tyrrell, 3 February 1914, F.O. 800/241.
78. Spring Rice to Tyrrell, 30 December 1913, F.O. 800/241.
79. Spring Rice to Grey, 27 April 1914, F.O. 800/241.
80. Spring Rice to Tyrrell, 27 January 1914, F.O. 800/241.
81. Ibid.
82. Spring Rice to Tyrrell, 3 March 1914, F.O. 800/241.
83. Spring Rice to Grey, 22 January 1914, F.O. 800/241.

Chapter 5. Wartime Ambassador: 1914–1916

1. Spring Rice to Grey, 3 November 1914, F.O. 800/241.
2. George M. Trevelyan, *Grey of Fallodon* (London: Longmans, Green & Company, 1937), 305–7.
3. Edward Grey, *Twenty-Five Years*, 2 vols. (London: Holder and Stoughton, 1925), 2:160.
4. Spring Rice to Grey, 7 September 1915, F.O. 800/241. For details of the Morgan connection, see Charles C. Tansill, *America Goes to War*, (Boston: Little Brown and Company, 1938), Appendix A, 661–62.
5. Gwynn, *Letters and Friendships*, 2:212.

6. *The Intimate Papers of Colonel House*, ed. Charles Seymour, 4 vols. (Boston: Houghton and Mifflin, 1926–28), 2:101–2 (hereafter cited as *House Papers*).

7. Quoted in Arthur M. Link, *Campaigns for Progressivism and Peace, (1916–1917)* (Princeton: Princeton University Press, 1963), 263–64. Spring Rice's health is frequently commented on. See Patrick Devlin, *Too Proud to Fight* (New York: Oxford University Press, 1975), 154, for example. An extreme and highly dubious assessment appears in Hugh L'Etang, *Fit to Lead* (London: Heinemann, 1980), 10, 156–58.

8. *House Papers*, 2:108.

9. Gwynn, *Letters and Friendships*, 2:186.

10. Ibid., 247, 302, 372, 374.

11. Ibid., 220; Spring Rice to Sir Robert Cecil, 3 February 1915, F.O. 800/241.

12. Gwynn, *Letters and Friendships*, 2:223; Spring Rice to Grey, 8 September 1914, F.O. 800/241.

13. Grey to Spring Rice, 18 September 1914, F.O. 800/241.

14. Spring Rice to Grey, 22 September 1914, F.O. 800/241.

15. Spring Rice to Grey, 1 October 1914, F.O. 800/241; Spring Rice to Grey, 28 September 1914, F.O. 800/241.

16. Gwynn, *Letters and Friendships*, 2:233.

17. Spring Rice to Grey, 3 October 1914, F.O. 800/241.

18. Ibid., 28 September 1914, F.O. 800/241.

19. Ibid., 3 October 1914, F.O. 800/241.

20. Spring Rice to Wilson, 20 October 1914, ed. Arthur S. Link, *The Papers of Woodrow Wilson*, 61 volumes (Princeton: Princeton University Press, 1966), 31:194 (hereafter cited as the *Wilson Papers*).

21. Wilson to Spring Rice, 26 October 1914, F.O. 800/241.

22. Spring Rice to Chirol, 3 November 1914, SRPP.

23. Spring Rice to Foreign Office, 21, 22, 23 December 1914, F.O. 382/49; F.O. 800/84.

24. Spring Rice to Foreign Office, 4 January 1915, F.O. 382/49; Foreign Office to Spring Rice, 7 January 1915, F.O. 382/49.

25. Spring Rice to Nicolson, 3 November 1914, F.O. 800/376.

26. Spring Rice to Grey, 25 August 1914, F.O. 800/241.

27. *Foreign Relations of the United States*, 1915 Supplement, 682–83, 687–88, 777–79.

28. Spring Rice to Grey, 5 October 1914, F.O. 88/241.

29. *House Papers*, 2:75–76.

30. Spring Rice to Lord Newton, 21 October 1914, SRPC.

31. Ibid.

32. Spring Rice to Chirol, 10 October 1914, SRPC.

33. Spring Rice to Newton, 1 December 1916, SRPC.

34. H. C. Peterson, *Propaganda for War: The Campaign Against American Neutrality* (Port Washington, N.Y.: Kennikat Press, 1968), 12–70. See also Irene Cooper Willis, *England's Holy War* (New York: Alfred Knopf, 1928), 192, 198; Armin Rappaport, *The British Press and American Neutrality* (Stanford, Calif.: Stanford University Press, 1951), 144–49.

35. Spring Rice to Grey, 22 September 1914, F.O. 800/84.

36. Grey to Spring Rice, 24 March 1916, SRPC.

37. Newton to Spring Rice, 26 December 1916, SRPC.
38. Grey to Spring Rice, 24 December 1916, SRPC.
39. Spring Rice to Balfour, 5 January 1917, F.O. 800/241.
40. Spring Rice to Balfour, 19 January 1917, F.O. 800/241.
41. Godkin to Spring Rice, 19 July 1915, SRPC.
42. Crewe to Spring Rice, 12 June 1915, F.O. 800/84.
43. Spring Rice to Grey, 17 May 1915, F.O. 800/84.
44. Spring Rice to Grey, 10 June 1915, F.O. 800/241.
45. Ibid., 23 June 1915, F.O. 800/241.
46. Spring Rice to Foreign Office, 4 May 1915, F.O. 800/242.
47. Spring Rice to Theodore Roosevelt, 26 November 1915, SRPP.
48. Spring Rice to Grey, undated, SRPC.
49. Ibid.
50. Spring Rice to Grey, 25 October 1915, F.O. 800/241.
51. Spring Rice to Roosevelt, 10 December 1915, SRPC.
52. Spring Rice to Newton, 21 October 1914, SRPP.
53. Spring Rice to Bryce, 7 May 1915, SRPC.
54. Spring Rice to Chirol. 13 November 1914, SRPP.
55. Ibid.
56. Spring Rice to Grey, 3 November 1914, F.O. 800/241.
57. Spring Rice to Chirol, 13 November 1914, SRPP.
58. Oscar Straus to Spring Rice, 9 April 1915, SRPC.
59. Spring Rice to Grey, 1 April 1915, SRPP.
60. Ibid., 12 February 1915, F.O. 800/241.
61. Ibid., 13 November 1914, F.O. 382/465.
62. Spring Rice to Foreign Office, 15 August 1916, F.O. 800/241. See Ernest R. May, *The World War and American Isolation 1914–1917* (Cambridge: Harvard University Press, 1959), 177.
63. Spring Rice to Grey, 20 May 1915, F.O. 800/241.
64. Spring Rice to Dominik Spring Rice, 17 September 1915, SRPC.
65. *House Papers*, 1:465.
66. Plunkett to Spring Rice, 2 March 1916, SRPC.
67. *House Papers*, 1:328.
68. Spring Rice to Theodore Roosevelt, 16 September 1914, SRPP.
69. Spring Rice to Foreign Office, 20 June 1915, F.O. 800/3.
70. Spring Rice to Grey, 28 October 1915, F.O. 800/241.
71. Spring Rice to Foreign Office, 2 August 1915, F.O. 382/465.
72. Spring Rice to Grey, 2 August 1915, F.O. 800/85.
73. Ibid., 21 November 1915, F.O. 800/241.
74. Ibid., 19 August 1915, CAB (Cabinet) 371/133/2
75. Ibid., 25 October 1915, F.O. 800/241.
76. Spring Rice to Foreign Office, 5 September 1915, F.O. 800/241.
77. *House Papers*, 2:77.
78. Gwynn, *Letters and Friendships*, 2:301.
79. Sherrill Wells, "The Influence of Sir Cecil Spring Rice and Sir Edward Grey on the Shaping of Anglo-American Relations, 1913–1916" (Ph.D. diss., University of London, 1978), 232–33.

Chapter 6. Wartime Ambassador: 1916–1918

1. *Letters and Friendships*, 2:315–17.
2. Spring Rice to Grey, 16 April 1916, F.O. 800/85.
3. Ibid., 31 March 1916, F.O. 800/85.
4. Ibid., 31 July 1916, CAB 37/144/23.
5. Henry Hall to Spring Rice, 21 July 1916, SRPC.
6. Spring Rice to Foreign Office, 16 March 1916, F.O. 800/85.
7. Spring Rice to Grey, 31 July 1916, CAB 37/144/23.
8. Ibid., 10 May 1916, F.O. 800/242.
9. Ibid., 31 July 1916, CAB 37/144/23.
10. Ibid.
11. Ibid., 10 May 1916, F.O. 800/242.
12. Ibid., 2 August 1916, CAB 37/153/13.
13. *House Papers*, 2:312.
14. Wilson to House, 23 July 1916, *House Papers*, 2:312.
15. Spring Rice to Grey, 21 July 1916, F.O. 800/86.
16. Ibid., 16 October 1916, F.O. 800/86.
17. Ibid., 25 October 1916, F.O. 800/86.
18. Spring Rice to Foreign Office, 7 September 1916, F.O. 371/2795.
19. Spring Rice to Foreign Office, 11 September 1916, F.O. 371/2795.
20. For comment and interpretation of the House-Grey Memorandum, see Ross Gregory, *The Origins of American Intervention in the First World War* (New York: W.W. Norton, 1971), 81–82; Joyce G. Williams, *Colonel House and Sir Edward Grey* (Lanham, Md.: University Press of America, 1984), 86–88.
21. Spring Rice to Grey, 19 May 1916, F.O. 800/85
22. Ibid., 30 May 1916, SRPP.
23. Ibid.
24. Ibid., 10 September 1916, SRPP.
25. Gwynn, *Letters and Friendships*, 2:357.
26. Ibid.
27. Spring Rice to Foreign Office, 16 June 1916, F.O. 800/242.
28. Gwynn, *Letters and Friendships*, 2:331.
29. Spring Rice to Grey, 16 June 1916, F.O. 800/242.
30. Ibid.
31. Ibid, F.O. 800/338.
32. Ibid., 4 August 1917, SRPP.
33. Ibid.
34. Ibid., 31 July 1917, F.O. 800/241.
35. Ibid., 17 October 1916, F.O. 371/2794.
36. Spring Rice to Lord Robert Cecil, 17 November 1917, SRPC.
37. Spring Rice to Chirol, 31 October 1917, SRPP.
38. Spring Rice to Grey, 29 November 1916, F.O. 371/2796.
39. Gwynn, *Letters and Friendships*, 2:360.
40. Spring Rice to Balfour, 22 December 1916, F.O. 800/241.
41. Ibid., 5 January 1917, F.O. 800/85.
42. Ibid., 12 January 1917, F.O. 800/85.
43. Ibid., 19 January 19, 1917, F.O. 800/85.
44. Spring Rice to Grey, 1 June 1916, F.O. 800/242.
45. Spring Rice to Balfour, 26 January 1917, F.O. 800/242.

46. Ibid., 2 February 1917, F.O. 800/85.

47. Ibid., 1 March 1917, F.O. 800/85.

48. Ibid.

49. Spring to Balfour, 9 March 1917, Gwynn, *Letters and Friendships*, 2:385.

50. Ibid., 23 March 1917, F.O. 800/85.

51. Gwynn, *Letters and Friendships*, 2:390.

52. Spring Rice to Chirol, 6 June 1917, SRPP.

53. *House Papers*, 1:205.

54. Ibid., 465.

55. Wilton B. Fowler, *British-American Relations 1917–1918: The Role of Sir William Wiseman* (Princeton: Princeton University Press, 1969), 14, 20.

56. House to Wilson, 10 January 1917, *House Papers*, 2:399.

57. Wells, "The Influence," 385.

58. Crewe to Spring Rice, 1 June 1915, SRPC.

59. Spring Rice to Gerald Balfour, 30 December 1909, SRPC.

60. Reginald Pound and Geoffrey Northcliffe, *Northcliffe*, (London: Cassell, 1959), 531.

61. Lodge to Balfour, 9 January 1917, F.O. 800/85.

62. Wells, "The Influence," 368.

63. Drummond to Spring Rice, 16 January 1917, F.O. 800/85.

64. Bryce to Spring Rice, 21 March 1917, SRPC.

65. David P. Trask, *Captains and Cabinets: Anglo-American Naval Relations 1917–1918* (Columbia: University of Missouri Press, 1972), 76. Spring Rice to Foreign Office, 18 May 1917, F.O. 800/242; Balfour to Spring Rice, 22 August 1917, SRPC.

66. Willert, *Washington and Other Memories*, 102–4.

67. Gwynn, *Letters and Friendships*, 2:401–3.

68. Northcliffe to Spring Rice, 2 November 1917, SRPC.

69. Spring Rice to Foreign Office, 21 September 1917, F.O. 800/242.

70. Spring Rice to Cecil, 17 November 1917, F.O. 800/242.

71. Spring Rice to Hardinge, 25 October 1917, SRPP.

72. Spring Rice to Foreign Office, 28 December 1917, 4 January 1918, F.O. 800/242.

73. Gwynn, *Letters and Friendships*, 2:391–93.

74. Ibid., 401–3.

75. Spring Rice to Foreign Office, 7 September 1917, F.O. 800/242.

76. Spring Rice to A. J. Balfour, 4 January 1918; Gwynn, *Letters and Friendships*, 2:425.

Chapter 7. Last Days, Last Words

1. Spring Rice to Chirol, 26 January 1918, SRPP.

2. Shane Leslie, *Long Shadows* (London: John Murray, 1966), 194.

3. Spring Rice to Chirol, 1 February 1918, SRPP.

4. Spring Rice to Franklin Polk, 1 February 1919, quoted in Fowler, *British-American Relations 1917–1918*, 124.

5. Lady Spring Rice to Chirol, 12 March 1918, SRPP.

6. Gwynn, *Letters and Friendships*, 2:435.

7. Spring Rice to James Cardinal Gibbons, 24 December 1917, SRPC.

8. SRPP.

9. Chirol, *In Memoriam*, 35–54.

10. Gwynn, *Letters and Friendships*, 2:437.

11. Chirol, *In Memoriam*, 63–64.

12. Arthur J. Balfour to Spring Rice, undated, SRPP.

13. *House Papers*, 3:27–28.

BIBLIOGRAPHY

Primary Sources

UNPUBLISHED

Spring Rice Papers, Churchill College, Cambridge
Spring Rice Papers, Private
   Public Record Office (Kew)
   Foreign Office (F.O.) 371/2794
                         371/2795
                         371/2796
                         382/49
                         382/465
                         800/84
                         800/85
                         800/86
                         800/241
                         800/242
   Cabinet (CAB) 371/133/2
                   371/144/22
                   371/153/13

PUBLISHED

Spring Rice, Cecil A. *Songs from the Book of Jaffir*. London: MacMillan, 1900.
———. *The Story of Valeh and Hadijeh*. London: Duckworth, 1903.
———. *Poems*. London: Longmans, Green, 1929.
———. *The Adventures of James*. London: privately printed, n.d.
Gwynn, Stephen, ed. *The Letters and Friendships of Sir Cecil Spring Rice*. 2 vols. London: Constable and Company, 1929.
Ford, Worthington C., ed. *Letters of Henry Adams, 1892–1918*. 2 vols. Boston: Houghton Mifflin, 1938.
Foreign Relations of the United States. 1915 Supplement. Washington, D.C.: Government Printing Office, 1916.
Lewis, R. W. B., and Nancy Lewis, eds. *Letters of Edith Wharton*. New York: Charles Scribners' Sons, 1988.

Link, Arthur S., ed. *The Papers of Woodrow Wilson*. 61 vols. Princeton: Princeton University Press, 1966–present.

Morison, Elting E., ed. *The Letters of Theodore Roosevelt*. 8 vols. Cambridge: Harvard University Press, 1951–54.

Seymour, Charles, ed. *Intimate Papers of Colonel House*. 4 vols. Boston: Houghton Mifflin Co., 1926–28.

Secondary Sources

BOOKS WITH PARTICULAR REFERENCE TO SPRING RICE

Burton, David H. *Theodore Roosevelt and his English Correspondents*. Philadelphia: American Philosophical Society, 1973.

Chirol, Valentine. *Cecil Spring Rice In Memoriam*. London: John Murray, 1919.

Cooper, John M., Jr. *The Vanity of Power: American Isolation and the First World War, 1914–1917*. Westport, Conn.: Greenwood Press, 1969.

Devlin, Patrick. *Too Proud to Fight*. New York: Oxford University Press, 1975.

Dumba, Constantin. *Memoirs of a Diplomat*. London: Allen and Unwin, 1933.

Fowler, Wilton B. *British–American Relations 1917–1918: The Role of Sir William Wiseman*. Princeton: Princeton University Press, 1969.

Grey, Sir Edward. *Twenty-Five Years*. 2 vols. London: Holder and Stoughton, 1925.

Leslie, Shane. *Long Shadows*. London: John Murray, 1966.

L'Etang, Hugh. *Fit to Lead*. London: Heinemann, 1980.

Pound, Reginald, and Geoffrey Northcliffe. *Northcliffe*. London: Cassell, 1959.

Trevelyan, George M. *Grey of Fallodon*. London: Longmans, Green, 1937.

Wells, Sherrill B. "The Influence of Sir Cecil Spring Rice and Sir Edward Grey on the Shaping of Anglo-American Relations, 1913–1916." Ph.D. diss., University of London, 1978.

Wharton, Edith. *A Backward Glance*. New York: Appleton Century, 1934.

Willert, Arthur. *Washington and Other Memories*. Boston: Little, Brown & Co., 1972.

GENERAL STUDIES

Allen, H. C. *Concord and Conflict: The Anglo-American Relationship Since 1783*. New York: St. Martin's Press, 1959.

Bailey, Thomas A., and Paul B. Ryan. *The Lusitania Disaster*. New York: Free Press, 1975.

Beale, Howard K. *Theodore Roosevelt and the Rise of America to World Power*. Baltimore: Johns Hopkins University Press, 1957.

Campbell, A. E. *Great Britain and the United States, 1895–1903*. New York: Longmans, Green, 1960.

Campbell, C. S. *Anglo-American Understanding 1898–1903*. Baltimore: Johns Hopkins University Press, 1957.

Clymer, Kenton J. *John Hay, The Gentleman Diplomat.* Ann Arbor: University of Michigan Press, 1975.

Cooper, John M., Jr. *The Warrior and the Priest.* Cambridge: Harvard University Press, 1983.

Dangerfield, George. *The Strange Death of Liberal England.* New York: H. Smith and H. Haas, 1935.

Ellis, John Tracy. *The Life of James Cardinal Gibbons.* 2 vols. Milwaukee, Wis.: Bruce Publishing Company, 1952.

Ensor, R. C. K. *England 1870–1914.* Oxford: Clarendon Press, 1936.

Ferrell, Robert K. *Woodrow Wilson and World War I.* New York: Harper and Row, 1985.

Garraty, John. *Henry Cabot Lodge.* New York: Alfred Knopf, 1968.

Gelber, Lionel M. *The Rise of Anglo-American Friendship.* New York: Oxford University Press, 1938.

Gregory, Ross. *The Origins of American Intervention in the First World War.* New York: W. W. Norton, 1971.

Hearnshaw, F. J. C. *Edwardian England.* Freeport, N.Y.: Books for Libraries Press, 1968.

Heindel, Richard H. *The American Impact on Great Britain, 1898–1914.* New York: Octagon Books, 1968.

Hinsley, F. H. *British Foreign Policy under Grey.* Cambridge: Cambridge University Press, 1977.

Hyde, H. M. *Lord Reading.* New York: Farrar, Strauss, 1967.

Koss, Stephen. *The Rise and Fall of the Political Press in Britain: The Twentieth Century.* Chapel Hill: University of North Carolina Press, 1984.

Lansing, Robert. *War Memories.* Westport, Conn.: Greenwood Press, 1970.

Link, Arthur S. *Wilson the Diplomatist.* New York: New Viewpoints, 1957.

Lloyd George, David. *War Memories.* 6 vols. Boston: Little, Brown & Co., 1933–37.

May, Ernest R. *The World War and American Isolation 1914–1917.* Cambridge: Harvard University Press, 1959.

Monger, George W. *The End of Isolation: British Foreign Relations 1900–1907.* London: T. Nelson, 1963.

Morgan, K. O. *The Age of Lloyd George.* New York: Barnes and Noble, 1971.

Morris, James. *Pax Britannica: The Climax of Empire.* New York: Harcourt Brace Jovanovich, 1980.

Neale, R. G. *Great Britain and United States Expansion.* East Lansing: Michigan State University Press, 1966.

Neary, Peter. "The Bryce Embassy to the United States, 1907–1913." Ph.D. diss., University of London, 1965.

Perkins, Bradford. *The Great Rapprochement: England and America, 1895–1914.* New York: Atheneum Press, 1968.

Peterson, H. C. *Propaganda for War: The Campaign against American Neutrality.* Port Washington, N.Y.: Kennikat Press, 1968.

Rappaport, Armin. *The British Press and Wilsonian Neutrality.* Stanford, Calif.: Stanford University Press, 1951.

Rowland Peter. *David Lloyd George*. New York: MacMillan, 1976.

Schmitt, Bernadotte E. *The Coming of War*. 2 vols. New York: H. Fertig, 1958.

Steiner, Zara S. *The Foreign Office and Foreign Policy, 1898–1914*. London: Cambridge University Press, 1969.

Tansill, Charles Callan. *America Goes to War*. Boston: Little, Brown & Co., 1938.

Trani, Eugene. *The Treaty of Portsmouth*. Lexington: University of Kentucky Press, 1969.

Trask, David F. *Captains and Cabinets: Anglo-American Naval Relations 1917–1918*. Columbia: University of Missouri Press, 1972.

Watt, D. C. *Personalities and Policies*. South Bend, Ind.: University of Notre Dame Press, 1965.

Williams, Joyce G. *Colonel House and Sir Edward Grey*. Lanham, Md.: University Press of America, 1984.

Willis, Irene C. *England's Holy War*. New York: Alfred Knopf, 1928.

Wilson, Trevor. *The Myriad Faces of War: Great Britain and the Great War*. London: Polity Press, 1986.

INDEX

229